Contents

The Missing Credits vii
Introduction 1

Part 1: Preparing for Home Ownership

Chapter 1
The Benefits and Drawbacks of Home Ownership. **11**
   The Pluses of Owning a Home 12
   The Minuses of Owning a Home 18

Chapter 2
How Much Home Can You Afford? **25**
   How Much Can You Invest in a Home? 26
   Get Prequalified or Preapproved 34
   What Lenders Look For 36
   Improve Your Chances of Getting a Loan 48

Part 2: Finding Your Home

Chapter 3
Choose Your Style of Home and Neighborhood **51**
   Your Lifestyle—Now and Down the Road 52
   Your Style of Home 52
   The Condition of Your Home. 65
   Find Your Neighborhood 72
   Create a Wish List 77

Chapter 4
Assemble Your Real Estate Team **79**
   Real Estate Agents. 80
   Your Mortgage Provider 96
   Your Real Estate Attorney 99
   Your Home Inspector. 102
   Other Real Estate Professionals 104

Chapter 5
Shop for Your Home **107**
    Select Homes to Tour. 108
    Bargain Hunting 121
    What to Look for on the Tour. 132
    Evaluate the Neighborhood 141
    Compare Homes. 142

Part 3: Financing Your Home

Chapter 6
Finance Your Down Payment **143**
    Why a Down Payment? 144
    Calculate Your Down Payment 144
    Alternatives to Paying 20 Percent Down 148

Chapter 7
Compare Mortgages and Other Financing Options. **151**
    Mortgage Basics 152
    The Mortgage Process 161
    Types of Mortgages. 163
    Choose the Term of Your Mortgage 176
    Government Financing Programs 180
    Creative Financing Options. 186

Chapter 8
Choose and Apply for a Mortgage. **193**
    Find the Right Lender 194
    Get the Best Mortgage. 197
    Gather Documents and Information 206
    Do the Paperwork. 207

Chapter 9
Know Your Closing Costs **225**
    Kinds of Closing Costs 226
    Add It All Up. 233
    How Much Will You Pay?. 234
    Reduce Your Closing Costs 236

Part 4: Negotiating and Closing the Deal

Chapter 10
Make an Offer

Make an Offer **239**

Figure Out What the Home Is Worth. 240

What Goes Into an Offer. 249

Negotiating: The Art of the Deal 256

Chapter 11
Prepare for the Closing

Prepare for the Closing **261**

Check Off Contingencies 262

All About Titles and Deeds 267

Survey the Property. 273

Homeowner's Insurance. 273

Get a Home Warranty 279

Prepare to Move 282

Take the Final Walkthrough. 286

Chapter 12
Inspect the Property

Inspect the Property. **291**

What a Home Inspector Does 292

Find a Good Home Inspector 292

What Happens at an Inspection 293

Understand Your Home Inspection Report 302

Specialized Inspections 304

If Problems Turn Up. 310

Chapter 13
Close the Deal

Close the Deal **313**

Countdown to Closing: 24 Hours to Go 314

What If the Closing Gets Delayed? 317

What Happens at a Closing. 319

A Mountain of Paperwork: What It All Means 322

Your HUD-1 Form 325

What If Something Goes Wrong?. 330

After the Closing. 331

Index **335**

The Missing Credits

About the Author

 **Nancy Conner** is the author of several Missing Manuals. She and her husband Steve live in upstate New York where they write books and invest in rental properties. Nancy fulfilled all the New York state requirements to become a licensed real estate agent. When she's not writing or looking at investment opportunities, Nancy enjoys visiting local wineries and listening obsessively to opera.

About the Creative Team

Peter McKie (editor) is an editor at Missing Manuals. He bought his co-op before this book came out, and was pleased to find that, through blind luck, he refinanced after his break-even point (see page 158 in Chapter 7 for details). He graduated with a master's degree from Boston University's School of Journalism and lives in New York City, where he researches the history of old houses and, every once in a while, sneaks into abandoned buildings. Email: *pmckie@gmail.com*.

Nellie McKesson (production editor) is (as of this writing) in the process of buying her very first home, in Brockton, Mass. When not filling out mortgage-related forms, she spends her spare time studying graphic design and building her t-shirt business (*www.endplasticdesigns.com*). Email: *nellie@oreilly.com*.

Marcia Simmons (copy editor) is a freelance writer and editor living in the San Francisco Bay Area. In addition to writing about technology, design, and cocktail culture, she maintains a personal blog at SmartKitty.org.

Ron Strauss (indexer). When Ron is not indexing books, he is on the lecture circuit educating people in how to become radiantly healthy with Natural Healing and a mostly raw vegan diet!

Jay Neeley (technical reviewer) is a cofounder of EasyImpress (*http://www.easyimpress.com*), a website developer for real estate agencies. As a Boston entrepreneur, when he's not putting the Silicon Valley startup scene to shame, he's working from coffee shops, creating odd constructions in the snow, and adventuring in and around the city.

Arwen O'Reilly Griffith (technical reviewer) is an editor at *Make* magazine and blogs at *Craft* online magazine. She's the mother of a rambunctious 1-year-old and just bought a teeny-tiny house on a hill in San Francisco with her equally crazy husband, Saul. She has big plans for her small garden.

Acknowledgements

A book like this requires the knowledge, skills, and talents of many people to take it from initial idea to finished product. I was fortunate to work with a world-class team. Thanks to Pete Meyers for suggesting the project. Editor Peter McKie helped me shape the outline and offered invaluable feedback. Thanks to technical reviewers Jay Neely and Arwen O'Reilly for their suggestions, comments, and corrections. Thanks also to copyeditor Marcia Simmons for rooting out typos, inconsistencies, and other mistakes.

Stephen Shore of InsideOut Inspections (*www.housewiz.com*) in Ithaca, New York, graciously provided the Missing CD's sample home inspection report. I've worked with Steve many times, and he's a first-rate home inspector. Thanks, Steve, for sharing your expertise here.

As always, my husband Steve Holzner was loving and supportive throughout the many long hours it takes to write a book. (He's written more than 130 himself, so he knows better than most what the process requires.) Thanks to him for hand-holding, back-patting, and providing me with a cozy fire and a glass of wine on Sunday evenings. He's the best!

—*Nancy Conner*

Introduction

Welcome (almost) to the world of home ownership! The fact that you've picked up this book and flipped it open to the Introduction says you're serious about buying a home, and you're looking for step-by-step guidance through the process—from finding the right home to signing the papers that make it yours. Either way, you've come to the right place.

Buying a home is a big step. In fact, it's many big steps—to the first-time homebuyer, the process can seem long, complex, and more than a little confusing. This book takes the confusion out of buying a home, guiding you through each step of the process and offering tips and information along the way. And if you've bought property before, this book serves as a step-by-step refresher course with information on all the current real-estate practices. Neophyte or veteran, you'll feel confident about one of the biggest decisions you'll ever make.

Should You Rent or Buy?

Home ownership is a big step, and many people worry whether they're ready to take it. If you currently rent your house, you may wonder if you can even afford to buy a home. Just looking at real estate listings online or in the Sunday paper can make you break out in a cold sweat. Yes, homes are expensive. But they're also an *investment*—and for many homeowners, it's one of the smartest investments they'll make. Depending on how much you currently pay for rent, how expensive homes are in your area, what your credit score looks like, and how long you plan to live in the house (among other factors), buying a home is often less expensive than renting in the long run. After all, when you rent, you just pay for a roof over your head. When you buy, you become the owner of that roof—and everything beneath it.

 Tip To see whether renting or buying makes better financial sense for you, use myFICO's "Am I better off renting?" calculator. You can find it at *http://tinyurl.com/yagk6lr*.

Renting does have its advantages. Here are some:

- **Renting offers more flexibility.** If you like knowing that you can pack up and move at a moment's (or a month's) notice, it may make more sense to rent. Depending on the terms of your lease, you're not tied to a residence for more than a year or two at most. When you own a home, on the other hand, you need to sell the property or find a suitable tenant before you can move—or else you'll end up paying a mortgage on an empty house.

 Tip If you know you're likely to move within three or four years, you're probably better off renting than buying. That's because you won't have time to build up much equity in your house (its cash value as you pay off your mortgage's principal) or break even on your closing costs. (Chapter 9 gives you an overview of the many costs associated with buying a home.)

- **Maintenance is someone else's headache.** When you rent, you call the landlord if a pipe bursts or the furnace quits. He sends someone to fix it—and takes care of the bill. When you own, all the maintenance—from keeping everything in good repair to mowing the lawn and shoveling snow—is your responsibility.

- **You can move in faster.** Buying a house takes time. If you're in a hurry to move to a new neighborhood, you might want to rent for a year and look for a place to buy during that time. Renters can usually move in soon after getting their rental application approved. Buying a home, on the other hand, takes months. You'll be living in your new house for years, so you want to take your time finding just the right home. Then you may spend a couple of weeks negotiating with the seller before you agree on a price and conditions. And getting financing and preparing for the property transfer can take 30 days or longer.

- **Your move-in costs are lower.** Renting a house usually involves no more up-front costs than two months' rent and a security deposit. Buying a home is far more expensive. You need a down payment of anywhere from 3.5 to 20 percent—or more—of the home's purchase price and thousands of dollars more for the fees and costs associated with getting a mortgage (Chapter 9 gives you a rundown of what those are).

- **You can keep your money in the bank.** Being a first-time homeowner frequently means scraping together all the money you can find to afford a down payment and closing costs. Once you buy a house, your money is tied up in your home. After you built up some equity (cash value in the house as you make principal payments), you can tap into it with a home equity line of credit (page 15). But if you want your money readily available (especially within the next few years), or if you want to invest in something other than real estate, it may make more sense for you to rent.

If you're thinking about buying a home, you're already aware that buying has its own advantages. Here are some major ones:

- **Say goodbye to your landlord.** It irks some people to pay good money each month and not get anything more in return than the right to live under someone else's roof. When you own your home, each mortgage payment builds up your equity in the house—not much at first, but it increases with time (page 12 explains how that works). Some landlords are great, but others are slow to make repairs—and quick to raise the rent. If you want to feel like your home is your own, you might be ready to buy.

- **Take advantage of tax breaks.** You can deduct mortgage interest, property taxes, and some closing costs from your federal income taxes. (For the tax savings to make a difference, the deductible items must add up to more than the standard deduction—and you'll have to itemize all deductions to claim this tax break.)

- **Beat inflation.** As the cost of living goes up, the cost of rent goes right up with it. If you use a fixed-rate mortgage (page 163) to buy a home, however, your principal and interest payments stay the same for as long as you live in the home. The longer you stay there, the more pronounced this benefit.

- **Build equity.** Renting is pay-as-you-go; as long as you pay your rent and abide by the terms of your lease, you can live in your home. But if you buy, as you make mortgage payments and as home values rise, you gain equity in your home. You can treat your home's equity like a savings account, cashing out when you sell the home and using the money for a down payment on your next home. Or you can borrow against it using a home equity line of credit (page 15).

- **Have your own place.** For many people, the main reason to buy a home is to have a place that's truly their own. You're not paying off the landlord's mortgage—you're investing in a home with your name on the deed. That's a great feeling, whether you buy a one-bedroom manufactured home or a many-roomed mansion.

About This Book

You may have heard that now is a good time to buy a home. In many parts of the country, prices are down and the number of homes for sale is up, creating a buyer's market. At the same time, news stories of foreclosures and other home-buying disasters may have you nervous about taking such a big step.

That's where *Buying a Home: The Missing Manual* comes in. It takes the mystery and confusion out of buying a home. This book guides you through the process, from the moment you wonder whether home ownership is for you until the moment you walk through your new home's front door. Along the way, you'll get clear explanations, tips, and practical advice about finding the right home, evaluating neighborhoods, choosing the right professionals to work with, making an offer, selecting a mortgage and applying for financing, negotiating with the seller, getting a home inspection, and making sure closing goes smoothly. There's a lot to cover, and this book will be with you every step of the way.

 Real estate laws vary widely from one state to another. Nothing in this book is intended to serve as legal advice. If you have legal questions related to buying a home, consult a qualified real estate attorney who's familiar with your local laws and practices.

About the Outline

Buying a Home: The Missing Manual is divided into four parts. Each one corresponds to a phase of the home buying process and contains several chapters:

- **Part 1, Preparing for Home Ownership** helps you get ready to set out on your journey. Before you start looking at homes, you should know whether home ownership is the right decision for you, and you should establish your target price range. Part 1 has two chapters:

  - **The Benefits and Drawbacks of Home Ownership (Chapter 1)** offers a clear-eyed look at the pluses and minuses of owning a home. For many people, it's a cherished dream. To keep that dream from becoming a nightmare, make sure you understand the drawbacks of home ownership as well as the many advantages. This chapter fills you in.

  - **How Much Home Can You Afford? (Chapter 2)** helps you figure out how much money you can afford to invest in a home. If you've never drawn up a monthly budget that lays out your recurring income and expenses, this chapter's for you. You'll use that information to estimate what you can afford in monthly mortgage payments, taking into account related expenses like taxes, maintenance, and utilities. You'll find out how lenders see your finances and decide whether you're qualified to borrow. You'll also get tips on raising your credit score and learn why it's a good idea to get preapproved for a loan *before* you start house hunting.

- **Part 2, Finding Your Home**, helps you clarify what you want in a home—and then shows you how to find it. This part has three chapters:

  - **Choose Your Style of Home and Neighborhood (Chapter 3)** describes different types of houses, from traditional single-family homes to duplexes to condos and co-ops. You'll create a wish list of all the features you want in your home and identify the neighborhoods where you'll concentrate your search.

  - **Assemble Your Real Estate Team (Chapter 4)** identifies the professionals who'll help make your dreams of home ownership a reality. It describes the roles of your real estate agent, mortgage broker or loan officer, real estate attorney, and home inspector—and tells you how to interview each to find the best one.

  - **Shop for Your Home (Chapter 5)** gives you a strategy to make house hunting more effective and efficient. Use your wish list to focus on "must-haves" and "would-likes" as you tour and compare homes.

- **Part 3, Financing Your Home**, looks at how and where you get the money to buy your house. Find your way through the financing maze with the help of these chapters:

  — **Finance Your Down Payment (Chapter 6)** is all about the biggest up-front expense you'll face: the 3.5 to 20 percent you need to pay up front so a lender will finance the rest. When you're thinking of buying a home that costs hundreds of thousands of dollars, coming up with the down payment can be daunting. This chapter explains how the size of your down payment affects your mortgage and suggests ways to come up with the money you need.

  — **Compare Mortgages and Other Financing Options (Chapter 7)** demystifies mortgages, explaining basic terms and showing you the wide variety of loans available. Learn the difference between fixed-rate, adjustable, hybrid, and balloon loans—to name a few—and decide which is best for you. Learn about how your loan's repayment schedule affects how much you pay each month and over the life of your loan. And see whether creative financing, such as renting to own, may be a good option for you.

  — **Choose and Apply for a Mortgage (Chapter 8)** walks you through the part of the process that many homebuyers find most intimidating: getting a mortgage. Learn how to find the right lender, get the best interest rate, and gather the papers and information you need to apply for a loan. Familiarize yourself with the forms lenders must send you in return, such as the Good Faith Estimate, which shows you the total cost of the loan, and the HUD-1 form, which breaks down your closing costs.

  — **Know Your Closing Costs (Chapter 9)** reminds you that the down payment is only part of the up-front money you need to buy a house. This chapter outlines the other costs, including fees related to getting a mortgage, inspecting the house, and transferring the house's title from the seller to you.

- **Part 4, Negotiating and Closing the Deal**, is all about making your dream home yours, from making a formal offer to closing the sale—and the 1,001 tasks needed to make that happen:

  — **Make an Offer (Chapter 10)** tells you how to make a formal offer and negotiate with the seller. An offer is a promise to buy—backed up with an "earnest money" deposit—so you need to make sure that your offer is written in a way that protects you if you discover a problem with the home or can't get financing.

- **Prepare for the Closing (Chapter 11)** lists what you need to do between the time the seller accepts your offer and the time you transfer ownership: deal with contingencies you wrote into the purchase agreement, decide how you'll hold title, buy insurance, get ready to move, and do the final walkthrough just before you make the deal official.

- **Inspect the Property (Chapter 12)** goes over one of the most important tasks in buying a house: getting a professional inspection to make sure there aren't any hidden structural or other defects that will cause you trouble (and cost you money) after you move in. See your home through the eyes of a professional home inspector—and find out what to do if there's a problem.

- **Close the Deal (Chapter 13)** takes you through the culmination of all your hard work: the closing, when the home finally becomes yours. There's a lot more to a closing than getting a set of keys. You have to understand and sign a mountain of paperwork, some of it related to your loan, some of it related to transferring the property, some of it related to squaring payments with the seller. This chapter tells you what to expect.

About the Missing CD

This book helps you buy a house. As you read through it, you'll find references to websites that offer property listings, real estate forms and calculators, current interest rates, and more. Each reference includes the site's URL, but you can save yourself some typing by going to this book's Missing CD page—it gives you clickable links to all the sites mentioned here. To get to the Missing CD page, go to the Missing Manuals home page (*www.missingmanuals.com*), click the Missing CD link, scroll down to *Buying a Home: The Missing Manual*, and then click the link labeled "Missing CD."

While you're on the Missing CD page, you can find updates to this book by clicking the link at the top of the page labeled "View errata for this book." You're invited and encouraged to submit corrections and updates. To do so, click the link, "Submit your own errata" on the same page.

To keep the book as up-to-date and accurate as possible, each time we print more copies, we'll include any confirmed corrections you suggest. We'll also note all the changes to the book on the Missing CD page, so you can mark important corrections in your own copy of the book, if you like.

Tiny URLs

This book mentions lots of great websites you can turn to as you buy a house. Sometimes that info is on a very specific page of a site, and the web address that takes you there can be awfully long.

The geeky name for a web address is *URL* (short for Uniform Resource Locator). For example, *http://www.google.com* is a URL—it tells your web browser to go to Google's home page. But not all URLs are as concise as that. To learn about Bankrate. com's free household budgeting worksheet (page 27), for instance, you have to go to *http://www.bankrate.com/finance/money-guides/free-household-budgeting-work-sheet.aspx*. That's a lot of gobbledygook to type in, and you have better ways to spend your time. That's where TinyURLs come in.

In 2002, a guy named Kevin Gilbertson started the website TinyURL.com. The site's mission is simple: to shorten ungainly website addresses, like the one for Bankrate. com. Highlight and copy the address you want to shrink, head over to *http://tinyurl. com*, and paste the address in the box. Click the Make TinyURL button and voilà— the site gives you a much shorter address (which starts with *http://tinyurl*.com) that takes you to the same spot as the long one.

Throughout this book, you'll see TinyURLs used in place of giant, clunky ones. To get to the Bankrate.com page mentioned earlier, for example, type in *http://tinyurl.com/ yeshrvk* instead. Better yet, head to this book's Missing CD page at *www.missing-manuals.com*, where you'll find clickable links to all the sites referenced in this book.

About MissingManuals.com

To see the latest Missing Manuals videos, the most recent blog posts by Missing Manuals authors, the most recent community tweets about Missing Manuals, and special offers on Missing Manuals books, go to the Missing Manuals home page (*www.missingmanuals.com*).

While you're online, you can register this book at *www.oreilly.com* (you can jump directly to the registration page by going here: *http://tinyurl.com/ yo82k3*). Registering means we can send you updates about this book, and you'll be eligible for special offers like discounts on future editions of *Buying a Home: The Missing Manual*.

You might also want to visit O'Reilly's Feedback page (*http://missingmanu-als.com/feedback.html*), where you can get expert answers to questions that come to you while reading this book, write a book review, and find groups for folks who share your interest in *Buying a Home: The Missing Manual*.

We'd love to hear your suggestions for new books in the Missing Manual line. There's a place for that on missingmanuals.com, too.

Safari® Books Online

 Safari® Books Online is an on-demand digital library that lets you easily search over 7,500 technology and creative reference books and videos to find the answers you need quickly.

With a subscription, you can read any page and watch any video from our library online. Read books on your cellphone and mobile devices. Access new titles before they're available for print, and get exclusive access to manuscripts in development and post feedback for the authors. Copy and paste code samples, organize your favorites, download chapters, bookmark key sections, create notes, print out pages, and benefit from tons of other time-saving features.

O'Reilly Media has uploaded this book to the Safari Books Online service. To have full digital access to this book and others on similar topics from O'Reilly and other publishers, sign up for free at *http://my.safaribooksonline.com*.

1 The Benefits and Drawbacks of Home Ownership

When you buy a home, you open a new chapter in your life. It's a time of both excitement and trepidation. You tour potential houses and picture yourself in a new environment. But you also worry about how you'll pay for everything. It's easy to feel overwhelmed by the home-buying process.

This chapter gives you a bird's-eye view of the benefits and challenges of buying a home so you know what to expect. In subsequent chapters, you'll work through these challenges in a logical, step-by-step fashion until you get the keys—literally—to your future.

The Pluses of Owning a Home

For many people, home ownership is the ultimate dream. It means you've got a permanent place in the world—somewhere you can raise kids, gather family and friends, and unwind from a hectic day. Whether you're in a one-bedroom condo or a turreted mansion, owning your own home means comfort, safety, and pleasure.

Owning your own home comes with practical benefits, too. You can borrow against the value of your house, take impressive tax breaks, and treat your house as a long-term investment.

A Place of Your Own

People buy homes for a number of reasons, but "I want a place of my own" tops the list. When you own your own home, you don't have to ask a landlord if you can wallpaper the dining room, install a luxurious tub in the master bath, or paint clouds on the ceiling of your daughter's bedroom. You can create an environment that reflects your taste, lifestyle, and personality.

On the other hand, you may buy a home because you need more space—an extra bedroom, an office or family room, perhaps a yard with room for kids and pets to run around. Or maybe you're tired of hearing your neighbors through the wall.

Buying a home also lets you put down long-term roots. You can become a permanent part of your neighborhood instead of someone just passing through. Settling in may inspire you to become more active in your community—join the PTA, start a gardening club, or even run for local office. A sense of belonging can be one of the most satisfying aspects of home ownership.

Equity

Almost everyone takes out a loan to buy a house. As you pay that loan back, you build *equity* in your property. Equity is the difference between the market value of your home—what someone would pay for it if you sold it today—and what you still owe the lender on the loan. If your home has a market value of $275,000 and you currently owe the lender $200,000, you have $75,000 worth of equity. Congratulations!

You build equity two ways:

- **By paying back your loan.** Every month, when you pay back part of your home loan, you reduce a portion of your principal, the amount of cash you borrowed from the lender. (The rest of the monthly payment goes to paying interest, what the lender charges you for loaning you its money in the first place.) For the first few years, most of each payment goes toward interest. Over time, however, you pay back more of the principal than the interest. And the more you reduce the principal, the more equity you have in your house.

 Some loans let you make extra payments toward your principal each month. That reduces the *term* of your loan (the number of years you have to make mortgage payments) and builds your equity faster. See page 178 for the details.

- **By increasing the value of your home.** If your home is worth more now than it was when you bought it, your home gains in equity. The value of your house increases under two circumstances: when housing prices go up as a result of market conditions and when you make improvements to your house (because improvements may put your house in a higher price bracket).

These two factors usually work in tandem. Consider this example: Say you find a house you want to buy for $180,000. You pay 10 percent of the purchase price ($18,000) in cash as a down payment and borrow the rest, $162,000, from a lender in the form of a *mortgage*. A mortgage is the loan you get to buy a house, and it's defined as the home's purchase price minus your down payment.

A few years down the road, as you pay off your mortgage month by month, you've reduced the loan's principal by $4,500, to $157,500. At the same time, home values in your neighborhood have gone up, and your home is now worth $187,500. When you factor in your loan's reduced principal and the home's increased value, you have $30,000 worth of equity.

Housing prices can also *decrease*—as they did in many areas of the U.S. when the housing bubble burst in the late 2000s. So while homes historically increase in value over time, it's possible that your home could *lose* equity.

When you sell your home, you can profit from the equity it's gained over the years. If you sold the home in the example for its new market price of $187,500 and paid off the $157,500 remaining on your mortgage and the costs associated with sale, the rest would go straight into your pocket—or perhaps into the down payment on a new home.

 Normally, when you profit by selling an investment, you have to pay a *capital gains* tax on that profit. But when you sell your home, Uncle Sam gives you a break. Currently, the IRS exempts home-sale profits of up to $250,000 for a single homeowner or $500,000 for a married couple who owns a home jointly. That means that when you sell your home, you only have to pay capital gains tax on any profit over those amounts.

The beauty of equity is that you don't have to wait to sell your house to benefit from it. You can put it to use right away by borrowing against it through either a home equity loan or a home equity line of credit (HELOC).

 Keep in mind that borrowing against equity means that you're using your home as collateral for the loan, so make sure you don't borrow more than you can afford to pay back. It also means that you now have two loan payments to make each month.

Home equity loans

With a home equity loan, you borrow a fixed amount of money, usually at a fixed interest rate. You repay the loan over a set period of time, just as you do a mortgage. (In fact, this kind of loan is sometimes called a second mortgage.) Homeowners often use home equity loans to pay for a single large expense, like adding a room or remodeling a kitchen.

Home equity line of credit (HELOC)

For this type of loan, lenders extend you a line of credit based on your equity rather than giving you a lump-sum payment. Taking into account the amount of equity you have in your home, the lender establishes a maximum line of credit and gives you a book of checks or a special credit card that lets you draw on that credit. You can spend any amount at any time for any purpose, until you've borrowed the maximum. So if your HELOC gives you a line of credit of $50,000, you can draw $5,000 one month, $20,000 the next, and so on until you reach the $50,000 maximum.

Most HELOCs have a term of 20 years. Lenders call the first 10 years the draw period. That's because you can tap your line of credit any time during that first 10 years. You can pay back some or all of what you borrow during the draw period, or you can make interest-only minimum payments. After the draw period, your borrowing privileges end. And if you have an outstanding balance, your lender amortizes your payments, which means she figures out how much you need to pay each month to pay back the HELOC's principal plus interest over the remaining term of the HELOC (the remaining 10 years in this example).

HELOCs usually have an adjustable interest rate. That means that the interest you pay goes up and down in conjunction with an established financial index, such as the prime rate (the interest rate lenders charge their best customers for loans). Some HELOCs have an initial fixed-rate period, during which the interest rate stays stable. When that period expires, however, your interest rate can change quickly. Your payments also fluctuate depending on how much money you borrow. If you draw $5,000 one month and then $15,000 the next, for example, your minimum payment increases after the second month.

 Tip Some or all of the interest paid on home equity loans and HELOCs is tax deductible. The total amount of your home equity debt can't exceed $100,000 ($50,000 if you're married but file income taxes separately), and all mortgages on the home can't add up to more than 100 percent of the home's fair market value. Check with your accountant or tax adviser to find out how much home equity loan interest you can deduct.

Tax Advantages

Uncle Sam loves homeowners—and shows you how much by giving you a break on your income taxes. Here's what you can deduct from your federal income tax when you own your home:

- Certain costs related to buying the home, such as points you paid (see page 157)
- Some or all of your mortgage interest
- Local property taxes
- In some cases, private mortgage insurance (see page 39)
- Other home-related costs, such as a home office or improvements you make to boost your home's energy efficiency

Of course, tax laws change frequently, and not everyone qualifies for each deduction. Check with your accountant or tax preparer to find out how homeowner tax breaks can best benefit you.

Long-Term Investment

Short-term home ownership—say of three years or less—doesn't always make a good investment. Over the short term, the real estate market can fluctuate significantly. Home prices can leap up one year, drop sharply the next, change a little, or stay flat. In fact, the real estate market can be so volatile that if you plan to stay in your house for just a couple of years, renting may be a better option. Also, the up-front costs of buying a home are high, and you've got to live in the home for several years before you break even on those initial expenses. Aside from the down payment on the house (Chapter 6), you have to pay a long list of other charges and fees to get financing and to transfer legal ownership of the house to you (Chapter 9 outlines these for you). The longer you live in the home, the more those initial costs are spread out over time, reducing their impact. For example, if you pay $6,000 in purchase fees and live in your house for only two years, the fees cost you $3,000 a year and, in all likelihood, your home hasn't increased in value in that short a time to make the investment worthwhile. If you stay in the home for 12 years, however, that initial $6,000 cost you only $500 a year (and all the while, presumably, your house has increased in value, making the investment a good one).

Finally, lenders calculate your repayment schedule so that, for the first few years you pay back the loan, a much bigger chunk of each monthly payment goes toward interest rather than principal. Unless you take out a shorter-term mortgage (page 177) or make extra payments toward the principal (page 178), you won't build much equity in those first few years.

To see an example of how much of each monthly payment goes toward interest and how much goes toward principal in the first year of a loan, check out the amortization table on page 156.

 Tip To get a sense of how long you have to live in the home before owning becomes cheaper than renting, try the "Is It Better to Buy or Rent?" calculator on the *New York Times* website at *http://tinyurl.com/2sdtvd*. Give the calculator information about how much you currently pay for rent, the home's purchase price, the size of your down payment, the interest rate of your loan, and the cost of property taxes. Click Calculate to get an estimate of the tipping point when buying becomes the better deal.

If you plan to live in your new home for a while—say, more than six or seven years—home ownership is almost always better than renting. According to the U.S. Census Bureau, the average price of a home has risen steadily over the past 40 years, as the following table shows.

Year	Average home price (adjusted for inflation to current dollar values)
1970	$81,650
1980	$116,780
1990	$126,400
2000	$149,500

The Census Bureau surveys home prices every 10 years, and the data isn't yet in for 2010. But in August 2009, the National Association of Realtors reported that the average sale price for an existing home was $177,700. So even though prices may slide in the short term, if you're in it for the long haul, your home remains a good investment.

 Note Historically, home prices rise less than other kinds of investments, like stocks and bonds. But you need a place to live, and owning your own home means that your mortgage payments do triple duty: They provide you with shelter, build equity, and offer tax breaks.

Trading Up

As you shop for a home, you'll probably encounter the phrase "starter home." Real estate agents use that term to describe property that may be of interest to first-time homebuyers. The home may be priced lower than others on the market, making it easier for buyers to come up with a down payment, or perhaps it's smaller, so it appeals to single professionals or couples without children.

"Starter home" also implies that second-time homebuyers move up to larger or pricier homes, using the profit from the starter home to beef up the down payment on their next home. It's a sensible strategy; thanks to the equity you build up over time, you can usually move up to a home you couldn't afford the first time you went house-hunting.

The Minuses of Owning a Home

There's a flip side to everything, of course, and home ownership is no exception. Don't go through the process of buying a home with your eyes shut and your fingers crossed.

When you figure out how much your new home will cost, purchase price is only part of the story—it's the biggest part, to be sure, but you need to expect other costs, too, both one-time and recurring.

One-Time Costs

One-time costs arise from financing your down payment and securing a mortgage:

- **The down payment.** This is money you pay up front toward the purchase of a home. Mortgage lenders see the down payment as a sign of your intent to buy the house and your ability to repay your loan. These days, lenders prefer a down payment of at least 20 percent. You may be able to qualify for a lower down payment (FHA-insured loans, page 180, are the best place to start looking).

 If your down payment is less than 20 percent, you'll probably have to buy private mortgage insurance (page 146), paying monthly premiums until you accrue at least 20 percent equity in your home.

- **Mortgage-related fees.** There are all kinds of costs associated with getting a mortgage, such as the application fee, the home-appraisal fee, and an origination or processing fee (what the lender charges for the administrative tasks involved in processing your application)—and that's just for starters, as you'll see in Chapter 9.

- **Other closing costs.** Mortgage-related fees are only part of the story. To legally transfer ownership of a house (what industry types call *closing* on a house), you'll also pay transfer taxes and recording fees, a title search and title insurance fee, settlement fees, and more. To prepare for the closing, you'll pay for a home inspection and buy hazard insurance as well.

Tip Chapter 9 gives you the details on closing costs, but in general, expect to spend 3 to 6 percent of your new home's purchase price on fees and other charges.

Recurring Payments

Of course, after you borrow money to buy your home, you have to pay the lender back. You do this by making a payment to the lender each month. Part of each payment goes toward paying back the money you borrowed (the principal), and part of it goes toward paying interest on the principal. But principal and interest aren't the only recurring payments you have to make; you also have to pay taxes and insurance. Some homeowners pay these once a year, directly to their tax collector or insurance agent. In other cases, the lender itself breaks the annual cost into 12 installments and adds them to your principal and interest payments. The lender holds the tax and insurance payments in an escrow account (basically, a special-purpose holding account), and then uses that money to pay your tax and insurance bills when they come due.

You may hear real estate professionals talk about PITI (pronounced *pity*, as in "It's a pity you have to pay it"). That acronym refers to the four components that may make up monthly payments to lenders:

- **Principal.** This is the amount of cash you borrowed from a lender to buy your house. You pay it back over the term (the total length) of your loan. Each month, part of your payment goes toward paying back the principal.

- **Interest.** Interest is the money you pay your lender for using their money to buy your house ("renting" their money is probably more accurate). For the first few years of your mortgage, most of your monthly payment goes toward paying interest.

- **Taxes.** This refers to your local property taxes, which support municipal services like sewage, trash pick-up, playgrounds, and the like.

- **Insurance.** This includes homeowner's insurance and possibly one or more of the following: private mortgage insurance (PMI), which lenders require when your down payment is less than 20 percent of the home's purchase price; flood insurance; and homeowners' association fees. Homeowner's insurance protects your home and its contents in case of fire, theft, vandalism, wind damage, and other disasters. It also covers you if someone is injured on your property. Page 273 has tips to help you choose a policy. And if you live in areas that have a high risk of flooding, your lender will require you to buy flood insurance in addition to your homeowner's policy. FEMA, the Federal Emergency Management Agency, administers the National Flood Insurance Program; you can get info about flood insurance at *www.fema.gov*.

 Tip You can find links to all the websites mentioned in this book on the book's Missing CD page. To get there, go to the Missing Manuals home page (*www. missingmanuals.com*), click the Missing CD link, scroll down to *Buying a Home: The Missing Manual*, and then click the link labeled "Missing CD".

Say you borrow $200,000 at an interest rate of 6 percent for a term of 30 years. Property taxes are $2,000 a year, your homeowner's insurance policy costs $750 a year, and you don't have to pay PMI. Based on those numbers, your monthly payment breaks down like this:

Principal and interest	$1,199.10
Property taxes	$166.66
Insurance	$62.50
Total monthly payment	$1,428.26

 Tip Use the mortgage calculator at *www.realestateabc.com/calculators/PITI.htm* to plug in your own numbers and estimate PITI for the home you're considering.

That's what you'll pay the first year. But keep in mind that the amount of your monthly payment can change from one year to the next, depending on several factors:

- **The type of mortgage loan.** If you opt for an *adjustable rate* mortgage (ARM; see page 164), your interest rate can change from year to year. When the interest rate goes up, so does the interest portion or your mortgage. Likewise, if the interest rate goes down, so does your interest payment.

- **Tax increases.** When your city, town, county, or school district hikes taxes, your monthly PITI payment reflects that. You have to pay more each month to make sure there's enough in escrow to pay next year's taxes. Your lender calculates the tax portion of your PITI once a year.

- **Inflation.** This can affect the cost of your homeowner's insurance, causing that portion of your payment to rise from year to year.

- **Increased equity.** If you put down less than 20 percent to buy your house, you can request cancellation of PMI after you build 20 percent equity in the home—whether the equity bump came from rising home values, payments toward the principal, or both. Getting rid of PMI lowers your monthly payment and can save you hundreds or even thousands of dollars. By federal law, your lender must cancel PMI when your equity in the home reaches 22 percent.

Utilities

When you figure out whether you can afford a home, don't forget to take utilities into account. Ask the seller about monthly costs for electricity, heating fuel, cable, Internet access, water, trash removal, and so on. Make sure that you can afford these charges along with the PITI.

 Depending on the terms of your loan, your monthly payment may comprise PITI (principal, interest, taxes, and insurance) or just principal and interest. If you pay PITI each month, the lender holds the money for taxes and insurance in a special account and pays these costs on your behalf when they come due. If you pay just principal and interest, staying current with tax and insurance payments is your responsibility.

Maintenance

Whether you buy a brand-new home or an old fixer-upper, sooner or later you'll have to pay maintenance costs. With all the rewards of home ownership comes responsibility—and that means you're the one who pays the bills when the lawn needs mowing, the shutters need painting, or there's a foot of snow in the driveway. You'll invest your time or your money—and probably both—in routine upkeep.

 In some areas, you may have to pay a one-time connection charge to set up utilities. If that's the case in your neck of the woods, add those connection charges to your one-time costs.

Repairs

Aside from routine and seasonal maintenance, be prepared for other expenses. You may have to replace the water heater, buy a new dishwasher, fix a leaky roof, or replace rotting trim. When an appliance dies without warning or other issues crop up unexpectedly, you need to find the money to fix the problem. Once you have sufficient equity in your house, you may decide to borrow against that equity. But it's a good idea to have an emergency fund that you can tap when things go wrong.

Remodeling

You may decide to remodel. Whether you replace carpets, redesign the kitchen, build an addition, or wallpaper a room, this can be a significant expense. On the plus side, remodeling can increase the value of your home and build equity faster, so it not only adds to the enjoyment of your home, it's a good investment.

Homeowner's Fees

Finally, some kinds of homes require monthly fees for maintenance and other costs:

- **Condominiums.** As page 60 explains, a *condominium* is a housing arrangement where specific parts of a piece of real estate are owned individually (such as apartment-style units in a building or complex of buildings) and shared areas and facilities are owned in common and controlled by a board that represents all the individual owners. These shared areas and facilities include walkways, hallways, elevators, staircases, building exteriors, heating and cooling systems, and perhaps a pool and parking lot. Monthly condo fees (sometimes called *common charges*) pay for all this—maintenance to the grounds, exteriors, and common areas; lighting in entries, hallways, and the parking lot; insurance; and sometimes a long-term fund for emergencies.

- **Co-ops.** Short for *housing cooperative*, in a co-op, residents own shares in a corporation—and the corporation itself owns the real estate. (See page 61 for more on the legal ins and outs of co-ops.) If you buying a co-op—or, more accurately, shares in a co-op—you pay a monthly fee for maintenance and other building-related expenses, just as condo owners do.

Note If you buy a condominium or co-op, your monthly fees will minimize out-of-pocket costs for routine maintenance. But these kinds of housing also may require unanticipated repairs, such as fixing a crack in the community pool, resurfacing the parking lot, or scrubbing away graffiti. Or a storm may damage the building or complex, and even though insurance will cover most of the damage, the deductible has to be paid. In such cases, a special assessment, charged to each unit, pays the tab—which means you'll have to chip in.

- **Homeowners' associations.** Some developments of traditional single-family homes include lots of attractive amenities, such as a community pool, tennis courts, a clubhouse, and so on. In such communities, a homeowners' association (HOA) collects monthly or annual dues to pay for these amenities. Some HOAs charge the same dues for each home in the development, others base fees on each home's square footage or purchase price, with the owners of bigger and more expensive homes paying more.

Potential for Lost Value

As any investor or Lotto player knows, there's no such thing as a sure thing. When you invest your money, you take a risk, and that's true when you buy a home. Even though houses tend to gain value over time, sometimes (especially in the short term) they can lose value. A recent example is the U.S. housing bubble that peaked in 2005, popped in 2006, and continues to deflate in some parts of the country now. Some people who bought at the height of the bubble now find themselves with *negative equity*—they owe the lender more money than their home is worth.

Fluctuating markets represent one way a house can lose value, but other factors can have the same effect. For example, crime rates could increase in your neighborhood, or the city could build a sewage-treatment plant a block away. Developers could saturate the market with new housing developments, or a major employer could lay off employees or go out of business. You could lose your job and be unable to afford to keep the house in good repair.

Reduced Flexibility

When you're a homeowner, you can't just pack up and move when wanderlust strikes or your company transfers you to a different city. You have to continue to pay the mortgage or pay off your home altogether. That means you either open your wallet far enough to keep paying the mortgage after you move, find a tenant to pay you rent so you can pay the mortgage, or sell the house.

So now, with eyes wide open, it's time to find your new home.

2 How Much Home Can You Afford?

Now that you've decided to buy a home, your next step is to determine just how much home you can afford. Figuring out your price range can take a little time, but it's important to know what you can afford. After all, you'll be living in your house for years, and you want to sleep soundly in it, without worrying about how you'll make your next mortgage payment.

To get a price range, you have to take a look at your finances: how much income you have each month versus how much you spend. Taking a good, hard look at your budget not only helps you save for a down payment, it tells you how much you can afford in mortgage and other home-related costs each month. Reviewing your budget has another benefit. It helps you see your finances through a lender's eyes. You can see whether you look like a high-risk or a low-risk borrower and take steps to increase your chances of getting a mortgage when you're ready to buy a home.

How Much Can You Invest in a Home?

Before you start shopping for a home, you need to get a realistic sense of what you can afford. There's no point in putting your time, energy, and effort—not to mention your emotions—into looking at houses that would break your budget. Aside from the sizable down payment (Chapter 6) and closing costs (Chapter 9) that you pay up front, owning a home means recurring expenses—principal, interest, taxes, insurance, utilities, maintenance, homeowners' association fees—and occasional emergency expenses. Flip back to page 18 for an overview of what it costs to own a home.

To get a sense of what you can afford, take the time to get a clear-eyed picture of your current finances: develop a monthly budget and look at the factors that determine how much you can afford in a mortgage. With a monthly budget in hand, you can see how much you can save each month toward a down payment (and look for ways to save even more) and get a sense of how much you'd be comfortable paying in monthly mortgage payments and other recurring costs.

 Tip For a lender's opinion about how large a mortgage you can afford, get prequalified or preapproved for a loan. Page 34 tells you more.

Figure Out a Monthly Budget—and Stick to It

Sitting down to budget your monthly expenses sounds about as much fun as scrubbing the kitchen floor, but taking a realistic, clear-eyed look at your household finances is essential to understanding how much you can afford in a new home.

And don't forget that a mortgage is just one element of home-buying. You also need a down payment (Chapter 6), closing costs (Chapter 9), and funds for insurance, taxes, maintenance, and repairs. Creating a budget helps you plan for these expenses, too.

Creating a budget isn't as painful as it sounds when you break it down into these main steps:

1. Determine your current income and expenses (how much money you earn and spend each month).

2. Analyze how you spend money now.

3. Identify long-term goals (such as saving enough for a down payment on a home).

4. Reevaluate current spending in light of those goals.

5. Track your spending from month to month to measure your progress toward your goals.

So sharpen a pencil, open a new spreadsheet, or fire up your favorite money-management software and get started. Although you don't need anything more than a pencil, a piece of paper, and a calculator to figure out your budget, a spreadsheet or a money-management program can make the task easier. Mint (*www.mint.com*) and Quicken (*http://quicken.intuit.com*) both offer free online money-management tools.

 Tip You can download free household budget templates for Microsoft Excel from many websites. Try the ones at Bankrate.com (*http://tinyurl.com/yeshrvk*) and Spreadsheet123 (*http://tinyurl.com/yb3aabs*).

Determine your current income and expenses

The first step in budgeting is to figure out how much money comes into your household each month. The second step, of course, is to determine how much goes out. To do so, you need this information:

- **Your household's monthly income.** Find some recent pay stubs to get your after-tax income. (If you get paid biweekly, multiply your after-tax pay by 26—because there are 52 weeks in a year—and then divide by 12 to figure out your monthly pay.) Or you can figure out the amount by looking at your most recent income tax return: Subtract total tax (line 61 on form 1040) from your adjusted gross income (line 38) and divide by 12. And don't forget to include other sources of income: alimony, child support payments you receive, interest, or any other funds that come into your household regularly.

Tip If you're self-employed or you receive income that changes from month to month (tips, bonuses, overtime, and so on), figuring out your monthly income is a little harder than just looking at a pay stub or two. Calculate your monthly income the way lenders do, by figuring out your average monthly earnings based on the past two years. Get out your W2 or 1099 forms from the past two years, add up all the income received during that time. (If you're using 1099s, look at your last two federal and state income tax forms, and subtract the tax you paid from the total.) When you've got your total income, divide by 24. The result is your average monthly income.

- **Your household's recurring monthly expenses.** These are the bills and other expenses you pay each month: rent or mortgage payments, utilities, insurance premiums, student loan payments, car loan payments, credit card payments, tuition, alimony/child support, groceries, and so on. Some of your expenses, such as utility bills, will vary from one month to the next. In cases like that, add a year's worth of bills and divide by 12 to get the monthly average.

Tip Scrutinize recurring monthly expenses to see if you can trim some back, such as asking your credit card company to reduce your interest rate or shopping around for cheaper auto insurance. And if you can afford to pay off a loan (such as a student loan), you'll save money on interest and improve your credit score (page 39).

- **Your household's discretionary monthly expenses.** *Discretionary expenses* are the optional ones—the money you spend because you want to, not because you have to. It includes items like entertainment, eating out, clothing, gifts, and recreational shopping. This is the budget category you'll scrutinize to see where you can cut back and funnel money into a down payment.

Tip Many people are unaware of just how much money goes toward discretionary spending. Your credit card statements can help you remember where your money went, but it's also a good idea to keep a log of your spending for a week or a month. When you buy anything, from a cup of coffee on your way to work to an impulse purchase at the mall, write down what you bought and how much it cost. You might be surprised to see where your money goes.

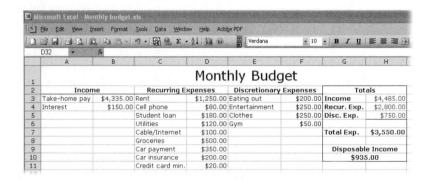

Analyze how you spend money

Add up all your sources of income, and then add up all your expenses (both recurring and discretionary). Subtract expenses from income and the result is your *disposable income*, the amount of money you have to do with as you please:

- If the number is positive, you're saving more than you spend each month. You can put this money toward your long-term financial goals.

- If the number is negative, you're spending more than you earn. You need to make some changes if you want to buy a home.

 Tip Besides cutting back on spending to save money, you can also look for ways to bring more money into your household. A second, part-time job, for example, could be a way to make your savings grow faster. Or maybe it's time to ask your boss for a raise (explain that you're saving to buy a home).

Identify long-term goals

What are your long-term financial goals? You may have several, such as saving for a wedding or a vacation, paying college tuition (for yourself or your kids), or beefing up your retirement funds. For the sake of simplicity, assume that your primary long-term goal is saving for your down payment (Chapter 6) and the closing costs (Chapter 9) you need to buy a new home, which can easily add up to 25 percent of the purchase price.

What's your timeframe for buying a home? Multiply your monthly disposable income by number of months between now and your target purchase date. Add that number to any savings you've already set aside. This gives you an idea of how much you can put toward a down payment and closing costs (see page 233 for a breakdown) if your current financial picture remains unchanged. (Page 146 offers strategies for finding money for your down payment.)

Reevaluate current spending

If you're spending more than you earn each month, or if you want to save more quickly, you need to identify ways to spend less. Determine how much you want to save each month, and adjust your current spending so you can reach that goal.

Start with your discretionary expenses. What can you trim or do without? You might eat out less often, trade movie night for a night of videos at home, or give yourself a monthly clothing budget to prevent impulse buying. You might be surprised at how much you can save once you start looking for ways to limit spending on nonessentials.

But don't stop there. Scrutinize what you spend on necessities, too. You won't be able to reduce some of them, like car payments, but others offer opportunities to save. Here are a few examples of ways to spend less on the things you have to buy each month:

- Switch to a lower-tier cable package with fewer premium channels—or cut out cable altogether.
- Switch to a less costly cell phone plan.
- Adjust your thermostat by a few degrees to minimize heating and cooling costs.
- Cancel subscriptions to magazines that pile up unread on the coffee table.
- Buy cheaper cuts of meat or replace some meat with less expensive but filling alternatives, such as pasta and vegetarian dishes.
- Avoid overpriced and nutritionally poor convenience foods.
- At the grocery store, compare unit prices and buy the economy size or store brand when it's cheaper than a national brand.
- Save gas by eliminating unnecessary trips and by walking, cycling, or taking public transportation when possible.
- Review your insurance policies to make sure you're not buying more coverage than you need.
- If you rent your current home, move to less expensive quarters.

These suggestions should get you thinking about other ways you can lower your monthly bills and put the savings toward your long-term financial goals.

Track your spending

To stay within your budget, keep track of what you spend each month (see the sample budget on the next page). Set aside time to sit down and compare your actual expenses with what you budgeted for the month. Then, tweak your budget as necessary. If you're not quite reaching your savings goal, go over your expenses again and look for places where you can spend less. If you're spending less than you budgeted, you can either add the surplus to your savings or splurge a little—just for this month.

 Tip To track your spending, try the free budget planner spreadsheet from Spreadsheets123 at *http://tinyurl.com/y9cl92k*.

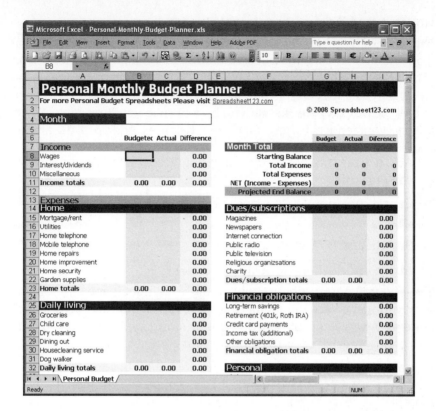

	B	C	D	E	F	G	H	I
Personal Monthly Budget Planner								
For more Personal Budget Spreadsheets Please visit Spreadsheet123.com								
						© 2008 Spreadsheet123.com		
Month								
	Budgetec	Actual	Difference			Budget	Actual	Diference
Income					**Month Total**			
Wages			0.00		Starting Balance			
Interest/dividends			0.00		Total Income	0	0	0
Miscellaneous			0.00		Total Expenses	0	0	0
Income totals	0.00	0.00	0.00		NET (Income - Expenses)	0	0	0
					Projected End Balance	0	0	0
Expenses								
Home					**Dues/subscriptions**			
Mortgage/rent			0.00		Magazines			0.00
Utilities			0.00		Newspapers			0.00
Home telephone			0.00		Internet connection			0.00
Mobile telephone			0.00		Public radio			0.00
Home repairs			0.00		Public television			0.00
Home improvement			0.00		Religious organizsations			0.00
Home security			0.00		Charity			0.00
Garden supplies			0.00		Dues/subscription totals	0.00	0.00	0.00
Home totals	0.00	0.00	0.00					
					Financial obligations			
Daily living					Long-term savings			0.00
Groceries			0.00		Retirement (401k, Roth IRA)			0.00
Child care			0.00		Credit card payments			0.00
Dry cleaning			0.00		Income tax (additional)			0.00
Dining out			0.00		Other obligations			0.00
Housecleaning service			0.00		Financial obligation totals	0.00	0.00	0.00
Dog walker			0.00					
Daily living totals	0.00	0.00	0.00		**Personal**			

How Much Mortgage Can You Afford?

You may have heard of a formula for determining the maximum amount you can afford in a mortgage: Take your household's gross annual income and multiply it by 2.5. It's quick, it's easy—and it's probably misleading. The "two-and-a-half-times-income" formula isn't a bad guideline if you can afford a 20 percent down payment and you don't have much debt. But it leaves out important variables that affect how much you can realistically pay back each month. This section shows you what to ask yourself when you sit down to estimate your price range for a home.

What's your monthly gross income?

Lenders look at this number to figure out your debt-to-income ratio (page 36). To do this, they consider your monthly gross income—that's the amount you earn before taxes and other payroll deductions are taken out. So grab your pay stubs and check out your gross income; you can also get the amount from your latest federal income tax return (line 38 on form 1040) or W2 form (box 1). Divide by 12 to get your monthly gross.

How much debt do you currently have?

This amount is the other side of the all-important debt-to-income ratio (page 36). Using your most recent credit card, bank, and other financial statements, see how much you currently owe on outstanding loans and credit card balances. Or check your credit report, which tallies your existing debt. (The box on page 45 tells you how to snag your free copy.) You can also call your lenders to get your current balances. Add up all the amounts you owe to figure out your total debt.

 Tip When you know your gross monthly income and your current debt, you can figure out your debt-to-income ratio. This is how lenders determine how much you can afford to borrow. Page 37 shows you how.

What are your other monthly expenses?

If you figured out your household's monthly budget (page 26), you know what you spend each month for basic necessities, entertainment, and other items. When you subtract your rent or mortgage payment, you get an idea of how much it costs to maintain your current lifestyle.

Homeowners have several expenses to cope with beyond their monthly mortgage payments, as page 18 lists. Estimate those amounts in your monthly expenses to make sure you'll have money for maintenance and other costs.

How much can you afford to pay up front?

When it comes to your down payment, size does matter, as Chapter 6 explains. These days, people continue to default on their loans, and many lenders require a down payment of 20 percent of a home's purchase price. But the down payment is only part of the cash you need to get a mortgage. You need to budget an additional 3 percent to 6 percent of the loan amount to pay closing costs and other home-buying–related expenses (Chapter 9 details these expenses).

 Tip Chapter 6 lists strategies for coming up with a down payment. If a 20 percent down payment seems out of reach, you might qualify for an FHA-insured loan, which lets you buy a home with as little as 3.5 percent down. Page 148 explains FHA loans.

What's the property tax rate?

Besides the principal and interest you pay your lender each month, you also have to pay local property taxes. Property taxes pay your share of local services—police, fire, schools, road maintenance, government administration, social services, and so on. The amount is usually figured as a percentage of a property's value as assessed by your local government—that percentage is the *property tax rate*. You might pay property taxes to your city or town, your county, the school district the property occupies—or a combination of these entities.

Property tax rates vary widely around the country. Even neighboring towns or counties can charge very different property tax rates. Find out the local tax rates for the area you want to buy in—ask your real estate agent or contact the local tax assessment office. And bear in mind that the tax amounts paid by the current owner might not be a good estimate of your property taxes after you buy the house. Many locales reassess properties when they change hands, and they do so based on current market rates. So if the current owner has been living in her home for a while, property taxes could take a big jump when you get the front-door key. Call the local tax office to find out whether they assess taxes on the full purchase price or a percentage. Then, multiply a property's price (or whatever percentage the taxman uses) by the tax rate to find out how much property taxes will cost.

 Note According to Kiplinger.com, Alabama, Arkansas, Louisiana, Mississippi, and West Virginia have the lowest median real-estate taxes in the country, while Connecticut, New Hampshire, New Jersey, New York, and Rhode Island have the highest.

What are current interest rates?

Along with the principal repayment, a loan's *interest rate* determines the size of your monthly payments (as well as how much you'll pay the lender for the privilege of borrowing the money). The lower the interest rate, the lower your monthly payments—and the less you'll pay over the life of the loan.

If you opt for a fixed-rate mortgage (page 163), your interest rate remains steady for the life of the loan. If you choose an adjustable-rate mortgage (ARM, page 164), the interest rate fluctuates over time. And when the interest rate increases, so do your monthly payments.

What are your future plans?

Polish up your crystal ball and peer five years into the future. Do you antici-pate any major lifestyle changes? If you plan to go back to school or start a family, you'll have some hefty additional expenses. By looking ahead now (and maybe going for a smaller mortgage), you can plan for future expenses and avoid being squeezed down the road.

 Tip Use an online calculator, such as Homefair's (*http://tinyurl.com/ydgkmbf*) or Bankrate.com's (*http://tinyurl.com/yjgnoxf*) to get an idea of how much you can afford to borrow to buy a home.

Get Prequalified or Preapproved

You wouldn't go on a shopping spree with nothing but a checkbook and no idea of how much money is in your account. For first-time homebuyers, shopping for a home without getting preapproved (or at least prequali-fied) amounts to the same thing. It's hard to shop for something when you don't know what you can afford.

To *prequalify*, you give a loan officer information about your income and finances. Based on that information (without checking it), the loan officer estimates how much you can afford to borrow. Because prequalification is an informal process, without verification of the information you submit, it's not binding on the lender—in other words, there's no guarantee that the lender will approve the amount for which you've prequalified when you formally apply for a mortgage. But prequalification doesn't cost anything, and it gives you a ballpark idea of what you can afford.

Getting *preapproved* is a lengthier process that takes a closer look at your finances. When you apply for preapproval, the lender verifies the financial information you give—info about your employment, cash on hand, credit, debt, and so on—and gives you a letter that specifies the maximum loan amount you qualify for. To get preapproved, you may have to pay a fee, and the lender will check all the information you submit. But preapproval is the lender's guarantee that, as long as you don't make any drastic changes to your financial picture (such as losing your job or taking out a large loan), you can get a mortgage up to the stated amount.

Both prequalification and preapproval give you an idea of your price range when shopping for a home. The difference is in the level of commitment: prequalification is a "maybe"; preapproval is a "yes."

Preapproval offers some real advantages to home buyers:

- **It shows you mean business.** If a seller is deciding among multiple offers, a preapproval letter carries some weight, especially if the seller is in a hurry to sell. Preapproval means that the seller won't encounter a nasty surprise when the chosen buyer can't qualify for a mortgage.

- **You can shop realistically.** When you're preapproved, you won't waste time looking at homes outside of your price range—and that can save you the heartache of falling in love with a house, only to find out later that you can't afford it.

- **It can speed up the closing process.** Because your financial information is already verified, closing can happen faster than if you hadn't been preapproved. You'll still have to get the home appraised and inspected, but you can shave a couple of weeks off the mortgage processing time.

For most house hunters, preapproval is a great idea. But if you decide to get preapproved, keep these issues in mind:

- **Preapproval isn't forever.** Your preapproval letter expires after a set period of time, often 90 days. If you're still shopping after that, you have to get the letter updated. If your financial situation changes, your preapproval amount may change, too.

- **You've been approved, but the property may not be.** Before a lender gives you a loan, you have to get an independent appraisal to confirm the home's value. If the lender determines that you've offered more than the home is worth, you may not get the loan—even though the purchase price is within your preapproved range.

- **Preapproval specifies a maximum loan amount.** Just because the bank has approved you up to a certain amount doesn't mean you should apply for the maximum. You get preapproved for the amount the lender determines you can afford, but you may not be comfortable paying that amount. Keep in mind other expenses associated with home ownership (page 18 gives you a rundown of those) and don't stretch yourself to the limit just because the lender said you could afford it.

Tip When you make an offer on a house (Chapter 10), it's a good idea to include a copy of your preapproval letter, because it shows the seller that you've already got financial backing. If your lender has preapproved you for more than you're offering, ask the lender to write a preapproval letter that mentions the *exact* amount of your offer—not the upper limit of your preapproval. If you're offering $200,000 and the seller sees that you're preapproved for $250,000, he might hold out for a higher price.

What Lenders Look For

In the previous sections, you looked at your finances from a consumer's (your) perspective. Now it's time to look at those finances from a *lender's* point of view. After all, the lender makes the ultimate decision to approve or deny your loan.

Lenders collect a lot of information about you, but they really want to know just one thing: how likely you are to make your mortgage payments until you pay off your loan. Understanding how lenders evaluate mortgage applications helps you present your household finances in the best light—and keeps you from being disappointed by unrealistic expectations.

Income Stability

Lenders want assurance that your income is steady and sufficient to pay back your loan. Income includes your salary or wages, but also commissions, royalties, alimony you receive, Social Security payments, disability payments, and any other cash that comes into your home. Be prepared to submit copies of your W2 forms or federal income tax returns for the past two or three years.

Your Debt-to-Income Ratio

Your lender uses a formula to determine how much you can afford to pay for principal and interest each month, based on how much you earn and how much you owe. This formula starts with your monthly gross income; that's the figure you determined on page 31.

Next, the lender uses that income to determine the maximum monthly debt you can carry, both for your monthly mortgage payment (PITI, for principal, interest, taxes, and insurance, page 19) and for your other monthly debt payments, such as those for credit cards, student loans, car loans, and so on.

Most lenders use the 28/36 rule to identify low-risk borrowers, their favorite kind:

- Your PITI shouldn't exceed 28 percent of your monthly gross income.

- Your *total* monthly debt (including your PITI payments) shouldn't exceed 36 percent of your monthly gross income.

To figure out your debt-to-income ratio, start with your gross monthly income. Multiply that amount by 0.28 to find the maximum PITI you can afford. Now, go back to your gross monthly income and multiply it by 0.36 to find your maximum monthly debt. The following table gives you some examples, and the worksheets that follow will help you calculate your own debt-to-income ratio.

Gross monthly income	Maximum monthly PITI payment	Maximum total monthly debt
$2,500	$700	$900
$3,000	$840	$1,080
$4,000	$1,120	$1,440
$5,000	$1,400	$1,800
$7,500	$2,100	$2,700
$10,000	$2,800	$3,600

Because PITI is included in total monthly debt—which can't be more than 36 percent of your gross monthly income—the 28 percent ceiling on monthly PITI payments applies only if you have little or no existing debt. The more debt you have, lenders reason, the less PITI you can afford.

Affordability Worksheet 1: Monthly Income and Expenses

Monthly income (before taxes)			
	Borrower	Co-Borrower	Total
Employment income	$ _____	$ _____	$ _____
Overtime	_____	_____	_____
Commissions	_____	_____	_____
Interest/dividends	_____	_____	_____
Other	_____	_____	_____
Other	_____	_____	_____
Other	_____	_____	_____
Total monthly income			$ _____

Worksheet continued on next page

Affordability Worksheet 1: Monthly Income and Expenses (continued)

Monthly payments on existing obligations			
Automobile lease/loan	$ _____	$ _____	$ _____
Student loan	_____	_____	_____
Credit cards	_____	_____	_____
Automobile insurance	_____	_____	_____
Other insurance	_____	_____	_____
Alimony	_____	_____	_____
Child support	_____	_____	_____
Other	_____	_____	_____
Other	_____	_____	_____
Other	_____	_____	_____
Total monthly payments			$ _____
Monthly housing expenses for new loan			
Mortgage payment (principal & interest)			$ _____
Real estate taxes			_____
Insurance premiums			_____
Total monthly housing expense			$ _____

Affordability Worksheet 2: Your Debt-to-Income Ratio

Take the dollar amounts from Worksheet 1 and:	
For the housing expense ratio	
Divide "Total monthly housing expense" by "Total monthly income"	$ _____
For the all debt payments ratio	
Divide (the sum of "Total monthly payments" and "Total monthly housing expense") by "Total monthly income"	$ _____

Tip Lenders look at total debt and PITI when they determine your debt-to-income ratio. They don't take your other expenses into account—things like maintenance and repairs, food, clothing, and entertainment. But *you* can't ignore those expenses. Make sure you factor them in to your own assessment of how much you can afford to pay each month.

Your Home's Loan-to-Value Ratio

Another important factor lenders consider in deciding whether to approve your mortgage is the home's loan-to-value (LTV) ratio. This number, expressed as a percentage, indicates how much you're borrowing relative to what the home is worth. Basically, the LTV ratio reflects the size of your down payment (Chapter 6).

Lenders use this formula to figure out the LTV ratio:

```
LTV ratio = Mortgage amount ÷ Property's appraised value
```

So if you want to borrow $200,000 to buy a home worth $250,000, your LTV ratio is 0.8, or 80 percent.

The bigger the up-front investment you make in your home, the better you look to lenders. That's why many lenders look for an LTV ratio of 80 percent or lower: It means you're putting down at least 20 percent of the purchase price as your investment in the home. A higher LTV ratio (that is, a number above 80 percent) makes you look like a riskier borrower, because you're investing less of your own money in the purchase. In that case, if the lender approves your loan, you'll probably have to buy private mortgage insurance (page 146). With a lower LTV ratio (say, 70 percent or below), you may be able to streamline the approval process or get a more favorable interest rate.

For a lender to determine your LTV ratio, you need to have an independent appraiser determine your home's value based on the current market (page 227) and you need to provide documentation showing how much money you have for a down payment.

Your Credit Score and Credit History

Your borrowing and spending habits don't take place in a vacuum. Three major U.S. credit bureaus—Equifax, Experian, and TransUnion—track how you manage your credit. Financial institutions and other businesses rely on these companies to evaluate you as a borrower by looking at how much credit you have available, how much you owe, and how responsible you are about paying on time.

A credit report is an overview of your credit history, which documents how much money you've borrowed in the past and how good you are at repaying it. It also lists late payments, any bills referred to collection agencies, and any bankruptcies you declared. Your credit history is also the basis for your credit score, a number that rates your credit-worthiness based on past behavior and current debt. The higher your score, the more lenders see you as someone who's likely to repay their loan. No matter which bureau issues your credit report, it contains both your credit history and credit score.

Each credit bureau calculates credit scores differently, but the best-known and most widely used algorithm is the FICO method, devised by the Fair Isaac Corporation (a company founded by Bill Fair and Earl Isaac in 1956 and now known as FICO). FICO scores range from 300 to 850, and higher is better. Your FICO score gives you a quick snapshot of how lenders view you as a potential borrower.

Tip Your FICO score may differ among the three credit bureaus. That's because each has its own database, gets information from different creditors, and receives that information from creditors at different times. For this reason, it's a good idea to check your credit report from all three bureaus before you apply for a mortgage so you can catch and address any major discrepancies. The box on page 45 tells you how to get a free copy of your credit report.

What goes into your FICO score

Credit agencies figure your FICO score using several factors, and they assign each a particular "weight" in the final score (see the pie chart below). This section shows you what FICO takes into account.

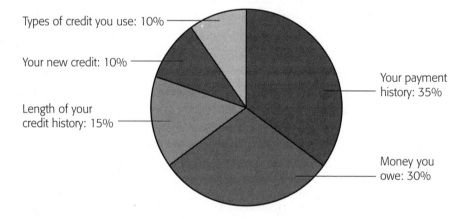

Your payment history

Understandably, the most important factor in determining your credit worthiness is your reputation for paying back the money you've borrowed—it accounts for 35 percent of your FICO score and takes the following into account:

- **Payment history for the different kinds of accounts you have.** Paying at least the minimum amount and paying it on time works in your favor in these categories. These accounts may include the following:

- — Credit cards you get from banks, such as Visa, MasterCard, and American Express.

- — Credit cards you have with retail stores like Macy's or Sears.

- — Installment loans, where you pay off a balance in regular increments, such as a car loans or a student loan.

- — Consumer finance loans, which are subprime loans given out by companies that aren't banks. Consumer finance companies don't accept deposits, and they provide loans (usually at higher interest rates) directly to consumers who don't qualify for bank loans.

 Note Too many consumer finance loans is a red flag that can lower your overall score, though paying them back responsibly over time can raise your score.

- — Existing mortgages (if any).

- **Delinquencies.** Missing payments for any of your accounts lowers your score. Your FICO score reflects:

  - — How much is past due.

  - — How long any delinquent accounts have been past due.

  - — How many past-due accounts you have.

- **How recently you've had delinquencies.** If you ran into a rough patch in the past and couldn't meet your payments, you need to show that you've resolved the problem and have stayed current on your payments since then.

- **Adverse public records.** FICO scoring looks for signs of legal troubles, including bankruptcies, foreclosures, any judgments against you, liens, lawsuits, wage attachments, and so on. On the plus side, the score takes into account how much time has passed since the infraction, the amount of money involved, and how well you've met your financial obligations since then.

 Note Bankruptcy filings stay on your credit history for 7 to 10 years, depending on the type of bankruptcy you declare.

- **Collection items.** If a creditor sends your past-due account to a collection agency, it's a mark against you. Again, if this happened in the past, your score improves if your payments stay current since then.

- **How many accounts you've paid as agreed.** Keeping the terms of an agreement with any creditor is important to your score.

Money you owe

How much money do you currently owe, and for what kinds of accounts? The answers to those questions add up to 30 percent of your FICO score. In this category, your score reflects these issues:

- **How much you owe.** FICO scores take into consideration how much money you owe on your various accounts. Even if you pay off your entire credit-card balance each month, be aware that your credit report may show that you owe something—in this case, it's usually the balance on your most recent statement.

- **How much you owe on specific types of accounts.** Your score takes into account how much money you owe for different kinds of accounts, such as credit cards and installment loans.

- **Whether some kinds of accounts have balances.** For certain kinds of accounts, having a small balance and making regular payments is better for your score than having no balance at all.

- **How many accounts have balances.** If you've got a lot of accounts and you owe money on all or most of them, this can be a red flag. Banks may think that you're trying to stretch your credit too far.

- **How much of your credit is revolving credit.** Revolving credit is an open line of credit that lets you borrow an amount up to a certain limit and pay it back from month to month—credit cards are an example. If you've got a lot of revolving credit on your report—for example, if you've got several credit cards and most of them are close to being maxed out—it can lower your score.

- **How much you owe on installment loans, compared to the amount you borrowed.** This is expressed as a percentage; for example, if you borrowed $20,000 for a student loan and you've paid back $5,000 of that loan, you currently owe 75 percent of the money you borrowed (plus interest). Steady payment of an installment loan tells banks that you can manage debt well.

Length of your credit history

The longer you successfully manage debt, the better a loan prospect you are; the length of your credit history counts for 10 percent of your credit score. You won't necessarily be penalized if you're new to the credit game—you can still get a high FICO score if these factors look good:

- **How long you've had credit.** Your score reflects how long you've had your oldest account and the average age of all your accounts.

- **How long you've had specific kinds of credit.** Showing that you can handle different kinds of credit over time—for example, a student loan plus a credit card or two—improves your score.

- **How much time has passed since an account was active.** A credit card account that's been inactive for a while carries less weight than a card you've used recently, even if you had the inactive card longer.

Your new credit

"New credit" comprises accounts you opened or loans you took out recently. From a lender's perspective, opening a lot of accounts over a short period of time is a red flag, so this kind of activity can lower your credit score. The new credit component of your FICO score weighs these factors:

- **How many new accounts you have.** If your wallet is bursting with lots of shiny new credit cards, you haven't yet proved that you can use those cards responsibly. This part of your score considers both the number of new accounts you have and the percentage of your overall credit history those new accounts represent.

- **How many times your credit report has been requested in the past year.** When you apply for credit and a financial institution requests your credit report, that request becomes part of your credit history. A large number of such requests in the recent past suggests that you may be getting ready to ramp up your debt—a warning sign that your score reflects.

 Note Smart consumers shop for the best rate when they look for a loan—and that can mean that multiple lenders request your credit report within a short time, even though you're planning to take out only one loan. FICO deals with rate shopping two ways. First, it treats all credit report requests within a two-week period as a single request, no matter how many lenders request your report. Second, FICO ignores all report requests made in the 30-day period before it calculates your score. That means report requests won't affect your score as you look for the best rate.

- **How much time has passed since you opened an account.** FICO breaks this information down by type of account (revolving credit, installment loan, and so on).

- **How much time has passed since a financial institution last requested your credit report.** You don't want to look as though you've been turned down for credit or applied for credit on a whim, so the longer the interval between credit applications, the better. This part of your score takes into account only those requests you made in the past year.

- **Whether you've corrected past problems.** If you've run into trouble with past-due accounts or had other credit-related problems, you're not doomed to a low credit score forever. By managing your credit responsibly and paying on time, you can rebuild your creditworthiness and improve your FICO score. Raising a low score takes time, effort, and careful attention to managing your money, but you can do it.

Types of credit you use

The type of credit you have (bank credit cards, store cards, installment loans, mortgages, and consumer finance accounts), how many accounts of each type you have, and recent information about those accounts make up 10 percent of your score.

What your FICO score *doesn't* include

By now, you may feel like FICO shines a searchlight into every corner of your life. But there *is* information FICO doesn't factor into your credit score:

- **Your race, religion, national origin, sex, or marital status.** The federal government doesn't allow any credit bureau to factor this information into a credit score.

- **Whether you receive public assistance.** If you get help from the government to make ends meet, such as food stamps or housing assistance, credit companies can't factor that information into your score; the federal government prohibits it.

- **Your age.**

- **Your salary, occupation, title, employer, date employed, or employment history.**

- **Where you live.**

- **The interest rate charged on a particular account.**

- **Child/family support obligations.**

Getting Your Free Credit Reports

The Fair Credit Reporting Act of 2003 entitles you to one free copy of your credit report *each year* from *each* of the three big credit bureaus: Equifax, Experian, and TransUnion. Get a copy of yours at least six months before you plan to apply for a mortgage so you can check for errors or other problems and take steps to correct them before you apply (see page 48 to learn how to do that).

There are three ways to request a copy of your credit report:

- **Online.** Visit *www.annualcreditreport.com* and fill out the online form. Note that this site is the only authorized website for getting your free credit report. Others (try Googling "free credit report" and see how many hits you get) will try to sell you a service or collect confidential personal information—don't fall for it.

- **By phone.** Call 1-877-322-8228 to order your free credit report by phone, and you'll receive a copy in the mail.

- **By mail.** Fill out the official Annual Credit Report Request Form and mail it to Annual Credit Report Request Service, P.O. Box 105281, Atlanta, GA 30348-5281. You can download and print out the form from the FTC's website: Go to *www.ftc.gov* and click Consumer Information, then select Credit & Loans, choose Your Rights: Credit Reporting, and click the Annual Credit Report Request Form link. (For a more direct route to the Annual Credit Report Form link, go to *http://tinyurl.com/43e6mo*.)

The big advantage of requesting your credit report online is that you get the report immediately. Phone and mail requests take up to 15 days to process, so you may have to wait two or three weeks for your report.

Whichever method you use, you need to provide your name, address, Social Security number, and date of birth. In addition, if you moved in the last two years, you'll have to give your previous address. If you're ordering online or by phone, for security reasons you may be asked for a piece of information that only you would know, like your most recent payment to a credit card or utility account, so have your bills, checkbook, or bank statement handy.

Whether you request your free report from each bureau simultaneously or spread them out over time depends on why you're checking your score. If you want to compare reports to look for discrepancies, order all three at once. If, on the other hand, you want to see how your score changes over time without having to pay for additional reports, spread out your requests over a few months. (Just keep in mind that there are likely to be variations in the scores produced by the different bureaus.)

- **Rental agreements.**

- **Certain kinds of requests for your credit report.** Not all requests for your credit report get factored into your score. These are exempt:

  - **Requests made by you to check your credit report.**

  - **Requests from employers or potential employers.**

  - **Promotional inquiries.** You know those offers for preapproved credit cards that show up in the mail? You didn't apply for that credit—a lender was hoping you'd be tempted to apply.

  - **Administrative inquiries.** Sometimes a lender with which you already have an account will request your credit report while reviewing your account.

- **Any information that's not found in your credit report.** FICO scores information that's present in your credit report. It doesn't collect any information beyond what's in the report.

- **Any information that is not proven to predict future credit performance.** An example is your income. Although people with higher incomes may be better able to pay back debt, income alone is not a good predictor of whether you'll pay back a loan according to the credit terms you agree to.

- **Whether you're getting credit counseling.** The mere fact that you're getting credit counseling to better manage your debt cannot affect your FICO score. Be aware, though, that the situation that caused you to seek credit counseling (such as late payments or defaults) and actions that you take as a result of credit counseling can both affect your score.

How Lenders Use Your FICO Score

Your FICO score is just one little number but, as the previous section details, a lot goes into that number. Lenders take your FICO score into account along with numerous other factors—your income, savings, credit history, and all that other information they ask for on the application (page 208). But the score alone is a good indicator of how creditworthy you appear to potential lenders. The following table shows score ranges, along with their associated ratings and what they mean for you.

FICO score	Rating	If your score falls within this range...
760–850	Excellent	You may qualify for the best financing terms.
700–759	Very good	You may receive favorable financing.
660–699	Good	You should qualify for most loans.
620–659	Fair	You may qualify for a loan, but you'll pay significantly higher interest.
Below 620	Poor	You may not qualify for a loan.

 Note Your credit score may affect the size of the down payment a lender requires. If your score falls below 700, lenders may require a larger down payment before they'll approve your loan.

Mortgage interest rates increase as credit scores drop. The following table and chart (based on rates from December 2009) show a difference of nearly 1.6 percentage points between the highest and lowest credit scores.

FICO score	Annual Percentage Rate (APR)
760–850	4.605
700–759	4.827
680–699	5.004
660–679	5.218
640–659	5.648
620–639	6.194

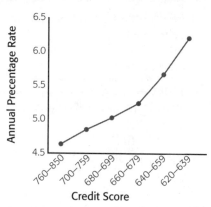

While a difference of 1.6 percentage points may not sound like much, those points make a huge difference over time. The table below shows how much it would cost you to pay back a $200,000 loan over 30 years at the APRs associated with each FICO score range. Over the life of the loan, that 1.6 percent difference will cost you more than $70,000.

Annual Percentage Rate	Monthly payment	Total interest paid over 30 years
4.605	$1,026	$169,319
4.827	$1,053	$178,935
5.004	$1,074	$186,688
5.218	$1,100	$196,161
5.648	$1,154	$215,519
6.194	$1,224	$240,697

Note Here's a compelling reason to check your score. In a 2004 study, U.S. PIRG (the national federation of state-level Public Interest Research Groups) found that 79 percent of credit reports contained at least one error, ranging from minor mistakes in personal data (such as a misspelled name) to serious errors that, if uncorrected, could lead to being turned down for a loan.

Improve Your Chances of Getting a Loan

Before you apply for a mortgage, improve your chances of approval by putting your financial house in order.

- **Improve your FICO score.** If you've got a blot on your credit history that's pulling down your score—or if you just want to bump up a "good" score to a "very good" or "excellent" rating—take steps to improve your score well before you apply for a loan. Because your FICO score reflects your behavior as a borrower over time, it can take months or even years for a score to improve. Follow these tips to move up the FICO scale:

  - **Pay your bills on time.** If you tend to forget exactly when each bill is due, set up automatic withdrawals to make sure payments get made when they should.

  - **If you're behind in your payments, get caught up as soon as possible—and then pay on time.** The longer you keep your accounts current, the more your score improves.

  - **Reduce your credit card balances.** High balances on revolving accounts pull down your score. If you're carrying a high balance on one or more cards, pay down the amount you owe.

  - **Reestablish a good payment record.** If you've run into trouble with credit accounts in the past, open a new account and be meticulous about using it responsibly—don't borrow too much and be strict about making payments on time. It takes time to rebuild good credit, so be aware that it may take years for your score to recover.

- **Don't quit your job.** Lenders look for income stability. If you're a job-hopper, or if you leave a job shortly before you apply for a mortgage, you may look like a higher risk than if you've been employed consistently for the last several years.

- **Reduce your overall debt.** As page 36 explains, lenders don't like total monthly debt that exceeds 36 percent of your gross monthly income. If you carry a lot of debt, the bank will scale back the amount of money it's willing to lend you. Reducing your debt makes you look like a better risk, and the debt won't squeeze your monthly PITI too far below its 28 percent ceiling.

- **Spend small.** The flip side of reducing your debt is making sure you don't increase it. For at least six months before you apply for a loan, avoid buying big-ticket items, such as a new car or a washer/dryer set or anything else you need to buy on credit.

- **Boost your down payment.** As you'll see in Chapter 6, lenders like to see hefty down payments, because the greater the investment you make out of your own pocket, the less likely you are to default. If you can put down more than 20 percent toward the purchase of your home, you'll find it easier to get a loan than with a lower down payment.

- **Don't apply for a lot of new credit.** As page 43 explains, lenders look at how long you've maintained your accounts and want to see responsible repayment over time. Opening a lot of new accounts at once may make you look desperate for some quick cash. It also affects your debt-to-income ratio (page 36).

- **Don't cancel existing credit cards.** Lenders are interested in how much money you currently owe in relation to the credit you have available. This is called the credit-utilization ratio. Say you've got three credit cards, each with a $10,000 credit limit. That means you've got $30,000 in available credit. If you have a $7,000 balance on one of those cards, a $2,000 balance on the second, and a zero balance on the third, you're using 30 percent of your available credit. But if you cancel the zero-balance card, your available credit drops to $20,000, which makes your credit-utilization ratio soar to 45 percent. Using a higher percentage of your available credit makes you look riskier to lenders.

 Tip Watch free videos with advice from a former FICO executive about how to improve your credit score at *www.videocreditscore.com*.

3 Choose Your Style of Home and Neighborhood

Before you head to the grocery store, you probably make a shopping list of all the items you want. That helps you stay focused, limits impulse buys, and ensures you don't forget to pick up milk, eggs, or the necessary ingredients for Friday's dinner party.

You need to be similarly prepared when you shop for a house. After all, you can't run back to the store to pick up another bedroom, and you can't return your house for a refund if you find it doesn't fit your lifestyle.

This chapter helps you figure out what you want in a new home. You start by looking at how you live now and how your lifestyle might change over the next several years. Then you'll consider the housing options available and what you want in a neighborhood. From there, you'll create a wish list and prioritize it. Then, as you begin touring homes, you'll have a clear sense of what you're looking for.

Your Lifestyle—Now and Down the Road

How do you live? Do you thrive on the energy of a city—the restaurants, culture, shopping, and nightlife? Or do you prefer the peace and privacy of a country home? Do you have (or are you planning to have) kids who need room to play, friends down the block, and good schools? Do you have animals to care for or hobbies (like woodworking or restoring cars) to accommodate? Are you an avid gardener, or would you rather have someone else do the yard work?

Take out a piece of paper and note the things you like best about where and how you live now, along with the things that drive you nuts. The former are aspects of your current home that fit with your lifestyle that you'll want to add to your wish list (see page 77). The latter are just as important negatives that you want to add to your "don't want" list later in this chapter (see page 78).

Once you do that, think about your long-term plans. On average, homeowners stay in their homes for five to seven years. How you live today is likely to change during that time. If you're single, will you marry and have kids? If you have kids now, will they be leaving home in a few years? Thinking about how your life may change helps you choose a home that accommodates those changes.

Your Style of Home

When you're in the market for a new home, you face a bewildering variety of choices. There are single-family houses in a huge variety of styles; you need to know the difference between a condo, a townhouse, and a co-op. And what do "stick-built," "manufactured," and "modular" mean?

This section describes your choices in the style of your home, explaining the look, types of ownership possible, and advantages and disadvantages of each.

Single-Family House

Close your eyes for a moment and conjure up your idea of the word home. If you picture a house with a yard surrounded by a white picket fence, two-car garage, garden, and swing set, you're probably in the market for a single-family house. This freestanding structure (no neighbors over your head or on the other side of a wall) sits on its own piece of land (called a *lot*). For many buyers, the emphasis in single-family homes is on family: It's the place you raise your family, from furnishing the nursery to celebrating holidays and birthdays to taking prom photos in front of the rose trellis.

In urban areas, you may see single-family homes referred to as detached (standalone homes), semi-detached (side-by-side homes that share one internal wall), or row houses (townhouse homes like those described on page 61).

Single-family homes come in many styles. Here are some popular ones:

- **A-frame.** A two-story house that gets its name from the steep-sloped roof that gives the building a triangular shape, making it look like the letter A. The roof plunges from a peak almost to the ground. A-frames frequently have many large windows and are popular vacation homes (think ski resorts).

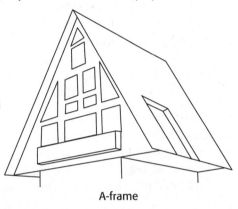

A-frame

 As you shop for a home, you'll encounter many architectural terms, some of which may be unfamiliar to you. Page 112 defines common architectural terms.

- **Bungalow.** Bungalow comes from the Indian word bangalo, which means "in the Bengal style." In India, a bungalow is a single-story thatched or tiled house surrounded by a wide veranda. In the U.S., bungalow refers to a small house of one or one-and-a-half stories, often without a basement.

Bungalow

- **Cape Cod.** As its name implies, this house style originated in New England, but you'll find it throughout the country today. A Cape is a wood-framed house with a square or rectangular footprint, with one-and-a-half stories and a steep, sloping roof. Capes often have a central chimney and, sometimes, dormer windows to let in light upstairs. A Cape's exterior is often finished with clapboard siding or shingles.

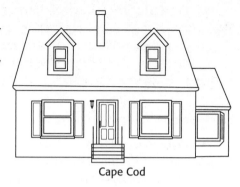
Cape Cod

- **Craftsman.** This architectural style, popular during the first three decades of the 20th century, reflects the American Arts and Crafts movement, which emphasized handcrafted, rather than mass-produced, goods. Craftsman homes feature low-pitched rooflines with overhanging eaves and often have a front porch with square columns supporting its roof.

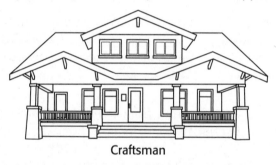
Craftsman

- **Colonial.** In general, this term refers to early American architecture from the British colonial period. Colonials are two-story, rectangular houses built of wood or brick, with a pitched roof. Colonial encompasses several distinct styles, often influenced by the colonizers of a particular region:

  — **Dutch colonial.** This style has one-and-a-half or two stories and a gambrel roof (the style of roof you find on a barn), often with dormer windows.

Dutch Colonial

— **French colonial.** You find this style in parts of North America that were originally colonized by the French, including Louisiana, the Mississippi River valley, and parts of the Caribbean. Porches are central to the design, as are low-pitched roofs that flare at the ends and cover the porch.

— **Garrison colonial.** The second story of a garrison colonial juts out slightly over the first.

— **Georgian.** With a rect-angular footprint, these symmetrical homes usual-ly feature three or five tall windows across the up-per story's front, a center door, a pitched roof with little or no overhang, and a central chimney (or one at each end of the house).

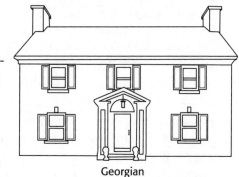
Georgian

Georgians are often made of brick or have clapboard siding.

— **Saltbox.** This type of home has two stories in front and, thanks to a steeply sloping back roof, one story in the back. Saltboxes get their name from their resemblance to the containers early Americans used to store salt.

— **Spanish colonial.** Popular in the south and southwest, Spanish colonial-style homes feature stucco walls; a low-pitched, ceramic tile roof; arched windows and doorways; and wrought-iron details.

Spanish colonial

- **Prairie style.** This design, best expressed in the architecture of Frank Lloyd Wright, features strong horizontal lines, including rows of small, high windows and a low-pitched, overhanging roof. Inside, an open floor plan makes the house great for entertaining.

Prairie style

- **Pueblo revival.** Inspired by Native American pueblos and Spanish missions, this style has thick walls with rounded corners (made of adobe or stucco), flat roofs, and projecting wooden beams. If the home has more than one story, it's often terraced. Homes in this style are popular in the southwest.

Pueblo revival

- **Ranch.** For those who don't like to trudge up and down stairs, the popular single-story home comes in endless incarnations. Ranches often have low-pitched roofs, a basement, and a garage. A raised ranch builds up the foundation so that the basement is only partially underground, giving this traditionally one-story style two floors of living space.

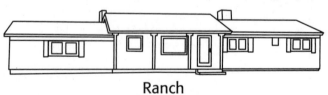

Ranch

A *shotgun house* is a kind of ranch house that flourished in the southern U.S. from the end of the Civil War to the early 20th century. Shotgun houses are narrow (just 10 or 12 feet wide) and without hallways; one room opens onto the next. They got their name because this straight-through arrangement let you fire a shotgun through the front door and the bullet would fly out the back door.

- **Split level.** Split-level houses have three floors (they're sometimes called tri-level houses). A single-story section of the house is attached to a two-story section, with the floor of the single-story part about halfway between the lower

Split level

and upper floors of the two-story section. Two small sets of stairs connect the sections. In the one-story section, you'll usually find the kitchen, living room, and dining room. The two-story section often holds a family room, den, or master bedroom downstairs and additional bedrooms upstairs.

- **Tudor.** This style evokes the buildings of 16th-century England, with decorative half-timbering, steeply pitched roofs, dormers, and tall, narrow windows (which often have small or diamond-shaped panes).

Tudor

- **Victorian.** This term refers to both an historical period (the mid- to late 19th century) and an architectural style that continues to thrive today. Victorians encompass a range of styles, including these:

  — **Italianate.** Tall houses with two, three, or even four stories and sometimes a cupola perched on a flat or low-pitched roof. Italianates may have arched windows and doors, and decorated brackets support the roof's overhang (which is why some people refer to this as the bracketed style).

  — **Mansard.** Mansard homes have a distinctive roof that slopes on all four sides, often with rounded dormer windows.

  — **Queen Anne.** The most ornate Victorian style, Queen Anne houses feature an asymmetrical shape, often with a tower or turret and features such as bay windows and gingerbread trim. The roofline is steep and complex. Porches often wrap around the house.

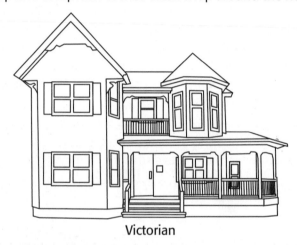

Victorian

If you're looking for privacy and space, you probably want a single-family home. The whole building is yours, and this kind of home usually has a yard, giving you outdoor living space as well.

The main disadvantage of single-family homes is the time and money it costs to maintain an entire building—inside and out—as well as the land it sits on (page 21). If you've never owned a single-family home, you can easily underestimate how much repairs and routine maintenance affect your wallet and your free time.

Duplex

A duplex is a two-unit building—think of it as two homes for the price of one. The units may be side-by-side, with each having its own front door, or they may be upstairs-downstairs, with one unit stacked on top of the other (in that case, a single front door may serve as a common entrance). Some duplexes are purpose-built, designed to be two connected homes. Others are converted from large single-family homes.

Buying a duplex comes with a significant financial advantage: You can live in one unit and rent out the other to help pay your mortgage. But renting part of the building can bring problems, too, such as loud music in the middle of the night or a broken lease if a tenant suddenly moves out. Also, when you own a duplex, you're responsible for the maintenance of both units and the building's grounds, so take those costs into account.

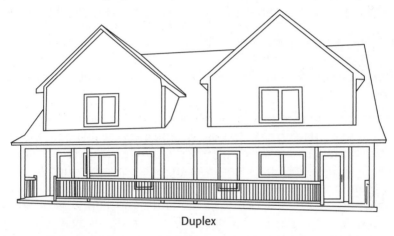

Duplex

 Note In some parts of the U.S., you may see homes described as "halfplexes." A halfplex looks just like a side-by-side duplex, but there's an important difference: Although a duplex has two units, it's a single piece of property that sits on one parcel of land and is covered by one deed. A halfplex is two separate pieces of property—each side is deeded separately. If you buy a halfplex, you buy a single unit in a two-unit building, including the land your unit sits on. This style of home is more like a townhouse (page 61) than a duplex.

Condominium

Condominiums—condos for short—are apartment-like homes in a multi-unit building. Unlike apartments, which are owned by a landlord who rents them to tenants, condos belong to the people who live there. When you buy a condo, you own your individual unit—you pay property taxes on it, and you earn equity over time. As a condo owner, you also own a share of the development's common areas: hallways, walkways, parking lots, elevators, and perhaps amenities like a club house. To keep these common areas in good shape, you pay dues to a condo association, which arranges for maintenance and repairs.

On the plus side, owning a condo lets you build equity in your home and frees you from much of the responsibility for maintenance: You never have to mow a lawn, weed a flower bed, shovel snow, or paint the exterior. In many condo developments, you enjoy amenities—tennis courts or a swimming pool, for example—that you might not otherwise be able to afford. And many condo owners appreciate the sense of safety and community that comes with living in a shared building. Condos are often less expensive than single-family houses, which make them attractive as starter homes.

But condos come with caveats, too. If you're looking for privacy, a condo in a multi-unit building may not be your best choice. In addition, condos tend to gain value more slowly than single-family homes (which slows the growth of your equity) and, when housing prices slump, condo prices drop faster than those of single-family homes. If disaster strikes and the building needs urgent or unexpected maintenance, your condo association will levy a special fee to pay for it. Finally, if you want to renovate your condo, you have to get approval from the condo association board before you can start work.

 Note A *loft*, a type of condo, is a residential unit in a building that wasn't originally intended to provide housing, such as a converted warehouse or factory. Lofts have wide-open interior spaces and a trendy urban or industrial feel. Loft conversions are often part of urban revitalization projects, and they're popular with professionals who work downtown and prefer an urban lifestyle to a long commute from the suburbs.

Townhouse

Townhouses sit in an uninterrupted row of houses, with their side walls connected to neighboring houses. They may be single-story buildings, but they're usually tall, narrow units of two or more stories. Each unit has its own entrance, and some may have a garage on the ground floor. You can find townhouses in cities, where they may line a city block, and in the suburbs, where they're usually part of a planned development. When you buy a townhouse, you usually gain title to an individual unit and the land beneath it. If the townhouse sits in a suburban development (as opposed to urban townhouses), the homeowners jointly own common areas, such as parking lots and public walkways.

Townhouses combine the benefits of single-family homes with those of a condo: They offer privacy (no one walks over your head, though you do have neighbors on the other side of the wall), and they're usually less expensive than single-family homes. Townhouses often require less maintenance than single-family homes as well. Urban townhouses don't have a yard to maintain, and the developer usually maintains the grounds of suburban townhouse developments. As with a condo, you pay taxes on your individual unit and a monthly or annual fee to the development's homeowners' association (page 23), which takes care of maintaining common areas and the building's exterior.

Townhouses

Co-operative Apartment (Co-op)

On the surface, a co-op looks just like a condo: It's an individual residence in a multi-unit building. The difference is in the ownership structure. A *coop building* is owned by a cooperative corporation—think of it as a company set up for the sole purpose of owning the building. Instead of buying a piece of physical real estate in the building, you buy shares in the corporation. With your share comes the exclusive right to live in a particular unit. Co-op owners pay fees to the corporation, and its board deals with day-to-day maintenance and management issues. The corporation pays the mortgage and property taxes on the building as a whole and includes your share in your co-op fees. Co-ops are prevalent in some large cities, such as New York (where about 85 percent of the apartments available for sale are co-ops) and Chicago.

Co-ops offer many of the same benefits as condos: shared amenities, freedom from maintenance, a feeling of safety, and a sense of community. You can deduct part of your monthly co-op fees from your income tax (the part you pay for property tax), and the value of your shares may increase over time as property values increase, just as with any other home. Co-op boards screen prospective shareholders carefully and often have stringent requirements for who qualifies as a shareholder, checking your employment, income, finances, credit history, and even personal background. This screening process gives residents a say in who their neighbors will be.

That same stringency can be an obstacle when you try to buy into a co-op, however. The application process can be time-consuming, may feel intrusive, and requires a lot of paperwork. And keep in mind that a highly selective co-op board can make it difficult to sell your shares and move on. Because many co-ops have strict rules about subletting your unit—or may even prohibit the practice altogether—this can be a real hardship later if you need to move.

Co-ops tend to have higher monthly fees than condos, because those fees include payments the corporation makes toward mortgage and taxes. And be aware that you may find it more difficult to obtain financing to purchase co-op shares: The corporation may deal only with certain banks and/or require a higher down payment than you need for a condo or single-family home.

Modular and Manufactured Homes

A home built piece-by-piece on the lot where it sits, from digging the foundation to nailing down the last shingle, is called a *site-built* or a *stick-built* home. But that's not the only way to construct a new home. Some homes are prebuilt in a factory and then shipped to the new owner's lot. There are two kinds of prebuilt homes: modular and manufactured. (See the table at the end of this section for the differences between these home types.)

Modular homes

Modular homes are made in sections in a factory and trucked to your lot, where a crane lifts the pieces from the truck bed and sets them on the foundation. Local contractors then assemble the pieces and do the finishing work, like hooking up the electricity and plumbing. So these homes are built partly in a factory and partly on site. You have to have a permanent foundation in place on your lot, just as with a stick-built home, and modulars are subject to local and state building codes—a local building inspector checks each new home to make sure it's up to code. Once the work is done, it's hard to tell that a modular began life as a group of factory-built sections.

Modular homes come in an eye-popping variety of styles and sizes, from simple ranches to a spacious and elegant two-story colonials and Victorians. You can choose a standard model or work with a manufacturer to create a customized home.

If you're interested in building a brand-new home, going modular may be a good choice for a couple of reasons. First, manufacturers and contractors can fabricate, assemble, and finish a modular home faster than they can a stick-built home. And it may cost less to buy and assemble a modular—building costs per square foot are often lower than for traditionally built homes, although that depends on the price of materials and labor in your area.

When it comes to financing, lenders treat modular homes just as they do stick-built houses, and existing modulars tend to grow in value at the same rate as other homes in the neighborhood, no matter the original construction technique.

Manufactured homes

A *manufactured home* is built entirely in a factory. Manufacturers build each home (or segment of a home) on a permanent steel chassis, and the home travels to its site on its own wheels. You can have a manufactured home attached to a foundation, but it's not required.

Another distinction of manufactured homes: Local building codes don't apply. Instead, manufactured homes must conform to the federal government's Manufactured Home Construction and Safety Standards code, called the HUD code. You can read about these standards at *http://tinyurl. com/yj7pxna*.

Manufactured homes are usually less expensive than other housing options, and you can trade in an existing one toward a newer model, just like you would trade in a car. Also like a car, you can buy this kind of home by getting a loan directly from the retailer, which you pay back in monthly installments.

Manufactured homes are eligible for FHA-insured loans (page 180) and VA loans (page 183).

Manufactured homes were built with mobility in mind (that's why they used to be called mobile homes), so when you move, you can take your home with you. Well, maybe. If you decide to move your manufactured home, keep these tips in mind:

- Manufactured homes are built to specifications that depend on the destination climate and other factors; a home built for the desert may not hold up well in frigid northern conditions or humid tropical climates. Check with the manufacturer to make sure that your model can withstand the weather at your new locale.

- Moving a manufactured home can be tricky. For the smoothest move, hire a transport company that specializes in hauling manufactured homes. Of course, this can be expensive, depending on the distance and the hauling company.

If you're considering a manufactured home, be aware of the downsides, too:

- You can't just buy a piece of land and plunk down a manufactured home. Many towns have zoning regulations that limit where manufactured homes can go. Before you buy, check local zoning laws, the property's deed restrictions, and neighborhood or development covenants. A real estate lawyer can help you with this.

- Most lenders won't finance a manufactured home unless you attach it to a permanent foundation (the home is their collateral, and they don't want it disappearing the middle of the night). If you don't want to anchor your home, you'll probably have to arrange financing with the home's retailer—and rates may be higher than for a mortgage.

- Manufactured homes aren't considered permanent structures, and this affects their long-term value. Over time, these homes are more likely than traditional and modular homes to decrease in value. So don't buy a manufactured home if equity is a priority.

	Modular home	Manufactured home
Transportation method	Transported on a trailer, from which the module is removed by a crane and set on a permanent foundation.	Transported on a permanent steel chassis that remains a structural part of the home.
Codes	Must conform to state and local building codes.	Must conform to federal codes mandated by HUD.
Size	May have multiple stories.	Limited to one story.
Location	Placed permanently on a private lot.	Often placed on a leased lot, as in a park. Placement isn't permanent.
Restrictions	Rarely restricted by zoning laws or neighborhood covenants.	Sometimes restricted by zoning laws or neighborhood covenants.
Cost	Often less expensive than stick-built homes, but more expensive than manufactured homes.	Less expensive than modular homes.
Value	Gains value over time, like a stick-built home.	Tends to lose value with age, like a motor vehicle.
Financing	Considered the same as a stick-built home for the purpose of getting a mortgage.	Often considered personal property (not real property). Many lenders require a manufactured home to be attached to a permanent foundation before accepting it as collateral for a loan. Dealers, rather than banks, often provide financing.

The Condition of Your Home

Besides the type of home you want, you need to think about its condition. Do you want to be the first person ever to sleep under its roof, or would you rather live in a house with history? Newer homes have modern central systems (heating, cooling, plumbing) and appliances, and they're more energy efficient. Older homes often exhibit character and charming period details. A newly built house comes with a warranty (page 281) that protects you if certain repairs become necessary, but you might be able to save some money by buying a fixer-upper, rolling up your sleeves, and getting to work.

 Read the fine print on your home warranty. Warranties sometimes offer less coverage than you might expect.

New Construction

You can pick out a home design and have it built for you, either on your own lot or in a subdivision that's being developed. Building your home from scratch gets you involved in every phase of its construction: choosing a floor plan, watching the walls go up, checking the finishing touches. A home built for you will conform to up-to-the-minute building codes and can incorporate modern, energy-efficient materials that reduce your heating and cooling costs.

On the other hand, a new home may be more expensive than an existing one (as much as 10 percent more, according to the National Association of Realtors), and the construction process may take six months to a year. So be prepared to pay for a place to live at the same time you're paying for the home's construction.

Hire a builder

You've spent hours poring over books filled with house plans to find a design that's perfect for you. You've bought the blueprints and found the lot where your new home will stand. Now all you have to do is hire a contractor, and your dream will become a reality. Right?

Not so fast. Hiring a builder can give you the home of your dreams, but if you're not careful, it can also be an experience beset with frustration and unforeseen expenses. If you decide to have a contractor build your new home, don't rush. Make sure you hire the best person for the job by following these tips:

- **Make sure the contractor is legit.** Before you hire a contractor, ask to see his or her license. You want to make sure that he has a current, valid license for your state. Also, ask for proof of liability insurance, which covers injuries and property damage during construction.

- **Check references.** Ask the contractor for the names of previous clients. Call them and ask about their experience with the contractor and how they feel about the final product. If you can, visit a few of the homes.

- **Compare bids.** Interview at least three contractors so you can compare their estimates.

- **Get everything in writing.** Make sure that contractors' estimates spell out everything you want in your home. If you want a fireplace, for example, make sure it appears in the estimate.

- **Read the final contract carefully.** Make sure that the document accurately describes your project and that you understand all its terms. If in doubt, show it to a real estate lawyer.

- **Expect delays.** A contractor's best estimate of how long it will take to build your new home may not match up with reality. All kinds of factors, including weather and availability of materials, can delay construction. If possible, be flexible about your move-in date so you're not putting your belongings in storage and living in a motel as you wait for your house to be finished.

Buy in a development that's under construction

In a new subdivision, the developer often begins by building one or more model homes for prospective buyers to tour. If you see a model you like, select an available lot and have the home built on it. When you buy a home this way, you get to choose your home's kitchen cabinets, paint colors, and carpets, and perhaps tweak the home's design to customize it. You also get a brand-new home with a warranty, so you can be confident that the home's major systems and appliances will work the way they're supposed to (or they'll be replaced).

 Tip After a developer has sold all or most of the homes in a subdivision, the model home often goes up for sale. Buying a former model home can be a great deal— you may be able to get a fully loaded showplace for less money than comparable homes in the neighborhood. Models have also seen a lot of traffic, though, thanks to home shoppers traipsing through them for months or years. If you're thinking of buying a model home, ask whether the builder will do paint touch-ups and clean or replace carpets before you move in. Also check to make sure that appliances and systems are still under warranty—and for how much longer the warranty will be valid.

On the flip side, when you buy a yet-to-be-built home, be aware of potential problems:

- When you base your decision on a model home, what you see is not necessarily what you get. Corner-cutting may leave you dissatisfied if the home doesn't match up to the model.

- New developments often have a cookie-cutter feel, with homes built from a limited number of designs. If individual style is important, you may be unhappy as identical houses spring up in your new neighborhood.

- Don't assume that the developer's agent, who works out of the subdivision's sales office, has your best interest at heart—no matter how charming or persuasive he may be, he represents the developer. Hire a buyer's agent (page 81) to represent your interests.

- Don't automatically apply for a loan through the developer's lender. You may feel some pressure to work with the developer's preferred lender to finance your purchase—but shop around before you decide. If the preferred lender offers you the best terms, great. But don't agree to not-so-great terms simply because you think you'll curry favor with the developer. Chapter 7 tells you how to choose the best mortgage.

- Developers' highest profit margins come from upgrades, so don't get carried away with options only to watch the cost of your new home soar. Double-check upgrade costs before you order them, and keep track of how much you're spending.

- Your move-in date may be pushed back by construction delays.

- A brand-new development isn't yet an established neighborhood. Streets may feel bare without mature trees, and you can't get a sense of your new neighbors if their homes aren't built yet.

Tip Ask the developer what kinds of trees he's planted in the development. To green the neighborhood, developers often plant fast-growing trees like poplars. These look nice, but because they grow so fast they can develop weak root systems for their heights, creating a danger that they'll fall over in a storm.

- Occasionally, a developer can't sell enough homes in a planned subdivision to make the project worthwhile. The developer may cancel the development—or even declare bankruptcy—leaving your dream home unbuilt.

Tip If a developer cancels a development or goes bankrupt, you could wait for months or years to get your deposit back—or even lose it. Before you hand over a deposit for new construction, make sure that the developer holds deposit money in escrow in a separate trust account. That protects your investment if the developer runs into financial trouble.

Preowned Homes

A lived-in home may be in move-in condition—thoroughly cleaned, dings in the walls filled in, paint touched up—or it may be a fixer-upper that requires significant work before you can move in (read the next section for more about buying a home that needs repairs or updating). Or it may fall somewhere in between, needing cosmetic work like new paint in the dining room or new carpet in the dining room before you're ready to call it home.

Newer homes, those built within the past 5 or 10 years, offer many of the perks of a brand-new home. Although these homes have been lived in, they're still likely to be up to modern standards of construction, materials, and energy efficiency. Newer homes may not feel as outdated in their interior design as older homes, and their floor plans and storage space are more likely to reflect the way people live now.

"Older homes" encompass everything from centuries-old structures to homes built a decade or two ago. These homes tend to be in established neighborhoods with settled neighbors, mature trees, and established zoning (municipal planners are unlikely to allow a factory in a residential neighborhood, for example). Older homes have a reputation for solid construction. Although new homes must pass an inspection, some modern construction techniques are more concerned with the bottom line than with quality craftsmanship. Older homes' yards may be larger if land was cheaper when the home was built. Finally, older homes can be appealing for their character, including period details like wide-board floors, hand-hewn beams, stained-glass windows, or detailed woodwork that would be prohibitively expensive in a newly built home.

Older homes come with their own potential problems, so if you consider an older home, keep these tips in mind:

- **A thorough home inspection is an absolute must.** When you tour an existing home, it's easy to focus on cosmetics—you love the pale-blue bedroom walls, but that shag carpet in the family room has to go—and overlook problems with the structure itself. An experienced home inspector will find potential problems before you buy. (Chapter 12 tells you what a home inspector looks for.)

- **An older home may require more maintenance.** With time, roof shingles loosen, concrete walks crack, window frames rot. If the house feels drafty, you may need to add insulation. Many houses built in the 1980s through the early '90s have polybutylene pipes (page 297), which can deteriorate with time and may leak.

- **There may be lurking health hazards.** Lead pipes, lead paint, and asbestos insulation are a few materials that used to be common in home construction but are now known to be unsafe. Your home inspector will look for hazardous materials (page 306) and let you know if they require remediation.

- **Appliances may be older and less energy efficient.** Ask about the age of appliances. Appliances have an average lifespan of 10 to 15 years, so be aware of when you might have to replace the dishwasher or fridge. Older appliances also tend to be less energy efficient than newer models—a difference that may show up in your utility bills.

- **Updating can be expensive.** You don't want to be held captive to the previous owner's taste, but the cost of updating a home's look can add up fast. Figure out the cosmetic changes you want and budget for them—or be prepared to live in the home as is for a while. And optional cosmetic updates are only part of the story: Systems or appliances may require updating to function properly. Your home inspector (Chapter 12) will let you know.

- **You may get fewer square feet for your money.** For the past 60 years, the size of the average American home has steadily increased from 980 square feet in 1950 to a peak of just over 2,600 square feet in 2008. Buying an older home may mean settling for smaller rooms and less closet space than you'd get if you bought new.

- **Watch out for tree damage.** Tall, mature trees cast inviting shade and look pretty, but they may also cause problems. Trees planted too close to a house, for example, can damage the roof, the foundation, or any underground pipes.

Fixer-Uppers

Whether it's called a fixer-upper, handyman's special, or a home in need of some elbow grease or a little TLC, this is an existing home that probably needs some work before you can move in. Buying a fixer-upper can be a good deal for these reasons:

- In a desirable neighborhood, a fixer-upper may be priced less than homes of similar size. Spending the time and money to renovate the home can give its value a huge boost, bringing it in line with those higher-priced homes.

- If you like historic homes, you can restore a poorly decorated or remodeled house to its original glory.

- Do-it-yourselfers get a sense of accomplishment and increase their pride of ownership when they fix up a rundown home.

- You don't have to live with someone else's decorating or design choices. A fixer-upper can be a blank canvas on which you create your vision of the good life.

Although the price discount and the potential to increase the home's value make fixer-uppers seem like a great deal, renovating a home isn't easy—and it isn't for everyone. Before you roll up your sleeves and open your toolbox, think long and hard about these questions:

- **Is the fixer-upper as good a deal as it seems?** It can be easy for your eyes to fill up with dollar signs as you contemplate the difference between the house's current price and its value once renovated. Don't guess; do the math. Talk to a real estate and find out how much similar homes in the neighborhood have recently sold for—that's your target value. Then, subtract the expected cost of renovations. Don't guess here, either; talk to contractors to get a firm idea. (Of course, the expected cost of renovations may not match the actual cost, so to be on the safe side, increase the estimate by 5 or 10 percent.) The home's expected value minus the adjusted renovation estimate is the break-even number, the maximum amount you should offer for the home.

- **How extensive are the required renovations?** To make sure you know what you're getting into, have the home thoroughly inspected (Chapter 12). If the property has serious structural problems—such as a crumbling foundation, significant dry rot, outdated wiring, or obsolete plumbing—the required repairs may be more than you should take on.

 Modern living uses a lot of electricity—for computers, appliances, air conditioning, and more—and an older home's electrical system may not be able to handle the load. Old electrical systems may also be a fire hazard. If you think the home's electrical system may need a substantial upgrade, get an electrician to inspect it and estimate how much the upgrade would cost.

- **Where will you live during the renovation?** Staying in your current home or temporary housing while you renovate can be expensive—remember, you're making payments on your new mortgage, paying for a place to live in the meantime, and racking up materials charges for the renovation. On the other hand, living in a home that's undergoing renovations can be a noisy, dusty, uncomfortable affair.

- **How long will renovations take?** Fixing up a place almost always takes longer than you think. Contractors may be delayed by other projects or simply fail to show up on the appointed date. If you're renovating the home yourself, be realistic in estimating how much time and energy you have to devote to the project. "I'll work on it evenings and weekends" may sound like a plan, but do you really want to spend every waking moment you're away from your job working on the house?

- **Are you prepared to keep a close eye on contractors?** The fixer-upper will be your house, so it's your job to make sure that the people you hire to renovate it do what they're supposed to and keep the project within budget.

- **What if the renovations go over budget?** Many things can drive a renovation's actual cost higher than the contractor's estimate: delays, increased costs of materials and labor, unforeseen problems uncovered during the work, and more. Leave some wiggle room in your budget for cost overruns.

Find Your Neighborhood

The building where you'll eat and sleep, kick back in the evenings, and wake up in the mornings is only part of what makes a home. The rest? Location, location, location. Choose your new neighborhood as carefully as you choose your new home. This section helps you find a neighborhood where you'll feel at home.

Schools

If you have kids (or plan to), local schools are a major consideration. Take some time to talk to school administrators, teachers, and local parents to find out more about the schools in the neighborhood you're considering. Attend a public parent-teacher association or school board meeting.

 Tip A visit to *www.education.com/schoolfinder* is a good first step in checking out local schools. Enter a school district or zip code, and you get information about local schools, including demographics, standardized test results, and reviews.

Here are some of the things you want to know about local schools:

- What grades do the schools cover?
- How many children attend the school?
- What's the average class size?
- What are the average scores on standardized tests?
- How does the school rank compared to others in the state?
- Are there any areas in which the school has received a "needs improvement" rating from the state?
- What does the school's music and art curricula include?
- What sports programs are available?
- What other after-school activities are available?
- What efforts does the school make to promote diversity?
- Are there problems with cliques or bullying?

If you've got high-school students in the family, ask these questions, too:

- What's the student attrition rate (that is, what percentage of students drop out)?
- What percentage of graduating seniors attend college?
- What is the school's college counseling program like?
- What percentage of teachers have graduate degrees in their subjects?
- Are there honors courses? In what subjects?
- Does the school have a chapter of the National Honor Society?
- Are there AP courses? In what subjects?
- How many students win state or national awards?
- What clubs and extracurricular activities are available to students?
- What team sports does the school offer?
- What levels of sports are available (varsity, junior varsity, intramural)?
- Does the school have any problems with gangs or vandalism?

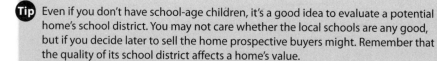

Tip Even if you don't have school-age children, it's a good idea to evaluate a potential home's school district. You may not care whether the local schools are any good, but if you decide later to sell the home prospective buyers might. Remember that the quality of its school district affects a home's value.

Services and Shopping

Some people prefer to live in a quiet, residential area devoted to homes. Others want to be within walking distance of services they use frequently. Consider how close you want to be to services such as these:

- Schools
- Post office
- Grocery store
- Malls
- Other shopping
- Dry cleaner
- Dentist
- Physician
- Hospital
- Veterinarian

Amenities

Amenities make life pleasant and enhance your sense of community. Decide how important it is to you to have easy access to:

- Parks
- Playgrounds
- Museums
- Places of worship
- Restaurants and cafes
- Music venues
- Performance theaters
- Cinemas
- Sports venues
- Hiking and biking trails
- Swimming pool or beach
- Skating rink

Make a list of the amenities most important to you and use it as you evaluate potential homes.

Neighbors

More than any other factor, people define a neighborhood. Your neighbors create a sense of community; they're the people you chat with across the fence, invite over for coffee, and sit with at kids' soccer games. When you buy a house, expect to interact with your new neighbors for a long time. Making and nurturing friendships is one of the joys of owning a home— and having neighbors you don't get along with can be one of its curses.

You want to live in a neighborhood where their lifestyles complement yours. If you have young children, for example, you probably want to be near schools and other families who have kids of a similar age. If your work schedule mandates an "early to bed, early to rise" regimen, you want a neighborhood that's quiet at night. If, on the other hand, you like to party until dawn, that quiet neighborhood may not be right for you.

Go into the neighborhood. Talk to people who live there. Drive or walk around at different times of day. Notice when people are out and about. Look for signs that neighbors share your interests—lush gardens, nice lawns, kids' play sets, and so on. Spending time in a neighborhood is the best way to get a feel for it.

 Tip Many multi-unit developments (condos, townhouses, and co-ops) have both owners and renters as residents. If you're considering buying in one of these developments, find out how many residents own their unit and how many rent. A high ratio of owners to renters indicates that your neighbors are likely to have pride of ownership in their residence, since they have a financial stake in it.

Commuting

How much time, at most, are you willing to spend traveling to and from work each day? How far is the neighborhood from your place of work? How will you get to work: using public transportation, walking, cycling, or driving? If you drive to work, does the route take you along highways or back streets?

 Tip Travel the route between your prospective neighborhood and your workplace during the hours you'd routinely make the trip to get a sense of rush-hour traffic— how busy are the roads, or how crowded are the buses and trains?

Economic Stability

Because the average homeowner moves within seven years, you want to find a neighborhood that's stable economically (or even better, one where home values are rising). Good economic stability will make it easier to sell your home quickly and make some money on the deal. Even if you plan to stay in your new home for many years, you should consider whether your new neighborhood is economically stable. Current home prices in your neighborhood affect the amount of equity you have in your home, so if values decline you may lose equity. Economic instability may lead to fore-closures (glutting the market with unsold homes) and an increase in crime.

No one can predict the future. A major employer whose business is boom-ing now may run into difficulty, laying off employees or closing altogether. Take a neighborhood's economic pulse by asking these questions:

- Is the neighborhood close to a diversity of employers? A wide range of employers, large and small, within commuting distance indicates greater overall stability in a community. If area employment relies heavily on one business or industry, how stable does the outlook for that industry appear?

- Are there a significant number of abandoned homes or empty storefronts?

- Is there a lot of graffiti?

- Do sidewalks and roads appear well maintained?

- Does the local news media feature stories about economic hard times? If you repeatedly come across stories about local businesses failing or unemployment increasing, this may be a risky time to buy.

Crime Rate

Nobody wants to move into a high-crime area, especially when you're making a significant financial investment in a home. There are two kinds of crime you need to be aware of: violent crimes (murder, assault, rape, and robbery with threat of force) and property crimes (burglary, larceny, auto theft, and arson). Call or visit the local police station or check out its web-site to review crime statistics. Read the local paper—you can subscribe or read it on the Internet—to see what kinds of crimes are reported and in which areas.

The website Sperling's Best Places breaks down a neighborhood's demographics, including a quick, by-the-numbers glimpse of its crime rate. Go to *www.bestplaces. net* and type a city, town, or zip code into the search box. Click Search, and then click the Crime link. The page that opens compares local incidences of violent crimes and property crimes with regional and national averages.

Zoning

You wouldn't want to settle into your new home and find out a year or two later that a company is building a huge factory across the street. Municipalities create zoning laws to minimize such problems; municipal planners divide a city or town into zones, each with restrictions on the kinds of buildings or uses within them. Examples of zones are residential, commercial, industrial, and mixed-use (which allows a mixture of buildings from different zoning categories). To be sure that your neighborhood will be filled with neighbors, not businesses or factories, look in areas zoned for residential use.

You can find out a prospective neighborhood's zoning classification—and what kinds of buildings and uses are allowed there—by talking to a real estate agent or checking with city hall.

 Ask your real estate agent whether the neighborhood you're considering has any *restrictive covenants* in place. These are deed restrictions, usually put in place by the neighborhood's original developer, that limit what you can do with the home or lot that you're purchasing. Covenants may cover a wide range of issues, from specifying the number of stories a house can have or how far it must be set back from property lines to spelling out acceptable paint colors and fence heights. There may also be restrictions on home businesses and the kinds of vehicles you can park in the driveway.

Create a Wish List

Now comes the fun part—putting together a list of everything you want in your dream home, from price range to style to amenities to your ideal neighborhood. The home you eventually buy may not meet *all* your criteria, but touring homes for sale with a list in hand (page 137) gives you the best chance of finding a home you'll love.

To create a wish list, follow the three steps below. The Missing CD has sample lists you can use for each of these steps. To find them, go to the Missing Manuals home page (*www.missingmanuals.com*), click the Missing CD link, scroll down to *Buying a Home: The Missing Manual*, and then click the Missing CD link.

1. **List what you want in a home.** Include all the features you want in your dream home, including style; size; condition; number of bedrooms and bathrooms; features like a garage, family room, fireplace, or pool; and neighborhood amenities. Don't worry about making your list too long; you'll narrow it down in step 3.

2. **Identify what you *don't* want.** Knowing the definite deal-breakers—what you're sure you *don't* want in a home—can be just as helpful as knowing what you do want. Creating a "don't want" list and sharing it with your agent will help your agent target your search better.

3. **Prioritize your preferences.** By the time you list everything you want (and don't want) in a home, your wish list might look so long that you wonder whether your dream home really exists. So look at the lists you've created and prioritize the items on them. Knowing what's most important to you, as well as what you could live without or add later, gives you an edge in evaluating homes.

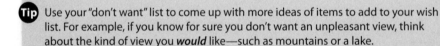 **Tip** Use your "don't want" list to come up with more ideas of items to add to your wish list. For example, if you know for sure you don't want an unpleasant view, think about the kind of view you *would* like—such as mountains or a lake.

4 Assemble Your Real Estate Team

A well-known African proverb says that it takes a village to raise a child. As a new homebuyer, you'll need nearly as many people to buy a home. Purchasing a home is a huge investment with many variables. It's an obstacle course you'll find tough to navigate on your own. You need the expertise of professionals who protect your interests as they take you through the process of finding a home, making an offer, getting financing, and finalizing the sale. This chapter introduces you to the real estate professionals who'll make up your home-buying team. For each of the main players—real estate agents, mortgage provider, attorney, and home inspector—you'll get tips on how to find the right one.

Real Estate Agents

In your quest for a new home, the person you'll interact with most is your real estate agent. She's a lot more than a smiling face in the classifieds, hovering over pictures of homes for sale. She's a licensed professional, authorized to negotiate and carry out the sale of real property on behalf of a buyer, a seller—or sometimes both simultaneously. Read on to learn the different roles real estate agents play, how they make their money, and—most importantly—how you find one who works well with you.

Agents and Brokers and Realtors

Every state and the District of Columbia require real estate agents to hold a license, but not all licenses are the same. Most states define two types of real estate professionals: broker and agent. But you may come across several other terms as well. Here's the lowdown:

- **Real estate broker.** This is an experienced real estate professional who's met state requirements to own, manage, or operate a real estate company. Licensing requirements usually include experience in the industry as a sales agent, advanced coursework, and passing an exam. (In some states, attorneys can become real estate brokers, even if they've never worked as real estate agents.) The broker in a real estate firm is its "boss," the person who takes responsibility for all the agents who work there. Depending on where you live, you may hear real estate brokers referred to as principal brokers or qualifying brokers.

 Note Some licensed brokers choose not to run their own firm but to work as agents for another broker in that broker's firm. These people are called associate brokers.

- **Real estate agent.** This is someone who's taken classes and passed a state-administered exam to get a license to sell property. The educational requirements cover the specific state's real estate laws and practices. Real estate agents are associated with a real estate broker and act under that broker's authority. Depending on where you live, real estate agents may be called subagents, sales agents, real estate salespeople, or, confusingly, brokers.

As you look for a home, you'll probably work primarily with a real estate agent. Real estate agents can represent the seller of a house, the buyer of a house, or both:

— **Seller's agent.** Also called a listing agent, this person works exclusively for the seller. Most often, you'll deal with the seller through the seller's agent. Except in cases where you have a specific agreement with an agent to represent you as a buyer (see the next item on this list), you should assume that any agent you work with is a seller's agent. Even if an agent didn't personally list the seller's property, any agent involved in the sale of a property is considered a subagent of the listing agent—unless that agent has a contract to represent only you, the buyer (see "Buyers' Agent" below).

 Agency means representation, and an *agent* is a representative. If you enter into an agency agreement with someone, it means that you've both agreed that that person will act as your representative.

— **Buyer's agent.** A buyer's agent works solely for you the buyer, and represents your interests throughout the real estate transaction, from initial house-hunting through closing the deal. Buyer's agency is a formal agreement, signed by you and a particular real estate agent, saying that the agent represents you and your interests in buying a home.

 In a transaction, the buyer's agent is called, confusingly enough, the selling agent. To keep from being muddled by the terminology, think of agents' roles this way: In transactions that have both a listing (seller's) and a buyer's agent, the listing agent puts a home on the market and represents the current owner; the selling agent facilitates the sale by representing the buyer who makes that sale possible.

— **Dual agent.** This is a single agent who represents both the seller and the buyer in the same transaction. In most states, dual agency is legal so long as the agent gets the consent of both the buyer and the seller. But as the box on page 83 explains, dual agency can lead to conflicts of interest.

 Dual agency can also occur when two agents who work for the same broker represent both parties in a real estate transaction. The box on page 83 tells you more.

Real Estate Agent vs. Realtor

What's the difference between a real estate agent and a Realtor?

REALTOR® is a registered trademark of the National Association of Realtors. Any real estate agent who claims this title must be a member in good standing of the NAR. To join the NAR, agents agree to abide by a code of ethics that includes honesty, putting clients' interests ahead of their own, and disclosing all relevant facts about a property.

As a homebuyer, you should work with a buyer's agent. You want to be sure that your interests are represented in negotiations and that your agent keeps your confidential information to herself. Later in this chapter, you'll find out how to choose a good buyer's agent.

 Note If a real estate agent fails to let you know that you're in a dual agency situation—that is, the agent represents both you and the seller or both your agent and the seller's agent work for the same firm—you may be able to revoke the purchase agreement you signed and sue the agent for concealing the relationship.

What a Real Estate Agent Does

Real estate agents are experts in local real estate: They monitor the market daily and look for housing trends (in prices, inventory, location, and so on). An agent tells you about available houses in your price range and takes you on tours of homes that interest you. Much of an agent's day is taken up by phone calls, meetings, and home tours.

For sellers, a listing (seller's) agent:

- Researches recent sales of comparable homes to help determine an asking price
- Helps sellers prepare their homes for sale
- Lists the home with the Multiple Listing Service (known in the trade as the MLS, a searchable list of homes for sale within a particular region)
- Advertises the home through various channels, which may include the Internet, classified ads, real estate magazines, and on-site advertising (the latter usually comprising a "For Sale" sign on the lawn and take-away information sheets about the home)

- Takes other real estate agents on a walkthrough so they can tell their clients about the home
- Hosts open houses
- Presents offers from interested buyers
- Negotiates the terms of the sale

Dual Agency

You're just starting to look for a new home and haven't yet selected a real estate agent. One weekend afternoon, you drive through the neighborhood where you want to live and see an Open House sign. You stop to take a look. Inside, everything is perfect. The house has the right number of bedrooms and bathrooms, the kitchen is a cook's dream, and the place is in move-in condition. "I love it!" you tell the smiling real estate agent who's hosting the open house. "I want to make an offer."

"Great!" she replies. "Let's write up the paperwork."

She looks nice. She's friendly and helpful. She's eager to help you buy the home. But there's just one problem. She's already representing someone: the seller.

Real estate agents have a *fiduciary duty* to their clients. That means that a real estate agent—whether a seller's or a buyer's agent—is legally bound to represent your best interests in any transaction. But when you start negotiating with a seller's agent, your best interests don't always line up with theirs. Yes, you want to buy the house and the seller wants to sell it. But you want to buy the house for the lowest price possible, and the seller wants to sell it for the highest price possible. See where the conflict comes in? In that situation, how can the same agent have the best interests of both of you at heart?

Most states allow dual agency, on the condition that the real estate agent tells both you and the seller that she's representing you both—and all parties sign a document agreeing to that. But before you agree to dual agency, think long and hard about whether you want the seller's agent representing you, too. For example, you might tell your agent confidentially that you've been preapproved for a mortgage of up to $250,000, but you don't want to bid more than $230,000 on a particular home. The agent knows that the seller wants to get at least $245,000 for that same home. Although a good agent always keeps your confidential information confidential, it may be tempting in this situation to try to convince you to raise your offer.

Dual agency also comes into play when a home buyer and seller are represented by two different agents who work for the same broker. This kind of dual agency may be called *designated agency*, and if your state allows it, you'll probably have to sign a statement saying you agree to have the same agency represent both you and the seller. Some agencies pay agents a bonus for selling in-house listings because the agency makes more money in such transactions—conflict of interest, anyone? If you want to buy a home that's listed with your buyer's agent's brokerage, make sure that your interests come before the broker's.

As a buyer, you can expect a real estate agent (either the seller's agent or your own) to work with you in these ways:

- Listen to your priorities in looking for a home, including your price range
- Contact listing agents to check availability and schedule showings
- Show you suitable properties
- Notify you as new properties appear on the market
- Suggest sources of financing

Tip You're not bound to work with any lender recommended by an agent. Page 197 has tips for finding the best mortgage.

- Help you write a purchase offer and present that offer to the seller
- Negotiate with the seller on your behalf
- Write a purchase-and-sale agreement (page 250)
- Set up and attend the home's appraisal and inspection
- Review disclosure statements and let you know about problems with a property

Tip Agents know what to look for in disclosure statements and other documents. Although it's important to find an agent you like, the most important quality an agent has to offer is his expertise.

- Deal with contingencies (page 251)
- Provide information to your mortgage officer, real estate attorney, and escrow officer
- Coordinate with other parties to schedule the closing
- Attend the closing

There are some things a real estate *can't* tell you by law. If you have questions about a neighborhood's character, diversity, crime rate, or schools, you have to look elsewhere for the answers. Federal fair housing laws prevent real estate agents from "steering" clients toward one neighborhood or away from another one. The idea behind the law was to prevent discrimination—to prevent real estate agents from deciding whether a client is a good or bad fit for a particular neighborhood. Despite the law's good intentions, it can be frustrating to have basic demographic questions go unanswered. Chapter 3 suggests ways to find those answers.

How Real Estate Agents Get Paid

Real estate agents earn their money by commission: When a property sells, they get paid, usually 4 to 7 percent of the purchase price. If a property fails to sell, the agent doesn't get paid—no matter how much time and money she's invested in showing and advertising the home.

The seller usually pays the agent's commission from the proceeds of the home's sale. Of course, sellers are aware of this and take the commission into account when they determine their asking price and decide whether to accept an offer. If you use a buyer's agent, he and the seller's agent split the commission (each side may get half, or the percentages may vary somewhat).

Here's an example of how buyer's and seller's agents typically get paid. Suppose you buy a house for $250,000 and the seller pays a 6 percent commission. In this case, the commission works out to $15,000. The listing agent and your agent split that commission down the middle, each earning $7,500. Each will probably pay a percentage of the individual commission to his broker, up to 50 percent—in this example, that's $3,750.

 The commission split between agent and broker varies depending on the agent's experience. For a new agent without much of a track record, the split may be 50/50 with the broker (his boss), while an experienced agent who generates lots of business can get a much sweeter deal, keeping 70 to 80 percent of the commission.

Sounds like easy money, doesn't it? Well…keep in mind that agents do a lot of work behind the scenes. On average, for each hour your agent spends with you, she's putting in a full, eight-hour workday doing tasks you don't see: making phone calls, checking listings, screening homes, setting up tours, filling out paperwork, coordinating with others on your team, and more.

 Note Some buyer's agents charge their clients a retainer, which may or may not be refunded if the agent fails to help you buy a home. Page 87 tells you more about working with buyer's agents.

Frequently Asked Question

Going It Alone

I think real estate commissions are too high. How much money would I save by skipping the agent and buying a home by myself?

The short answer: Not as much as you might think. Remember that commissions are based on an agreement between the seller and the listing agent. If you don't bring in an agent to work on your behalf, the listing agent simply keeps the whole commission.

If you're interested in a home that's for sale by owner (FSBO, pronounced *fizz-bo*)—a situation in which the seller forgoes an agent and handles all the details of the sale—you might be tempted to do without an agent, too. When the seller doesn't offer a commission, you have to pay your agent out of your own pocket. If no agent is involved on either side, there's no commission to pay. You could save thousands of dollars.

But for most buyers—especially new buyers—this isn't a good idea. Look over the list on page 84 of what an agent does for you. Negotiating, setting up appointments, writing documents, opening an escrow account—all this requires knowledge and a major time commitment. And you may not have the legal expertise to understand the documents related to your purchase. You can get assistance with that from your real estate attorney—and you'll definitely need an attorney if you don't work with an agent. Remember, though, that attorneys charge you for each and every hour (or part of an hour) they work. So relying on a real estate attorney to help you with paperwork that an agent customarily takes care of may end up costing you quite a few bucks.

If you're a new buyer, the best route is to go with an experienced buyer's agent.

Working with a Buyer's Agent

The whole point of working with a real estate agent is to have a knowledge-able professional represent your interests throughout the home-buying process, from identifying possible homes to closing the deal. So you want to find an agent who has your best interest at heart.

The concept of a buyer's agent arose because of concerns about conflicts of interest between buyers and the agents. In the past, a real estate agent always represented the seller—whether the agent had listed the house himself or was simply showing it to buyers, he worked on the seller's be-half. So a buyer could go to an agent, explain what he was looking for and how much he was willing to pay, and grow to trust that agent. But the agent had no obligation to fulfill that trust. In fact, as a subagent of the seller, he was legally bound to give the seller any information that was in the seller's best interest to know. So if a buyer said, "Let's ask for a $5,000 credit to pay for roof repairs, but I'll buy the house even if the seller doesn't go for it," the agent would have to let the seller know that the sale didn't hinge on granting that credit. No one protected the buyer's interests.

By the mid-1990s, the idea of a buyer's agent was in place, and most states had disclosure laws that required real estate agents to tell you whom they represent: the seller, the buyer, or both. When you agree to work with an agent, the agent must clarify your relationship, spelling out her responsi-bilities toward you. In some states, a conversation is sufficient; others re-quire a written statement (as the next section explains).

Your buyer's agent may represent you in one of several ways:

- **Buyer's agent—single agency.** In this role, the agent works for a bro-kerage that represents both buyers and sellers. However, this agent represents only you, the buyer, as you shop for and purchase a home.

- **Buyer's agent—dual agency.** Dual agency happens when a single agent represents both the buyer and the seller (for example, when you call a home's listing agent to see a house and decide to work with that agent) or when the buyer's agent and the seller's agent both work for the same broker. The box on page 83 goes over some of the conflicts of interests that may arise in a dual agency.

- **Exclusive buyer's agent (EBA).** This kind of agent works for a real es-tate agency that represents only buyers. The agency doesn't list prop-erties, so the agents who work there never represent a seller. If you work with an exclusive buyer's agent, you may have to pay an up-front retainer—and you may not get a refund if the agent fails to find you a home.

As page 85 explains, buyer's agents usually get paid a commission, splitting the fee with the listing agent. But buyer's agents can be paid in other ways, so make sure you know how your agent earns his money. Here are some of the ways buyer's agents may get paid:

- **A percentage of the purchase price.** This is the most common method.
- **A percentage of the purchase price and a bonus based on the difference between the listing price and the purchase price.** In other words, the agent gets a bonus if she negotiates a sale price below the asking price. For example, you might give your agent a bonus of $100 for every $1,000 below the asking price you buy the home, up to whatever maximum you're willing to pay. This gives the agent an incentive to bargain hard on your behalf.
- **A flat hourly fee.**
- **An hourly fee plus an up-front retainer.**
- **An hourly fee with a specified minimum number of hours.**

 Tip Commissions and fees are always negotiable. Don't be afraid to ask for a lower commission or a lower hourly fee.

Although your buyer's agent has a fiduciary duty to represent your interests in a transaction, the commission system comes with a built-in conflict of interest: The more you pay for a home, the more money the agent makes. So some unscrupulous buyer's agents may steer a buyer toward certain listings or advise you to overbid.

 Note *Fiduciary duty* means a legal responsibility to act in the best interests of another party.

A good buyer's agent puts your interests first because it's the law. But smart buyer's agents also realize that a satisfied client (and the good word of mouth that comes with it) is more important than a few hundred bucks. An extra $10,000 in the purchase price puts between $150 and $300 in the agent's pocket. Ethical agents realize that a client's trust in them has value far beyond that.

Signing with a Buyer's Agent

To formalize your relationship when you hire a buyer's agent, you'll most likely sign a buyer's agency or buyer's brokerage agreement. (In some states, agency can be based on a verbal agreement, but it's always a good idea to get it in writing.) This agreement specifies that the buyer's agent works for you and spells out each party's responsibilities.

There are countless variations on buyer's agency agreements depending on where you live and the policies and practices of the agency you choose, but a typical agreement addresses these issues:

- **Your relationship with the agent.** This may be exclusive or nonexclusive:

  An *exclusive* buyer's agency agreement specifies that you'll work only with this agent to look for a home.

  A *nonexclusive* buyer's agency agreement places no limit on the number of agents you can work with, but it usually specifies that you can't use one agent to buy a house another agent showed you first.

- **The term of the agreement.** This may cover a period of days from the date of signing or specify an end date. If the agent helps you buy a house within that time frame, the agreement ends when you close on the house.

- **The geographic area of the agreement.** If you're looking for a primary home in the city and a weekend home three hours away , the same agent probably can't help you. So this section lists the counties covered by the agreement.

- **The types of property covered by the agreement.** This typically says that the agreement covers any residential property you might buy, whether listed with an agency or by an owner (see page 121).

- **How the agent gets paid.** As page 88 shows, buyer's agents can get paid in a variety of ways. This section spells out the compensation model. For example, you might agree to pay a certain amount toward the agent's fee if the commission received from the listing agent falls below a minimum threshold.

- **Whether you'll accept dual agency.** Not all states allow dual agency because of potential conflicts of interest (as the box on page 83 explains).

- **Whether the agent is an exclusive buyer's agent.** EBAs (page 87) represent only buyers and will never represent a seller during the term of your agreement.

- **The agent's responsibilities toward you.** This section describes what the agent will do for you: find suitable properties, negotiate on your behalf, uphold fiduciary duties to act in your best interests, respect confidentiality, and so on.

- **How the agent will handle your earnest money.** When you make an offer, you back up that offer with earnest money (page 250) to show you're not just fooling around and wasting everyone's time. The agent may hold onto your check until the seller accepts your offer; after that, the agent deposits the earnest money in an escrow account.

Don't rely on a handshake to cement your relationship with a buyer's agent. Get it in writing. And if you have any concerns about your relationship with the agent that aren't addressed in the agreement, bring them up. Working with the agent, you may be able to amend the agreement.

Finding an Agent You Can Work With

Don't assume that you have to go house-hunting with the first real estate agent you talk to, whether that agent is a buyer's or a seller's agent. You'll be working with your agent for weeks or months, so take the time to find a good partner in your search for a home. Talk to several agents and to their former clients before you choose your buyer's agent.

Interview agents

Employers wouldn't dream of hiring a new employee without an interview. When you choose an agent to work with, you effectively hire that agent. After you contact several agents, choose three who seem like good candidates. Sit down with each for a heart-to-heart. During the conversation, take notes and pay attention to body language.

Here are some questions to ask during the interview:

- **Do you work as an agent full-time?** If not, find out how much time the agent devotes to his real estate practice. You want an agent who's available when you have a question or concern.

- **How long have you been selling real estate?** An experienced agent knows the local market and is both familiar and comfortable with the process of buying a home.

- **How many homes did you help buyers purchase last year?** Ask for a list of these homes, along with the listing price and purchase price.

- **Do you represent both buyers and sellers?** If the agent says yes, ask how she handles a dual agency.

- **What's your average list-price-to-purchase-price ratio?** As a buyer, you want to find an agent with a good track record of negotiating deals. Look for a ratio that shows the agent has helped buyers purchase homes for less than the asking price. For example, say the agent helped three clients buy houses that were all listed for $250,000: The first client paid $243,000 (97.2 percent of the list price), the second paid $248,500 (99.4 percent of the list price), and the third paid $241,900 (96.7 percent of the list price). That agent would have a list-price-to-purchase-price ratio of 97.7 percent, showing that, on average, his clients paid 97.7 percent of the sellers' asking prices. When you compare two agents, a lower list-price-to-purchase-price ratio may indicate a better negotiator.

- **How will we communicate?** Some agents will pick up the phone and call you when they see a listing you might like. Others will shoot you an email. Some contact clients frequently—possibly several times a day—others less so. Make sure the agent's preferred communication style is compatible with your own.

- **How many buyers and sellers do you represent right now?** What you're really asking here is whether the agent has sufficient time to devote to help finding you a home. A super-busy agent who's going to four or five closings a week and hosting open houses every weekend may not.

- **What's your assessment of the current state of the local market?** Find out whether the agent sees the current market as a buyer's market, a seller's market, or something in between—and how that will affect how she works with you.

- **What's your strategy for helping me find a home?** Listen to what the agent says about how he hunts down homes that look like a good match. If you're likely to be in stiff competition with other buyers, ask how the agent handles multiple offers on the same property.

- **Do you have access to homes that are For Sale by Owner (FSBO)?** Some homeowners decide to sell their homes themselves, without the assistance of a real estate agent (see page 86). If you're interested in FS-BOs, ask how the agent can help you find such homes. Ask, too, about how the agent gets paid when dealing with FSBOs.

- **Will you help me find the other professionals I need to buy a home?** Your agent can refer you to preferred lenders and title companies, home inspectors, and real estate attorneys. You don't have to take any of these recommendations, but you might find it helpful to get suggestions of people who've worked well with the agent in the past.

 Tip If the agent is "affiliated" with other real estate professionals, ask whether the agent receives a referral fee when someone becomes a client of those professionals. Be wary of any recommendation in which the agent has a financial interest—and perhaps of the agent who does business that way.

- **How do you find most of your clients?** Look for an agent who does lots of business with repeat clients and referrals.

- **Can you give me some references to contact?** The section below discusses what to ask people who've worked with the agent in the past. You want to know about *buyers'* experiences, so you don't have to contact people who sold their homes with this agent.

- **What happens if you don't find me a home?** If things don't work out with this agent, you need to be able to cancel the agency contract and move on.

- **What other question should I ask you?** How the agent answers this question indicates what she thinks buyers in your area need to know.

Check references

After you interview agents, you may have a strong sense of which you'd like to work with. Before you sign a buyer's brokerage agreement (page 89), though, call some buyers the agent has worked with in the past. Checking references can confirm your hunch—or send up a red flag. It can also serve as a tiebreaker if you're having a tough time deciding between two agents.

When you call references, be considerate. After all, the person is doing you a favor. Don't call at an inconvenient time, like dinner hours or late at night. Introduce yourself, explain why you're calling, and ask whether the person has a few minutes to talk to you (if you get "no" for an answer, ask if there's a more convenient time when you can call back). Keep the phone call brief, but try not to hang up with a lot of unanswered questions.

Ask these questions to get a sense of how well the agent worked with previous buyers :

- Describe your overall experience working with the agent.

- Would you describe the agent as honest and trustworthy?

- Did the agent devote sufficient time to working with you? Was it ever difficult to arrange a showing or a meeting because the agent was too busy? Did the agent deliver offers and complete paperwork on time?

- What did you like best about working with the agent?

- What did you find most frustrating about working with the agent?

- Would you work with this agent again?

- Looking back on your home-buying experience, do you think this agent helped you make the right choice?

Take notes during the conversation, and be sure to thank the person for her time before you end the call.

 Tip Go online to read reviews of real estate agents in your area at *www.homethinking. com* and *www.incredibleagents.com*.

Make a decision and make it legal

After you speak to references, you have the information you need to choose an agent. Take these factors into account:

- **Compatibility.** Is the agent someone you'd enjoy working with? You're not looking for a new best friend, but you'll spend a lot of time with your agent as you tour homes, discuss strategy, fill out paperwork, and do the myriad other activities involved in buying a home. Your agent should be compatible with you in terms of personality, approach, and communication style.

- **Understanding.** It's important that your agent "gets" what you're looking for in a home. Otherwise, you'll both waste your time looking at properties that aren't a good fit for you.

- **Availability.** Look for an agent who'll work with your schedule. You don't want to find yourself missing opportunities because you can never find a common time to meet.

- **Trustworthiness.** Your agent has a fiduciary duty toward you; that means your relationship is based on trust and confidence. You need to work with someone you trust to deal with you fairly, to keep a lid on your confidential information, and to represent you with both honesty and honor.

Once you decide on an agent, sign a buyer's agency agreement (page 89). A written, signed agreement clarifies the responsibilities of you and your agent both—so you can get on with the business of finding your dream home.

Helping Your Agent Help You

No matter how perfectly you can picture yourself in your future home, your agent isn't a mind-reader. To get the most out of your relationship with your agent, share information about what you want for your new home. You know to cover the basics—price range, neighborhood, style of home—but think broadly, too. Here are some questions to get you started:

- **What are your plans for the future?** You're probably thinking ahead to the day you'll move in to your new home. But living in a new home doesn't end with the excitement of moving day. How is your life likely to change during the years you'll be in the home? For example, you might start a family, send your last kid off to college, or have an aging parent move in. You might be planning to start a home business or go back to school. Look ahead 5 or 10 years, and then share that vision with your agent, who can help you find homes that have the potential to accommodate your plans.

- **How will you use the home?** Maybe you need a home office or workshop. If you entertain frequently, you might want a house with a formal dining room or an open floor plan. If you're an avid gardener, you need space for your garden to grow. Think about the activities you'll do in the home, and your agent can focus on homes that match your preferences.

- **What problems have you had in your past homes?** If you can complain for hours about the time you lived next door to a noisy nightclub or the drafty old barn where you shivered though an entire winter, your agent can help you avoid similar problems in the future.

Agents have tons of experience matching homebuyers with homes that suit their needs and their lifestyles. Your agent may be able to see the potential—and potential problems—in homes that you might not. The more your agent knows about you, the better she can focus on finding homes that are a good fit.

Firing Your Agent

Not all matches are made in heaven—and that goes for relationships between homebuyers and agents, too. If the thrill is gone and your agent isn't doing the job you expected, how do you move on?

It may not be easy. Agents do a lot of up-front work for free—usually they don't get paid until you close on a house. So they need to protect themselves from unscrupulous buyers who use up a lot of their time and then try to cut them out of a deal. You may have to request a clause in your agent agreement that lets you terminate your relationship with 48 hours' notice. Make it clear that you want to work with the agent and expect to have a mutually rewarding relationship, but you need a termination clause in case things don't work out. If the agent is unwilling to include such a clause, you might want to set up a trial period by limiting the term of the agreement to 30 or 60 days.

You should only fire your agent with good reason: if, for example, she doesn't show you appropriate homes or return your phone calls or emails. Before you fire an agent, sit down and have a talk; you may be able to work things out. If that doesn't happen, you have three choices:

- If your agency agreement has a termination clause, give notice that you're ending the agreement. Don't look at houses with the agent during the notification period. If you end up buying a home that you found while the agreement was still in effect, you may owe the fired agent her commission.

- If your agency agreement doesn't have a termination clause, explain to the agent why you feel the agreement isn't working out and that you want to end it. The agent may or may not agree.

- If the agent doesn't agree to end your relationship, talk to the agent's boss, the broker who manages the agency. If the broker won't end the agreement, you have to wait for it to expire.

 Note Don't fire an agent and then buy a house that the agent already showed you. You could be setting yourself up for a lawsuit.

Your Mortgage Provider

Not many people have enough cash on hand to pay for a house. So an important member of your team is the mortgage provider who fronts the money that lets you buy the home. You may find financing through a mortgage broker or deal directly with a lender.

Working with a Mortgage Broker

Think of a mortgage broker as a matchmaker. But instead of helping people find their soulmates, a broker matches homebuyers and lenders. If you choose a mortgage broker, you work directly with her, and she acts as an intermediary between you and the lender.

Mortgage brokers work for brokerage firms, and both federal and state laws regulate them; most states require these firms to be licensed. Many brokers are members of the National Association of Mortgage Brokers (NAMB), which offers three levels of certification:

- **General Mortgage Associate (GMA).** This entry-level certification shows a threshold level of professional knowledge about the mortgage industry. To receive GMA certification, a broker must pass an exam, but no industry experience is required.

- **Certified Residential Mortgage Specialist (CRMA).** Brokers with this level of certification have at least two years' experience under their belts. They must also pass an exam and earn at least 50 qualifying points, which are awarded for professional activities such as education, getting other certifications, experience, and leadership.

- **Certified Mortgage Consultant (CMC).** This is the highest level of certification NAMB offers. It requires five years of experience in the industry, passing an advanced exam, and a minimum of 100 qualifying points for professional education and activities.

Here's what you can expect a mortgage broker to do:

- Gather information about your finances, employment, and credit history (page 39) and assess your eligibility for a mortgage based on that information

- Identify loans from a variety of lenders that meet your needs

- Present those loans to you, along with a clear explanation of how they work and what the terms mean

- Help you get preapproved (page 34) for a mortgage
- Help you apply for a mortgage, from gathering documentation to filling out the paperwork
- Present your mortgage application to a lender
- Keep track of all the conditions you must meet before closing, acting as a liaison between you and the lender, home appraiser, surveyor, various insurers, and so on
- Facilitate the closing, making sure that all your documents are in order and that the lender transfers the funds

Mortgage brokers typically get paid 1 to 2 percent of the loan amount. They may collect money through direct fees (called processing, origination, or brokerage fees), a slightly higher interest rate on your loan, or a combination of the two. *You* pay the mortgage broker, so be aware that these fees are open to negotiation. A good mortgage broker should be able to match you up with a loan that pays her fees by finding a lower-cost loan that you could find yourself.

 Note About a two-thirds of American homebuyers get their mortgage through a broker; the rest work directly with a lender.

As with your real estate agent, talk with several mortgage brokers and check references before you agree to work with one. In fact, it's even more important to check out potential mortgage brokers thoroughly—in most states (California is an exception), mortgage brokers have no fiduciary duty toward their clients. In plain English, that means the broker has no legal obligation to put your interests before his own. Good mortgage brokers are ethical and do serve your best interests, but you don't want to find yourself in a situation where greed makes a broker steer you toward a loan that's not the best deal for you.

Before you agree to work with a mortgage broker, get the answers to these questions:

- **Are you licensed (this is not required in all states) and/or do you belong to any professional associations, such as NAMB?** Membership in one of these associations suggests a level of professionalism and industry experience.

- **How long have you worked as a mortgage broker?** You want to work with a broker who's successfully matched buyers and lenders for at least two years.

- **Do you specialize in residential mortgages?** For this question, "yes" is the answer you want to hear.

- **How many residential mortgages have you brokered in the past year?** Look for someone who's successfully brokered 10 or more mortgages.

- **I'd like to make sure the broker I work with has my best interests in mind. What kind of fiduciary duty do you feel you have to clients?** Make sure the broker convinces you that she's working on your behalf and not putting herself first.

- **Could you give me the names and contact information of three recent clients to serve as references?** If the broker can't provide references, move on.

Check references the same way you checked them for your real estate agent (page 92). Ask these questions:

- When did you work with the broker?

- Did she listen to your needs and concerns?

- How responsive was she? Did she answer your questions clearly and give you information in a timely manner?

- Did she present you with a variety of loan choices?

- Are you happy with the loan you chose?

- Did the broker help you throughout the process of getting a loan?

- What did you like about working with this broker?

- What frustrations did you experience in getting a mortgage?

- Would you choose this broker again if you were in the market for a loan?

Satisfied clients are a good indication that you've found a good broker.

Working with a Mortgage Lender

Some homebuyers prefer to work directly with a lender. You might want to deal with a local bank or credit union that has a thorough understanding of your area, or you might prefer to use the Internet to research the best rates yourself (page 197). If you go directly to a bank or other financial institution, you'll deal with a *loan officer*. This person works with you just as a mortgage broker does, identifying appropriate loans, analyzing your financial information, and guiding you through the mortgage process from application through closing. Unlike a mortgage broker, who searches different lenders' products to find you the best loans, a loan officer is employed by a particular lender. That means she'll present only mortgages offered by that lender.

If you work directly with a mortgage lender, you probably won't get to choose your loan officer the way you choose a mortgage broker. Because loan officers work for a particular financial institution, you'll most likely get an appointment with whoever is available. Even so, if a friend or family member had a good experience working with a loan officer, see if you can set up an appointment with that person.

What about a loan officer's fiduciary duty? The situation here is more clear-cut than when you work with a mortgage broker. A loan officer is an employee of a bank, credit union, or other financial institution. The lender—not you—pays the loan officer. So never forget that your loan officer, no matter how nice and friendly, is working for the lender.

Your Real Estate Attorney

Buying a home means scaling a small mountain of paperwork—over and over again, you have to sign your name on the bottom line. It's essential to understand each and every piece of paper you sign. Your real estate agent and mortgage broker or loan officer can explain many of the contracts and forms involved in your transaction—but neither of these people is a lawyer. It's a good idea to have a qualified real estate attorney on your side to scrutinize the fine print, answer questions, and explain difficult concepts.

Every state has its own real estate laws. In some, such as New York, a real estate attorney is a normal and expected part of the home-buying transaction: Only an attorney can prepare the home purchase documents, perform a title search, and close the deal. In other states, such as California, your agent will help you fill in the blanks on standard forms that have already been approved by the state bar association. An escrow officer (see Chapter 13) handles the closing, so you may not need an attorney. But even if your state doesn't require an attorney, consider bringing one on board early in the process. If things go wrong, it's better to have an attorney who's familiar with your situation than to rush around looking for one who might be able to salvage a deal.

What an attorney can do for you

If you're a first-time buyer, a real estate attorney can give you peace of mind as you go through an unfamiliar and complex process. Here are some of the services a real estate attorney provides:

- Reviews the purchase agreement before you sign it and, if necessary, revises it. Or, if you already signed a purchase agreement and worry there's a problem, an attorney can void a purchase contract if it violates your state's laws.

- Reviews (or in some cases performs) a title search for the property, which confirms that the seller is its legal owner. (Page 268 tells you all about title searches.)

- Reviews all other legal documents related to the purchase, including the deed. If there are mistakes in the deed, such as misspelled names, the attorney can correct them.

- Prorates costs you split with the seller. For example, the seller may have prepaid a year's worth of property taxes, and you have to reimburse her for that money from the date you take ownership.

- Coordinates among agents, your mortgage broker or loan officer, the lender's attorney, and the seller's attorney to make sure all documents are ready for the closing.

Even experienced homebuyers should consult an attorney in certain situations:

- **For complex transactions.** If legal issues arise and your real estate agent doesn't know how to address them, you definitely need a real estate attorney. For example, say the current owner converted his garage into a studio apartment that doesn't have a certificate of occupancy; you want to know whether you can legally rent out the apartment. Or you want to buy a home with a partner who's not a relative, or through a trust. If your situation doesn't fit the language of standardized real estate forms, an attorney can get the wording right.

- **When you don't have a real estate agent.** If you buying a FSBO home (page 86) directly from a seller, you definitely need an attorney to help you with the paperwork and make sure everything is legal.

- **When your state requires it.** As mentioned earlier, some states require an attorney to prepare certain documents related to the purchase of a home. Ask your real estate agent if that's the case in your area.

Choose a real estate attorney

It's important to pick an attorney with expertise in real estate law. A lawyer might be a whiz at tax or probate law or corporate mergers, but unless she has significant experience with residential real estate transactions, you don't want to hire her for this job. So before you hire an attorney, ask these questions:

- **How much experience do you have in residential real estate transactions?** Look for an attorney who has five or more years of experience. An attorney who specializes primarily in commercial or rental real estate may not be the best person to represent you in a home purchase.

- **How many homebuyers have you represented in the past year?** At least 10 shows that representing home buyers is a significant part of the attorney's practice.

- **How do you charge for your services?** Some attorneys charge a flat fee for real estate transactions, others charge by the hour. Ask how much in attorney's fees a typical home purchase costs. Fees may vary widely; for example, hourly fees may range from $150 to $350 for each hour of the attorney's time.

- **Have you ever been sued for malpractice or disciplined by a bar association?** It's in your interest to hire a competent attorney with a clean ethical slate.

- **Will you provide me with a list of recent clients?** Get at least three names.

 Tip Before you hire an attorney, check with your state's disciplinary agency to make sure that the attorney hasn't been in trouble for ethical or other violations. You can download a list of state disciplinary agencies, complete with addresses, phone numbers, and website information, from the American Bar Association at *www.abanet.org/cpr/regulation/directory.pdf*.

References don't mean much unless you check them. So talk to some of the attorney's previous clients to get their opinions and their answers to these questions:

- How did you choose this attorney? Did someone recommend her or had you worked with her before?

- What services did she provide?

- Did she meet deadlines and return your phone calls and emails promptly?

- Did she explain concepts and answer your questions clearly?
- Were you satisfied with her work?
- Would you work with her again?

Your Home Inspector

In the movie *The Money Pit*, a young couple buys what looks like a beautiful home at a bargain price—until the house starts to fall down around them. A home inspector makes sure you don't meet the same fate.

When you tour a home, it's easy to notice the cosmetics—you like the carpet in the living room, but the kitchen cabinets have got to go. But how do you know whether the home's foundation is solid and the central systems (electrical, heating/cooling, plumbing) work the way they should? No matter how well-maintained a home appears, it can hide problems that require a trained eye to spot.

A home inspector gives your prospective property a thorough going-over, from roof to foundation, checking the structure and its systems. Chapter 12 shows you what a home inspector does, step by step.

The purchase offer (page 249) your real estate agents writes up should include a contingency (page 251) that tells the seller the offer is valid only if you're satisfied with the results of the home inspection. Typically, this contingency gives you 17 days to withdraw your offer or move forward with your purchase: 14 days to conduct a home inspection and 3 days to make your decision. You should interview inspectors and choose the one you want to work with *before* you make an offer on a house. At busy times of the year or in areas where the real estate market is hot, you may find your preferred home inspector has a waiting list. So find an inspector and call her as soon as your offer is accepted.

 Tip Some sellers have a home inspection done before they put their home on the market. Even in that case, you should still hire a home inspector to look over the property. The couple of hundred dollars you'll spend is worth it to get a second opinion.

As with the other real estate professionals on your team, you should interview home inspectors before you choose one. Ask these questions:

- **Are you a full-time home inspector?** This isn't a guarantee of competence, but it shows that the inspector is in enough demand to make a living at it and suggests dedication to the job and (perhaps) better availability.

- **How long have you been inspecting homes professionally?** You want an experienced home inspector, especially one who's familiar with your area and the problems that commonly occur there. Look for one who's been in the business for at least a couple of years.

- **Do you have training in home inspections?** Many home inspectors have a background in construction, but inspecting homes is a specialized discipline that requires specialized training. It's a good sign if the inspector has taken classes in home inspection.

- **Are you a member of any professional associations, and do you have any special certifications?** Some of the professional associations for home inspectors are the American Society of Home Inspectors (ASHI), the International Association of Certified Home Inspectors (InterNACHI), and the National Association of Home Inspectors (NAHI). Each of these organizations have standards of practice and a code of ethics that members must follow.

- **Do you have up-to-date professional liability insurance?** Sometimes called errors and omissions insurance, this policy covers the home inspector in case there's a mistake or oversight in the inspection report. If things go wrong and you end up having to sue the inspector over a faulty report, this insurance means you'll get paid if you win a judgment.

- **What does your inspection cover? May I see a sample report?** The inspector should assure you that your inspection meets state criteria (if applicable) and complies with the standards of practice and code of ethics of one of the major home inspectors' associations. Look for a report that goes into a lot of detail instead of a quick checklist. (For an example of a good inspection report, check out page 302.)

- **How many residential home inspections did you do in this area in the past year?** Look for one to two per month at a minimum.

- **How long does a typical inspection take?** A thorough home inspection takes two to three hours for a single-family home. If the inspector whizzes through it in less time, he may miss problems.

- **May I attend the inspection?** If you're on site during the inspection, you can ask questions and see potential problems for yourself. If the inspector doesn't want you around, choose someone else.

- **How quickly will I get the report after the inspection?** Most inspectors deliver a report within 24 hours. And find out how the inspector gets the report to you as well—via email, fax, or in print.

- **Can you give me the names and contact information of at least three references?** Homeowners know for sure how thorough a home inspection was only after they move in. It's a good idea to talk to previous clients to find out whether the inspector missed something important.

When you get a list of references, check them out (page 92 gives tips for checking references). Here are some questions to ask:

- When did you work with the home inspector?
- Did the inspector show up on time and deliver the completed report promptly?
- Did you accompany the inspector? If so, did he explain what he was doing and answer your questions?
- How much time did he spend going over the property?
- Was the home inspection report thorough, easy to understand, and supported with photos and/or documentation?
- Have any problems arisen that the inspector should have pointed out but didn't?
- Would you choose this home inspector again?

Watch out for inspectors who rushed through the inspection or who missed issues that later turned into problems for the buyer.

Other Real Estate Professionals

By now you've met the main players. Here are some other professionals you might want on your home-buying team:

- **Accountant.** Your accountant or tax preparer can clue you in on the tax breaks associated with buying a home.
- **Appraiser.** Lenders need to know that a house is worth at least as much as you're paying for it. An appraiser inspects the house and compares it to similar properties in the area to determine its worth.

 Later, after you build some equity in your home, you may hire an appraiser when you apply to cancel private mortgage insurance (page 146).

- **Contractor.** If you're thinking about buying a fixer-upper or making significant renovations to a home, it's a smart move to have a contractor estimate how much the repairs and renovations will cost before you submit an offer.

- **Escrow officer.** Sometimes called an escrow agent or closing agent, this neutral third party makes sure that the transaction proceeds as it should—in other words, that both you and the seller are living up to your agreement. The escrow officer may be an attorney, a full-time escrow agent, or someone who works for a title agency. In a typical sale, the escrow officer has these responsibilities:

  — Sets up an escrow account to hold money related to the sale, such as your earnest money (page 250), until closing

  — Holds signed documents until all paperwork related to the sale is complete

  — Performs the title search and arranges for title insurance

  — Prorates costs, such as taxes and bills that the seller has already paid

  — Prepares the final paperwork

  — Distributes money due at closing

  — Ensures that the sale happens properly and legally

 Note In some states, such as California and Arizona, brokers and title companies are allowed to prepare legal contracts and title documents, hold money in escrow, and close real estate deals. These states are called "escrow states." In other states, such as New York, only attorneys can perform these tasks. These are called "title states." Your real estate agent can tell you whether you're in an escrow or title state. For more on how closings work in escrow states versus titles states, see Chapter 13.

- **Insurance agent.** At the closing, you need to prove to your lender that you've insured your property, so you need to find an insurance agent who specializes in homeowner's insurance. Page 273 has tips on how to shop for homeowner's insurance.

5 Shop for Your Home

You've laid the groundwork—taken a good, hard look at your finances, gotten preapproved for a mortgage, written a wish list for things you want in your new home, and started putting together your real estate team. Now, you're ready to look at some houses.

In this chapter, you'll learn the art of touring houses and how to reconcile your wish list with what's on the market. You'll find homes for sale from both traditional sources (real estate classified ads and working with a real estate agent) and nontraditional sources (websites that let you sort listings by your preferences). And you'll scour the market for bargains, like homes that are owner-offered, bank-offered, and in foreclosures or at auction. Read on to search for your new home and keep your priorities in mind, even as you face a bewildering choice of listings.

Select Homes to Tour

It's time to go house hunting! Before you get out the tape measure to see if your king-sized bed fits in the master bedroom, you need to put together a list of homes to tour—houses that fit your price range and meet your needs. In this section, you'll find out how to add houses to your list by working with your agent, searching the Internet, and pounding the pavement in your target neighborhoods.

Working with a Real Estate Agent

When you've got a buyer's agent on your team, real estate listings come to you. It's your agent's job to keep an eye out for houses that fit your price range and wish list. So after you choose an agent (page 90 gives you tips for doing that), sit down and discuss what you're looking for. Include these details:

- Price range
- Preferred style
- Number of bedrooms
- Number of bathrooms
- Preferred neighborhoods
- Any high-priority special requirements, such as a workshop, garage, or finished basement

 Tip If you wrote up a wish list (page 77), give your agent a copy. It will help her remember what you want as she scours listings for you.

Your agent will search the **MLS**, also known as the Multiple Listing Service, an exhaustive database of homes for sale in your region. Real estate agents subscribe to the MLS to pool their listings and make it easy for agents to find potential homes for their clients. A typical MLS listing includes one or more photos of the house, its asking price, its square footage, the number and types of rooms, the lot size, and other information. When your agent finds properties that look like a good fit, she'll send you the listings via email or call you to discuss them. If any of the listings look appealing, your agent sets up appointments to get you inside the houses so you can take a look around. She'll meet you at each home and give you a tour.

Tip Some agents walk with you from room to room; others hang back and let you explore on your own. If you have a preference, let your agent know.

These tips will help you get the most out of working with a buyer's agent:

- **Keep appointments and be on time.** Setting up tours of six or seven homes on a Saturday takes a lot of coordination: The current occupants need to vamoose so you can feel free to look around, and the listing agent may want to be there. If you're late, the carefully planned appointments topple over like a stack of dominoes—and you may not be able to tour all the houses you planned to see.

- **Don't waste the agent's time.** Remember that most agents work on commission (page 85)—if they don't close a deal, they don't get paid. So if you're not really sure whether you're ready to buy a house, don't sign up with an agent yet. Scratch your real estate itch by visiting open houses instead (page 120).

- **Be proactive.** Keep an eye on local listings yourself by reading the newspaper and checking Internet real estate sites (page 114). If you see a home you like, contact your agent to discuss the property and arrange a showing.

- **Don't call listing agents yourself.** If you see a For Sale sign in a yard or an ad in the paper, don't call the property's listing agent to set up a showing. If you do, the listing agent will expect to represent you in any negotiations—putting you in a dual agency conundrum (see page 83). Instead, call your agent, identify the property you're interested in, and let her handle things from there.

- **Ask questions.** They say the only stupid question is the one you don't ask. Your agent is a resource with a lot of experience helping people buy homes—make good use of that resource. If you have any questions about the process or the papers you sign, ask.

- **Communicate.** Agents can do a lot of things for you, but reading your mind *isn't* one of them. At every stage of the process, communicate clearly. Let your agent know what you're looking for, when you're available, and how you want her to contact you. If problems arise (for example, if the agent isn't staying in touch as often as you'd like), let her know. That's the only way you can work together to find a solution.

- **Give feedback.** After you tour some homes, talk to your agent about what you liked and disliked about each. This helps her narrow her focus in finding properties for you to tour. The more she knows about your preferences, the better she can target homes to show you.

 Tip When your agent has a clear idea of what you're looking for, she'll be able to contact you as soon as she hears about a good match coming on the market—sometimes before the house gets listed on the MLS.

- **Get referrals for other real estate professionals.** Your agent works with lenders, appraisers, home inspectors, insurers, and other professionals on a regular basis. Tap into her network by asking for a list of recommendations. It's still up to you, of course, to research the candidates and make a decision.

 Tip Chapter 4 lists questions to ask the real estate professionals you'll need on your team.

Decoding Real Estate Ads

Real estate ads—whether online, in the classified section of a newspaper, or in one of those free regional "homes for sale" magazines—have their own language. As a new homebuyer, you may feel like you need a crash course in real-estate-ese to make sense of them. Otherwise, you could be disappointed when you arrive at a house expecting "charming period details" and find scuffed hardwood floors and cracked plaster walls.

It's the listing agent's job to stimulate buyer interest in a home. Naturally, the agents write ads that make each house seem as enticing as possible. With just a few words, they try to create a picture in your mind's eye and a homey feeling that makes you want to pick up the phone and schedule a tour. Although some ads use descriptive terms like sunny and efficiency kitchen realistically, others use them as euphemisms to put the best spin on potential issues, trying to turn deficits into features.

The following table lists some common terms from real estate ads, along with translations of what the terms can really mean.

What the ad says:	What it may really mean:
Charming	Old
Close to everything	In a commercial district
Cozy	Small, cramped
Cute as a button	Small, cramped
Diamond in the rough	Requires repairs
Dollhouse	Small, cramped
Easy access to highway	You can hear trucks rumble past
Efficiency/galley/railroad kitchen	A very small, narrow kitchen
Grand	Expensive; inefficient to heat and cool
Grandma's house	Outdated appliances and interior décor
Great/terrific potential	Has significant problems you'll have to fix
Handyman's/contractor's special	Requires extensive repairs
Intimate	Small, cramped
Jewel box	Small, cramped
Low-maintenance yard	Small or paved yard
Must see inside	Home's exterior is unattractive
Needs TLC	Requires repairs
Not a drive-by	Home's exterior is unattractive
Private	Isolated
Ready to move in	Vacant
Sold "as is"	Requires repairs (and the seller won't help you pay for them)
Sunny	No trees to shade the house
Unique/custom design	May have oddities in the floor plan
Updated	Some kind of renovation was done some time between last week and the previous century—ask what and when
Winter views	Trees block the view during the other three seasons
Won't last long!	Seller considers the current price to be rock-bottom and won't accept lower offers

Of course, seeing these terms in an ad *doesn't* mean you should cross the house off your list without taking a look. Just don't let the wording of an ad influence you before you go into a house and judge it for yourself.

The Best Time to Go Househunting

Are some times of year better than others to shop for a home?

Conventional wisdom says that most homebuyers start shopping for homes in the spring—and conventional wisdom is right. Or mostly right. In many parts of the country, the cold, dark days of winter melting into flower-filled spring inspire people to get out and look for new quarters. Also, many people, if given the choice, prefer to move in the summer: The weather is less likely to cause moving-day problems, and parents want their kids to switch schools with minimal hassle. So if you shop in the spring through early summer, be aware that you'll probably have more competition than at other times of year.

Real estate sales tend to slow down in November, December, and January, and then gradually begin gathering steam again until they're in full force again in the spring and early summer. If you shop during the slower months, you may find that sellers are more flexible, especially if a home's been on the market for a while.

One caveat: In climates prone to hot, humid summers—especially those popular with retirees—the cooler winter months may be prime house-hunting season. Ask your real estate agent about local sales trends and whether some months are better than others for home shopping.

At the same time, of course, sellers are aware of the cyclical nature of the real estate market, and some wait until sales heat up before they list their homes. So even though you'll have more competition in the busy season, you'll have more choice as well.

The architectural terms that describe various features of a building may also seem mysterious if you're not familiar with them. Here are some you may encounter and their meaning:

Architectural term	Description
Bay window	A three-sided window that projects from the face of a building.
Bow window	A bay window that's curved, rather than angular.
Bulkhead	A slanted outside door over a stairway that leads to a basement.
Cathedral ceiling	A high ceiling that follows the line of the roof, often with the roof rafters exposed.
Clerestory windows	Pronounced "clear story," a row of windows high in a wall (above eye level) for admitting sunlight.
Cupola	A small structure, sometimes dome-shaped, that sits on the roof to admit air and (sometimes) sunlight.
Dormer window	A window that projects vertically from a sloping roof.
Eaves	The overhanging edges of a roof.

Fanlight	A fan-shaped window above a door or other window.
Gable	The triangular area formed by a sloping roof.
Gambrel roof	A barn-shaped roof, where a shallow pitch near the peak becomes a steeper pitch father down.
Gingerbread	Ornate exterior trim often found on Victorian-style homes.
Greenhouse window	A three-sided glass window with a glass roof and shelves for plants.
Hip roof	A roof that slopes from the peak to the eaves on all four sides of the house. Also called a hipped roof.
Mansard roof	A roof that slopes from all four sides of the house and has two pitches: shallower above and steeper below. The lower pitch usually has dormer windows.
Palladian window	A large window divided into three sections: an arched center window and two smaller side windows.
Skylight	A window in the roof, which may or may not open, to let in sunlight.

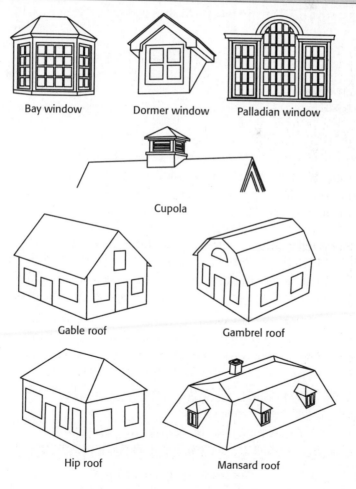

Bay window   Dormer window   Palladian window

Cupola

Gable roof   Gambrel roof

Hip roof   Mansard roof

Page 52 describes popular styles of single-family houses.

Shopping on the Internet

People shop for all kinds of items online: books, music, clothes, electronics, jewelry, furniture—and yes, even houses. You can't put a house in a virtual shopping cart and buy it with a single mouse click, but you can search the Web to find houses for sale. Looking at homes online is a great way to acquaint yourself with what's on the market, get a sense of prices, familiarize yourself with real-estate ads, and even take a peek inside available homes. Online research is particularly useful if you're relocating to an area far from your current home, because you can glean a lot of information and narrow your choices using online listings before you travel to tour homes in person. But even if you're searching locally, online real estate sites keep you abreast of the market and let you look at listings on your own time.

 A survey conducted by the National Association of Realtors showed that, in 2008, one-third of all homebuyers began their search online. And 87 percent of them used the Internet to shop for a home at some point in the process.

Realtor.com

A good website to start your online search is Realtor.com (*www.realtor.com*), sponsored by the National Association of Realtors. This site has access to information from more than 800 MLSes across the United States and Canada. You can search all the listings for an area by typing in a city and state or province and then clicking the Search button, or you can get specific and tell Realtor.com to look for homes that match your price range and wish list criteria: number of bedrooms, number of bathrooms, type of housing (single family, multi-family, condo, and so on), minimum size, and preferred features (fireplace, central air, laundry room, and so on).

After you tell Realtor.com what to search for, you get a list of available properties. You can sort this list by price or by number of photos per listing (to get a good sense of the way the place looks), or you can see the results on a map, letting you concentrate on listings in a particular neighborhood.

The listings vary in detail according to how much information the listing agent included, but most have at least one photo of the house (featured listings may have as many as 25), a rundown of its features and specifications, a way to contact the listing agent, and links to more of the agent's listings.

If you register (registration is optional and free), you can save your searches and individual listings to go back to them later—although the site automatically keeps track of your last five searches and the last five properties you view, even if you don't register. Registration also lets you opt in to receive email alerts when there's a change to one of your saved searches, or when new listings come on the market in the area you're searching.

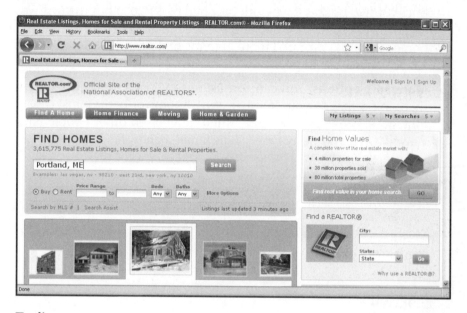

Trulia

Trulia (*www.trulia.com*) is a real estate search site brimming with useful data—and it's free. You search it just as described above: Enter information about the area you want to live in and (if you want) your price range and preferred features. Trulia's unique feature is the way it lets you sort the results. You get a plethora of options:

- **Newest.** Seeing new listings as soon as they come on the market can give you an edge over other buyers.

- **Number of photos.** Before you make an appointment to look at a house, you can check out the inside and the surroundings. Lots of pictures give you a clearer sense of whether this would be a good property to tour.

- **Price.** You can sort listings from lowest price to highest, or the other way around.

- **Price reduced date.** When a seller reduces a home's list price, it's a good indication that he's getting impatient to sell. You may be able to reach an agreement quickly or, if the price was reduced several weeks or months ago, find a seller who's open to counteroffers.

- **Price reduced $ (high to low).** This sorts reduced-price listings by dollar value—from those that have had the greatest drop in dollar value to those that have dropped the least.

- **Price reduced % (high to low).** You can also sort reduced-price listings by how much the price has dropped as a percentage of the original list price, from greatest percentage to least. For example, if the prices of two houses have both dropped by $10,000 but the first was originally priced at $600,000 and the second at $200,000, the second home's price has dropped more in terms of percentage: 5 percent vs. 1.5 percent for the more expensive home.

- **More sort options.** You can sort listings by just about any criterion that's important to you: Number of bedrooms or bathrooms, square footage, address, popularity of listing (how often other people have viewed it), and property type (single family, condo, land, and so on).

Tip Tell Trulia to find only listings with upcoming open houses or only listings that have been reduced in price (or both) by turning on the appropriate checkbox when you search.

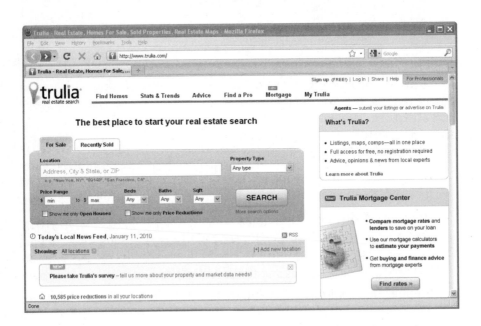

When you see a listing that looks interesting, click its address to get more information. The listing page has several tabs:

- **Home Facts.** This tab gives you the listing's basics: price, size, number of bedrooms and bathrooms, lot size, how long the listing has been on Trulia, and so on. Trulia calculates the price per square foot, which is useful when you want to compare how much living space different homes (and homes in different neighborhoods) offer for the price. Clicking the View More Details button takes you to the listing's page on the real estate agency's website.

- **Photos.** You can look at photos on the Home Facts tab, but the images are bigger and easier to scrutinize on this tab. Handily, this tab includes a number that tells you how many photos you can view. This tab may display both exterior and interior photos, depending on what the listing agent uploaded.

- **Maps & Nearby.** View the home in the context of its neighborhood by clicking this tab. You can see the home's location on a zoomable map and the locations of nearby schools, gas stations, grocery stores, restaurants, and banks. For many locations, you can see street-level photos of the neighborhood—especially helpful if you're searching at a distance and can't easily hop into the car and drive past.

- **Comparables.** Select this tab to see a map pinpointing other, nearby homes for sale in your price range. Hover your mouse pointer over any house location to open a box showing the comparable property and its price. Click "View more details" to open that property's listing page.

- **Sales Trends.** Trulia's strength is in giving you fast, useful information about local housing trends. Click this tab for an at-a-glance view of how a home compares to other listings in the area: its price in relation to those of similar homes and to those of all homes for sale in the town or neighborhood you're looking at. This tab also shows a graph charting the area's average listing price from week to week, so you can see whether prices are heading up or down.

- **Mortgage.** This tab includes a mortgage calculator so you can figure out a home's affordability. It also displays the current mortgage rates from a selection of banks. Keep in mind, though, that the mortgage payment calculator includes only principal and interest—taxes and insurance will be extra.

- **Schools.** This tab displays a map showing a house's location and its nearby schools. You can zoom in or out on the map. Click a school to see the school's address, phone number, and how many students and teachers it has. Click the name of the school to open Trulia's profile page for that school.

Yahoo Real Estate

One of the most popular real estate sites, Yahoo Real Estate (*http://real-estate.yahoo.com*) lists more than 4 million homes across the country. You can search for a home according to your preferences or restrict your search to just newly built homes or just foreclosures. Sort the results by price, size, number of bedrooms, or number of bathrooms.

Yahoo Real Estate gives a market snapshot of the city or town where you're househunting, including number of homes on the market, median price, and whether price trends are headed up or down. There's also information about mortgage rates in the area.

Zillow.com

Zillow (*www.zillow.com*) is helpful when you're looking at home values in a particular neighborhood (page 240), but it's also a great place to search for a home. Like other real estate sites, you can enter your search criteria and sort the results by price, size, and number of bedrooms or bathrooms. Zillow listings include some unique features:

- **Zestimate.** Zillow expresses its estimate of what a particular home is worth as both a specific price and a "value range," a high and low estimated market value. The smaller the value range, the more accurate the estimate.

- **Walk Score.** By looking at how close a home is to nearby amenities, Zillow assigns a score that indicates how easy it is to live a car-free lifestyle; the higher the Walk Score, the more walkable the home's neighborhood. The Walk Score has these categories and score ranges:

- **Car-Dependent, Driving Only (0–24).** You need a car to get from the home to just about anywhere else.

- **Car-Dependent (25–49).** There may be an amenity or two within walking range, but you need a car to get from this home to most destinations.

- **Somewhat Walkable (50–69).** You can walk to some stores and other amenities, but many errands require a car.

- **Very Walkable (70–89).** You can leave the car in the garage for most of your errands.

- **Walkers' Paradise (90–100).** Car? Who needs a car?

 Tip You can search for a new home on any of the real estate websites listed in this section; most of them have the same listings. Try each of them, and then work with the one that gives you the most useful information.

Agency websites

The big, national real estate agencies have websites you can use to launch your search for a house. Start with any of these:

- Century 21 (*www.century21.com*)

- Coldwell Banker (*http://coldwellbanker.com*)

- GMAC (*www.gmacrealestate.com*)

- Prudential Real Estate (*www.prudential.com/realestate*)

- RE/MAX (*www.remax.com*)

Each site lets you search by location, but the results show only homes listed with that agency's local office. You can also use these sites to find a buyer's agent and read articles about real estate.

Online classifieds

In ancient times (that is, before the Internet), people used to search for a home by getting the local paper and scouring the Real Estate section of the classified ads. You can still do that, of course, but it's a lot easier and faster to search the classifieds online. You'll get better results, too, because more and more classified advertising has moved off the page and onto the Web. Most newspaper websites have a Classifieds link or a Real Estate link (or both) that takes you to a page where you can view and sort current listings.

The best-known online classified ad side is craigslist (*http://craigslist.org*). Listing agents and "For Sale By Owner" sellers both use craigslist to advertise their properties. From the main craigslist page, select the region (state, city, province, or country) you're interested in. Then, under "housing" in the middle column, click "real estate for sale." Listings appear throughout the day; click any listing for more information and to contact the poster.

Cruising Neighborhoods

If you're moving to a different area in your city or to a nearby town, make an effort to drive, bike, or walk through the neighborhood where you hope to find a home. Sometimes an agent will plant a For Sale sign a day or two before the listing appears on the MLS, Realtor.com, or her agency's website. If you notice a sign in front of a house that interests you, jot down the listing agent's name and phone number. Then call your agent and ask her to set up a showing.

Asking Around

Tap into your network of friends and acquaintances; let everyone know that you're planning to buy a home. Spread the word among your friends, neighbors, coworkers, and other acquaintances. Someone may pipe up and say, "I know someone in that neighborhood who's planning to move." Getting an early lead on a potential listing can give you an edge—especially if you come recommended by a friend of the seller. Some people have bought homes this way before the properties ever made it onto the market.

Attending Open Houses

During an **open house**, usually held for a couple of hours on a Saturday or Sunday, you can tour a home at your own convenience and your own pace. An agent (or the seller of a FSBO) hosts. You can come in, pick up an information sheet listing the basics (number of bedrooms and bathrooms, square footage, and so on), look around, and ask questions. The host may ask you to take a business card or write your name and contact information on a guest sheet; the reason for the latter is so that, if you or your agent inquires about a listing and it turns out to be the same house, any eventual sale gets credited to the agent who hosted the open house.

Your buyer's agent doesn't have to accompany you to an open house. If you're thinking about making an offer on the home, though, be sure to let the listing agent know that you're already working with an agent—and get your agent involved ASAP.

An open house is an informal drop-in tour. But approach an open house the same way you approach a private tour (page 108): Bring along your wish list, take notes, look past the fresh flowers on the dining room table and the nice-smelling potpourri in the master bathroom, and evaluate the home as a place you might want to live.

Bargain Hunting

Thanks to eye-popping price tags and decades-long loan repayment schedules, homebuyers want the most for their money. Your buyer's agent will tell you which homes are a good deal and will negotiate with sellers and their agents to help you get the best price. But you might want to look beyond the MLS for bargain properties your agent might miss. This section explains how to find these homes—FSBOs, short sales, foreclosures, and auctions—along with their advantages and disadvantages.

For Sale by Owner (FSBO)

Some sellers decide to do without an agent and sell their homes themselves, often to avoid paying an agent's commission. They pound a For Sale sign into the front lawn, buy an ad in the classifieds or post one online, schedule an open house—and wait for buyers to come to them. A house that's For Sale By Owner is called a FSBO, pronounced *fizz-bo*.

It might surprise you to learn that somewhere between 15 and 20 percent of the homes on the market are FSBOs. For you, the buyer, that means you could come across a good prospect that your agent doesn't know about. Many buyer's agents don't spend much time looking for FSBOs for their clients (although some agents seek out these properties in the hope that they can convince the seller to list the home with them). So it's up to you to find FSBOs to tour.

FSBO sellers usually advertise by putting up a sign and taking out an ad in the local newspaper's Classifieds section. Online classified ads on sites like craigslist (page 119) are also popular. You may see notices tacked up on community bulletin boards (at a local coffee shop or bookstore). There are some websites that specialize in FSBO listings, although you'll find far fewer listings on these than on sites like Realtor.com and Trulia:

- ForSaleByOwner.com.
- FSBO.com.
- Owners.com.

 Note Keep in mind that a FSBO is not necessarily a bargain. Sellers who don't have an agent to advise them on sales of comparable properties and the current state of the market may overprice their homes.

Working with a FSBO seller through your agent

If you've been working with a buyer's agent, call him and let him know that you're interested in a FSBO. If you want to make an offer, the agent will get in touch with the seller to ask whether the seller will pay his commission from the sale's proceeds. This isn't as outrageous as it may sound: As page 85 explains, the seller usually pays the commission, and the agents involved split it. Your agent will ask the seller to pay a "co-operative" commission of 2 to 4 percent. A homeowner eager to sell may agree, especially in a slow market. After all, here's a buyer ready to move forward, and the seller may be willing to absorb your agent's fee to close the sale.

Of course, the seller may refuse. Many FSBO sellers are dead set against paying *any* commission (after all, that's why they're FSBOing). If that happens, your agent, who needs to get paid one way or another other, will discuss his fee with you—meaning you'll pick up the cost of the commission, so take it into account when you make your offer. Make sure you and your agent agree on that fee before you proceed, and get it in writing.

 Note If you decide to buy a FSBO, don't cut your agent out of the deal to avoid paying the commission. It's unethical and, depending on the terms of your agency agreement, you could get sued.

After you settle the commission issue, working with your agent to buy a FSBO is no different from working with your agent to buy any other home, except that your agent negotiates directly with the seller (or maybe the seller's attorney), rather than the seller's agent.

Working with a FSBO seller on your own

If you're not already working with a buyer's agent and you decide to buy a FSBO, you can do so on your own. The first thing you should do is find a real estate lawyer to help you with the paperwork, starting with your purchase offer. (In some states, only a qualified attorney can write certain real estate documents.) You need to be absolutely certain that whatever papers you sign conform to the laws of your state, that you understand what's in them, and that whatever you sign doesn't put you at some legal disadvantage. Only a qualified lawyer can advise you on legal matters related to real estate. So get one on your team.

 Tip Page 101 has a list of questions to ask real estate attorneys before you hire one.

When you work directly with a FSBO seller, these tips will help make the transaction as smooth as possible:

- **Know values for comparable houses in the neighborhood.** An agent can advise you about whether a home is reasonably priced for its size, condition, and area, but it's harder to judge that on your own. Compare prices using resources like Trulia (page 115), home appraisal site Zillow (*www.zillow.com*), City-Data.com (type in a zip code and scroll down the page that opens to the Recent Home Sales form), and local records of recent sales (the local newspaper often publishes them, sometimes online, or contact the office of your local city or county clerk and ask how to search recent sales).

- **Be a good negotiator.** Whether you're buying or selling, one excellent reason to work with an agent is to have an experienced professional handle negotiations on your behalf. Negotiating on your own can be trickier. You get emotionally involved, and tempers can flare. Some FSBO sellers have fixed expectations about their selling price and won't budge; others are more flexible. When you sit down with the seller to ask for concessions, be prepared. Have everything written down and back it up with solid reasoning. Be willing to compromise on the little things to gain more leverage on the big things. And approach negotiations with the goal of creating a win-win situation for *both* parties—that's the mark of a truly well-crafted negotiation.

- **Get a thorough home inspection.** You'll do this anyway (Chapter 12 explains why), but a home inspection is super-important when you buy a FSBO. Most states require sellers to disclose any known problems with a property, whether or not they're working with an agent. But a few states don't. Make home inspection a contingency (page 251) of your offer—and then protect yourself with the best home inspection you can get.

Buying a FSBO without an agent to guide you and look out for your interests will require extra time and effort on your part. And if you're a first-time homebuyer, you're more likely to have a lot of questions and make potentially costly mistakes (the latter's the reason you absolutely must hire a good real estate attorney). But it can be done, and it may save you some money.

Short Sales

A *short sale* happens when you buy a home whose purchase price is lower than what the seller owes on the mortgage. In other words, the amount you pay for the house "falls short" of the amount owed. Short sales usually happen when a homeowner has run into serious financial trouble—the loan may already be in default, and the homeowner is trying to avoid foreclosure.

Occasionally, a seller who's in a hurry to move will accept a short-sale offer and make up the price difference to fully pay off the loan. Usually, though, a short sale means that the home's mortgage holder is going to get less money than it's owed, and it's no shocker that financial institutions don't like losing money. So the lender must approve a short sale before you can move forward. Lenders accept short sales when paying foreclosure costs would be more expensive than what the lender loses on the sale. That's not just because a foreclosure racks up attorney's fees and saps lenders' time. After a foreclosure, the lender owns the house, and most would rather not be in the real estate business, pouring money into taxes, maintenance, insurance, and so on for the foreclosed homes sitting on their books.

To approve a short sale, lenders want the property and the seller to meet these conditions:

- **The home has lost market value.** When the real estate bubble burst in the late 2000s and house prices plummeted, many homeowners suddenly found themselves owing more on their mortgage than the house was worth. The lender will require proof (such as recent sales data for comparable homes) that the home is now worth less than what the seller owes on the mortgage.

- **The mortgage is in or near default.** A lender is unlikely to approve a short sale if the seller's mortgage payments are current—usually a lender approves a short sale only after it has sent a notice of default to the owner. So a seller in good standing can't drop the price below the mortgage balance just because she's in a hurry to sell (unless, of course, she pays the difference herself).

- **The seller is experiencing significant financial hardship.** The lender requires a letter from the seller explaining why he's unable to fully repay the bank's loan. Hardships might include unemployment, a medical emergency, or the death of a co-owner. If the seller isn't experiencing serious hardship (if, for example, the seller is simply in a hurry to move), the lender is unlikely to approve a short sale.

- **The seller has no assets.** From the lender's point of view, any asset the seller owns—such as a savings account, stocks or bonds, or other real estate—could go toward paying the difference between the selling price and the amount owed. The lender expects the seller to use such assets to pay back her mortgage in full.

As this list suggests, a short sale isn't a happy occasion for either the lender or the seller. The seller has gone through a difficult time to get to the brink of a short sale. It will damage his credit record (although not as much as a foreclosure would), and he's lost all the money he invested in the home.

A short sale also may not be as good a deal as it looks at first. If you consider only the difference between what the seller owes and what you offer, a short sale can seem like a terrific bargain. But there's a reason the seller's willing to sell short—find out what that reason is. For example, if area house prices have fallen sharply, the house may be worth less than you think it is (especially if the market hasn't yet bottomed out).

If you decide to pursue a short sale, make sure you cover all these bases:

- **Work with a buyer's agent who's experienced in short sales.** Because these sales require some finesse and extra work, you want an agent who knows the terrain.

- **Find out if the property is subject to any liens or second mortgages.** If so, all the lenders involved have to approve a short sale—and the more lenders involved, the harder it is to gain everyone's approval.

- **Be prepared to pay extra costs.** The lender is losing money in a short sale, so it'll do everything it can to keep transaction-related costs low. The lender may negotiate a lower agents' commission, for example, so if your agreement with your agent stipulates a minimum commission, whatever the lender doesn't contribute comes out of your pocket. And the lender will probably refuse to pay any closing costs, so you're on the hook for 100 percent of them.

- **Don't expect money toward repairs.** Short sales are as is. Be sure you include a property inspection contingency in your purchase agreement (page 252) so you have an out if the home needs significant repairs. For smaller problems, get an estimate of how much repairs will cost and decide whether you can afford them—or walk away from the sale. (Chapter 12 tells you all about home inspections.) Know in advance, though, that the lender will almost certainly be unwilling to contribute to the cost of repairs.

- **Become familiar with the phrase, "Patience is a virtue."** A lender considering a short sale weighs the money lost now against potential future losses. Doing the math can take a long time. On the one hand, the lender doesn't want to lose a chunk of the money it loaned the current owner. On the other hand, the costs of foreclosing and then maintaining the property (taxes, critical repairs, insurance, and so on) may be more than the lender is willing to shoulder. It can take time for the lender to sort all this out. It also takes time for the lender to verify the seller's claims of financial hardship and check for assets. Homes advertised as "Bank-Approved Short Sales" may close more quickly. After the lender has OKed the sale, though, it may expect you to move quickly, requesting settlement in as few as 30 days. So if you go the short sales route, be ready to move forward with your side of the transaction.

 Tip Give your purchase offer an expiration date. If your offer is open-ended, the lender may take its time approving the sale. Work with your agent to determine a reasonable termination date, after which the offer is invalid.

Foreclosures and Auctions

The skyrocketing foreclosure rate was one of the top news stories of the late 2000s. With the number of foreclosures hitting a new record in each quarter of 2009, the sheer volume of foreclosed homes has made bargain hunters perk up and pay attention. Buying a foreclosed home can save you some money on the purchase price, but the process is fraught with challenges, hassles, and costs that may outweigh the up-front price savings.

When a borrower defaults on mortgage payments, the lender may *foreclose* on the loan. That means the lender repossesses the property, taking ownership and reselling it to recover at least some of the money owed on the loan. Lenders aren't especially eager to foreclose, especially in an area with a high foreclosure rate—there's lots of competition, the property may sit on the market for a while, and maintaining a foreclosed property gets expensive. So a homeowner who's in default often gets a grace period during which she can try to catch up on payments. If she can't, though, the lender starts the foreclosure process. There are three ways you can buy a property that's in foreclosure (or heading there):

- **Preforeclosure.** During this phase, the lender has notified the homeowner of impending foreclosure but hasn't yet taken possession of the property. In many states, preforeclosure lasts only a month: the 30 days between the time the current owner receives a notice of foreclosure and when the bank takes ownership. When a home is in preforeclosure, you may be able to buy it in a short sale (page 124). When you buy during preforeclosure, you deal directly with the current owner or the owner's agent.

- **At auction.** When a bank owns a foreclosed property, it has to pay maintenance, property taxes, insurance, and so on. Lenders want to move foreclosed homes off their books quickly, and a popular way to do this is through a public auction (page 130 tells you more about buying a foreclosed home at auction). Third-party companies that specialize in real estate auctions usually conduct these sales (for example, see the "REDC" and "Williams and Williams" bullet points below).

- **As an REO.** Lenders call lender-owned properties REOs (for *real estate owned,* mimicking the line item on the lender's books). Usually, an REO is a property that failed to sell at auction, and the lender has listed the home on the open market. When you buy an REO, you're buying the property directly from a lender who's also the owner, so you'll deal directly with the lender or the lender's agent.

Finding foreclosures

If you want to hunt for foreclosed homes, ask your real estate agent to search the MLS for REOs. And if you visit an area with many foreclosures, you'll see yard signs that trumpet the property's status with phrases like *Bank Owned*, *Bank Repo*, or *Foreclosure*. Call the listing agent (or ask your agent to do so) and say you'd like to learn about foreclosures that aren't yet on the market—you may be able to get a jump on other bargain-seekers this way.

You can also discover foreclosures at these websites:

- **Bid4Assets** (*www.bid4assets.com*). This online auction site sells, among other things, property seized by the U.S. Marshals Service, including real estate.

- **Foreclosure.com** (*www.foreclosure.com*). This site charges a monthly fee to view its listings—more than 1.8 million of them across the country. Besides foreclosures, listings include preforeclosures, bankruptcy-related properties, FSBOs, and tax-lien seizures.

- **ForeclosureS.com** (*www.foreclosures.com*—note the "S"). This site also charges a monthly fee to give you access to its list of preforeclosures, auctions, and REO properties.

- **Government agencies.** Sometimes government agencies seize property due to back taxes or overdue payments. The agencies below list government-owned properties currently for sale:

  — **Department of the Treasury** (*www.treas.gov/auctions/irs*). Sometimes the Internal Revenue Service seizes property from people who owe back taxes and sells those properties at auction. On the site's home page, scroll down to the sections labeled Real Estate and Real Estate—Seeking Guaranteed Bids; click either section name to preview properties coming up for auction.

  — **Fannie Mae, the Federal National Mortgage Association** (*www. homepath.com*). This site lists homes owned by Fannie Mae, a government-sponsored company that finances a secondary market for home mortgages. You can search properties by state, county, city or town, zip code, and more.

  — **HUD, the U.S. Department of Housing and Urban Development** (*http://tinyurl.com/yex8dyh*). The Federal Housing Administration is part of HUD. If a borrower defaults on an FHA-insured loan (page 180), the lender files a claim with the FHA, which pays off the loan and turns over the property to HUD. This website lists HUD-owned foreclosures. Click a state to go to an authorized website that lists such properties in that state.

- **RealtyTrac** (*www.realtytrac.com*). This site lists over a million foreclosed properties, but you have to pay a subscription to get information about them.

 Tip All three subscription sites listed here—Foreclosure.com, ForclosureS.com, and RealtyTrac—offer a free seven-day trial, so you can see whether their listings are worth the cost.

- **REDC** (*www.auction.com*). The Real Estate Disposition Corporation conducts online and on-site auctions of real estate located all over the country (not all properties are foreclosures). If you decide to participate, be sure to read the site's excellent FAQ page carefully.

- **Williams and Williams** (*www.williamsauction.com*). This auction company sells REOs and other properties at in-person auctions and online.

 Tip Buying real estate in an online auction isn't for newbies or the faint-hearted. You're buying a property, possibly sight unseen, in a frenzied contest with other bidders. If you want to buy a house this way, take the time to read and understand the auction company's rules and policies. Be clear about everything you need to know about registration, inspection, down payment, financing, and the legalities *before* you bid.

Disadvantages to buying a foreclosed property

Foreclosures happen to all kinds of properties, from manufactured homes to suburban tract houses to condos to luxurious mansions. A foreclosed property may look like a great deal compared to other homes on the market, but before you buy, consider these caveats:

- **You're buying as is.** Lenders selling foreclosed properties generally aren't interested in negotiating reimbursements for repairs—they just want to unload the property and recoup as much of their money as they can. To make matters more complicated, you may not be able to tour the property or have it inspected before the sale. So you may have to pay for repairs that you don't even know about at the time of the sale.

- **You'll have to pay any existing liens or back taxes.** The previous owner may have used the house as collateral for other debts, fallen behind on taxes, or taken out a second mortgage to try to get caught up on the first. When you buy the home, these debts become your responsibility.

- **You're buying without any disclosures.** When you buy a bank-owned property, the bank can't provide disclosures about the home's history and condition. So there may be some nasty surprises after you move in.

- **The current owner or tenant may be uncooperative.** If someone's living in the property, you may have to evict them. Eviction can be an expensive and extremely unpleasant process. And it's not uncommon for angry former owners to damage the house or strip out items of value—such as plumbing fixtures and copper pipes—before they leave.

- **The current owner may get the house back.** Most states have laws that give homeowners some degree of protection in a foreclosure. Some states, for example, give former owners a grace period to buy back their auctioned home, a period that can last anywhere from 10 days (in New Jersey) to a whole year (in Alabama). So if you buy a house at auction, you might have to give it up if the former owner comes up with the cash to buy it back. (If this happens, you get your purchase price back, but not any funds you spent on repairs or improvements.)

 Tip To find out whether a former owner can buy back her house—and how long she has to do it—take a look at the chart on Innovest Resource Management's Foreclosure Forum at *www.foreclosureforum.com/basics.html*, or ask a real estate lawyer.

- **Expect delays and more delays.** Like short sales, foreclosures can move slower than molasses on a cold day. Lawsuits, paperwork, and other delays mean you can wait a long time (and face a lot of uncertainty) before you can call a home yours.

- **You're competing with experienced real estate investors.** Foreclosures are popular with real estate investors—they buy houses at low prices, fix them up, and flip them to make a profit. Some investors flip houses for a living, and they're aggressive in scooping up the best bargains. In addition, if bids at an auction come in low, the lender itself will probably buy back the home and sell it as an REO for a higher price.

- **You may not get clear title.** If you bid on a property at auction, it's your responsibility to research the state of the title (page 268) before you buy. (REOs listed with a real estate agency, on the other hand, come with clear title.)

Buying a property at auction

The process of buying an auctioned property differs from the real estate–buying process you read about in other parts of this book. Before you show up at an auction ready to bid, understand how real estate auctions work. This section explains.

Foreclosure auctions may take place at the property itself, on the county courthouse steps, or at another location. Bidders register on-site to participate. At the appointed time, an auctioneer appears, reads an opening statement, and starts the bidding. The first bid often comes from the lender that holds the foreclosed mortgage, in an amount that covers what's owed, along with any money the lender spent on the foreclosure. Other bids may follow, continuing until the auctioneer decides the bidding has peaked. At that point, the auctioneer declares a winning bidder.

 Tip On-site auctions often have an open house for a couple of hours before the sale, so get there early and take a good look around.

Although the auction itself is a simple, straightforward process, success at an auction requires both preparation and a cool head. If you've got your heart set on a particular property, it's easy to get carried away during the bidding—and end up buying the house for more than you intended. Keep these auction tips in mind:

- **Attend several auctions before you bid.** You'll be better prepared to participate if you've witnessed a few before you jump in with a bid.

- **Do your homework.** You may not be able to inspect a property before the auction begins, but you can—and must—do other kinds of research. What are the house's basic specifications: its size, number of bedrooms/bathrooms, age, and so on? Is it currently inhabited? Are there any liens on the property? How much is it worth on today's market? If you don't know the answers to these questions, you don't know enough to buy the property.

 Tip Use Zillow (*www.zillow.com*) and local records of recent sales of comparable homes to estimate value (page 118). As you figure out how much to bid, it's a good idea to subtract at least 10 percent from the market value in anticipation of repairs and updates.

- **Decide on your maximum bid ahead of time.** Once you know how much a house is worth, you've got a ceiling for your bid. During the auction, *don't bid higher than that ceiling*. In the excitement of bidding, it's easy to bid more than you intend—and more than the house is worth. Don't let your emotions land you in a bad deal.

- **Be aware of auction-related costs.** The auctioneer may charge a buyer's premium, due at the close of the auction. Contact the auction company ahead of time to find out what fees you'll need to pay if you win.

- **On the day of the auction, have the necessary cash on hand.** Some auctions require a minimum deposit immediately after the auction; others require payment in full, no financing allowed. Know what the rules are, and bring a cashier's check with you to the sale.

- **Arrange financing ahead of time.** If the auction lets you finance the property (not all do), get preapproved. After the auction, you have a limited window of time to come up with the full amount you owe—and if you can't, you lose your deposit.

 Note It can be surprisingly difficult to get a good buy at auction. For one thing, you're competing against experienced real estate investors who know enough to drop out quickly when a price moves out of bargain territory. In addition, the lender wants to recoup its investment. In a market where home values have dropped, the lender's first bid may price everyone else out of the sale, because the amount still owed on the house is more than it's currently worth.

What to Look for on the Tour

Touring houses can be both exhilarating and exhausting. You know that one of these properties will become your new home, and you're eager to find it. Yet you may have to visit many homes before the stars align and you're ready to make an offer.

Your real estate agent may chauffeur you to the homes you view, or you may meet her there. When you arrive, the seller's agent may be there to greet you, too, and to let you in; if not, your agent will remove a key from a secure lockbox to open the door. Your agent (or the seller's agent) will have an information sheet of basic facts about the house—this may be a brochure or a printout of the MLS listing. You may get other information too, such as a seller's disclosure form (see page 139 for what that is), utility cost estimates, and other facts that the seller thinks are useful to prospective buyers.

Once you're inside, you'll have the run of the house. You can walk through all the rooms, peek into closets and cupboards, measure windows, and explore the basement and attic. This section tells you how to get the most out of your tour.

Preparing to Visit Houses

As with so many other things, preparation is key to a successful house-hunting tour. If you have everything in place before you set out to look at houses, you'll be able to focus on how well each house meets your needs—and the visits will go much more smoothly. Before you venture out into the marketplace, keep these points in mind:

- **Don't overschedule yourself.** If you try to look at too many houses in one day: They'll all start to blur together, and you'll have a hard time remembering each house individually. Six or seven house tours in a single day is a good upper limit—after that your brain starts to turn to mush. If you're making a long-distance move, however, you may have to pack as many tours as you can into just a few days. That's when a camera, checklist, and good note-taking skills become even more important. (Keep reading for tips on how to get organized and remember the houses you tour.)

- **Get some rest.** Study after study has shown that people who are tired find it hard to focus and make decisions. That's not the condition you want to be in as you look at prospective homes. People with busy schedules may have to squeeze in a showing whenever they have time, and if you're moving a long distance you may have to pack a lot of showings into a few days' househunting trip. But if possible, try to get a good night's sleep before you tour homes.

- **Get a babysitter.** Parents of young children may find that the kids disrupt the tour, running through rooms, hiding in closets, and begging to try out the backyard swing set. Even well-behaved children can distract you as you try to evaluate a potential home. The best time to bring the kids into the process is later, when you've narrowed down the possibilities and want to get the kids' opinions on your choices.

- **Gather your gear.** Make sure you have a camera (page 136), your checklist (page 137) clipped to a clipboard, a list of questions to ask (page 138), a notebook, a pen or two, and a folder for collecting information sheets.

 Tip Before you start looking at houses, measure any large or unusually shaped pieces of furniture you want to move into your new home. Write down the measurements. When you visit homes, take along those measurements—and a tape measure.

Keep an Open Heart and a Critical Eye

Buying a home is an emotional experience. To buy smart, you need to engage heart and head alike. Although you should fall in love with the home you buy, you also want to be sure that you're getting a house that's a good value and will suit you and your family for the years you live there. These suggestions will help you see homes clearly as you tour them:

- **Don't be distracted by nice touches.** Smart sellers make their homes look as welcoming as possible. They take down family photos (because it's harder to imagine yourself living in a house with smiling strangers on the wall), remove pieces of furniture to make rooms look bigger, put out fresh flowers or bowls of fruit, and hang mirrors or position lamps to brighten dark rooms. This is called *staging*, and its purpose is to direct your attention away from a home's less attractive features through the use of props. Don't spend the tour admiring the dining room curtains or feeling tempted to relax on a pillow-covered sofa. Focus on the house, not its contents.

 Note Professional stagers make a living by helping sellers transform ordinary houses into showplaces to impress buyers.

- **Walk through the house as though you already live there.** No, that doesn't mean taking a quick nap on the owner's bed or putting your feet up on the coffee table as you watch TV. But do think about how you use your home and see whether this home fits the way you live. For example, imagine yourself preparing a meal as you look around the kitchen. Is there sufficient counter space? Where would you keep pots and pans? Is the dishwasher convenient to the cupboard where you'll store dishes and glassware? How about the bedrooms? Are they conveniently located relative to the bathrooms or will you have to walk halfway through the house in your bathrobe to get to the shower each morning?

- **Put on your home inspector's hat.** You'll hire a professional to do a complete home inspection and you'll do a thorough walkthrough if you decide to buy the house, but on this first look, simply keep your eyes peeled for potential problems. Here are some things to watch for:

  — **Light switches.** Flip them on and off to make sure they work.

  — **Water pressure.** Turn on faucets in sinks and tubs to check water flow.

  — **Toilets.** Flush toilets to make sure they empty and refill completely.

— **Floors.** Do they squeak (that's a sign of loose nails)? Are they level or slanted? Are there soft spots next to the toilet or tub (that indicates water damage)?

— **Walls.** Do you notice any cracks or bulges? They might be a sign of structural problems.

— **Doors and windows.** If they stick or don't close squarely, you may need to repair or replace them—or they could be a sign that the foundation isn't stable. Check exterior doors to see whether light gets through around the edges when the door is closed; if so, you may need to add insulation or refit the door.

— **Sills.** Look for signs of water damage, such as mildew or mold. Also check for peeling paint; in older homes, the paint may be lead-based.

 Federal law requires that sellers of homes built before 1978 give buyers a lead disclosure statement. See page 140 for more information about this form.

— **Drafts.** Check around windows and doors and along exterior walls. If the house is drafty, you'll probably have to add insulation.

— **Ceilings.** Are there any stains or signs of water damage?

— **Heating/cooling system.** If it's winter, is the ground floor warm or chilly around the edges? If the weather is warm, is the upstairs too hot?

— **Appliances.** Is the refrigerator cold? Do all of the burners work on the stove? If appliances come with the house, you'll want to do a quick check that they're in working order.

— **Cabinets.** Do the doors open and close easily? Are their shelves in good condition?

— **Odors.** If the house smells funny, you may have trouble getting rid of that odor after you move in.

— **Basement.** Are there cracks in the foundation? Those can indicate a need for expensive repairs.

— **Roof.** From the outside, check the roofline. Is it straight or does it appear to sag anywhere? Scan the roof for missing shingles or sagging areas. (Binoculars can help here.)

- **Remember that selling a home is an emotional experience for a homeowner.** If the seller is present as you tour, don't make disparaging remarks about decorating choices or funny smells (but do make a note of any odd odors in your notebook). The seller doesn't have to agree to sell to you—and if she takes a dislike to you, she probably won't. On the other hand, don't gush over the home, either. If you come across as desperate to buy the place, you'll put yourself at a disadvantage when it's time to negotiate. Finally, if the seller seems particularly proud of some aspect of the home, you can make a favorable impression by complimenting the seller on it. For example, if the home has beautiful landscaping, you can admire it and talk about how you'd maintain it if you owned the home.

- **When you're thinking about making an offer, visit the home again.** Try to visit on a different day and time. Write down any questions you have or things you want to double-check to make sure you don't forget any concerns during the second tour. Bring along your checklist and notes, and compare your impressions on this visit with the first.

 Tip Sometimes, you'll know that a home isn't right for you as soon as you set foot inside the front door. If that happens, you can go ahead with the tour if you want—maybe the property is a diamond in the rough—but don't feel obliged to tour a home you know you won't buy. Doing so is a waste of time, yours and the agents' alike.

Bring a Camera

A digital camera or camcorder can be your best friend on a home tour. If you visit several homes in one day, taking photos or shooting brief video clips to review later will help you remember which house had the tiny kitchen, which had built-in bookshelves in the family room, and which had that hideous avocado tile in the master bath.

 Note As a courtesy, ask permission to take photos or shoot video before you start. Unless a seller has specifically said, "No pictures," it's unlikely to be a problem.

When you arrive at a home, the first photo or video you take should be a close-up of the house number to indicate that the photos/clips that follow go with that property. Take lots of photos or clips. Capture the home's exterior, its grounds, and each room. If there's a feature you love, like a stone fireplace in the great room, get a record of it. If there's a feature you hate, like those avocado-colored tiles, capture that, too. Record anything you have a question about, as well. Seeing the image later will remind you to get an answer to that question.

Use Your Wish List As a Checklist

When you decided what you wanted in a new home, you created a wish list of preferred features and amenities (page 77). Now that you're actively shopping, turn that wish list into a checklist and keep track of which homes have the features you want.

Leave room at the top of the checklist so you can record the home's address, the date you saw it, how much the seller is asking, how long the house has been on the market, and who the listing agent is. Beneath that, list your preferred features and follow each one with three columns: Must Have, Would Like, and Y/N. The first two columns come directly from your wish list. The third is where you write "Y" if the home has that feature and "N" if it doesn't.

Bring along copies of the checklist—one for each house you visit. Write the address at the top of each sheet and, as you go through a home, note which features it has and which it's missing and write down explanatory notes. For example, maybe you'd like a fireplace in your new home's family room: Write "no fireplace, but wood stove."

Property address:		Date visited:	
List price:		Time on market:	
Listing agent:		Agency:	
Feature	Must have	Would like	Y/N
Single-family home	X		
Colonial style		X	
Brand-new		X	
Less than 10 years old	X		
Two stories	X		
Three bedrooms	X		
Four bedrooms		X	
Two-and-a-half bathrooms	X		
Eat-in kitchen		X	
Formal dining room		X	
Home office	X		
Fireplace		X	
First-floor laundry room	X		
Deck		X	

Forced-hot air natural gas heating	X		
Central air		X	
Hardwood floors		X	
Two-car garage	X		
Walking distance to playground		X	
In _____ school district	X		

Ask Questions

Touring a home gives you a chance to look around and decide whether you can picture yourself living there. But there's more to a home than a floor plan and color scheme. The seller can give tell you about the home's condition and history, which you need to consider before you buy.

Ask the seller or seller's agent the following questions (if just you and your agent tour the house, have your agent pass questions on to the seller's agent). Ask whatever questions occur to you, but use these to get started:

- **How long has this home been on the market?** Knowing how long a home's been for sale may help you get a sense of whether the seller would be open to offers below the asking price.

- **Why is the house on the market?** There are many reasons people put a home up for sale: moving out of the area, upsizing or downsizing to a different home, settling an estate or a divorce, financial difficulties, and so on. When you have a sense of why the owner is selling, you and your agent can discuss the best way to approach him if you decide to make an offer.

- **Are there any problems or disputes with neighbors?** If the next-door neighbors are embroiled in a lawsuit with the current owners over tree damage or property lines, you need to know about it.

- **What repairs or updates have you made recently?** Sellers are usually eager to highlight renovations as a selling point.

- **Are any repairs likely to become necessary within the next couple of years?** If the answer to this question is yes, be sure to take those repairs into account when you budget for your new home (see page 26).

- **How old is the roof? Are there any leaks?** If the roof is older than 15 years, you may need to replace it soon. Re-roofing can be a major expense, so if that's on the horizon, you need to know.

- **If the home has a basement, is it dry or damp?** A damp (or flooded) basement can cause mold growth and damage wood and masonry.

- **When was the heating and/or air conditioning system installed?** If it's well maintained, the average furnace lasts for about 25 years. An air conditioner is good for maybe 15. If the heating and cooling system in the home is getting close to that age—or older—you may need to spend a few thousand dollars to replace it.

- **Has the seller prepared a written disclosure statement?** A disclosure statement lists known problems with the home, past and present. Not all states require it, and among those that do the seller may not have to hand over a disclosure until after you make an offer. But ask for one anyway. The next section tells you more about disclosure statements.

 Tip Your home inspector will look for problems with the home's structure and systems, but it's a good idea to ask about known issues before the inspection. If the inspector knows about specific problems, he can spend extra time checking them out.

- **How much does the seller pay each month for utilities?** You need to take utilities into account as you plan your monthly budget (page 26). Ask about these:
    - Heating fuel (gas, oil, propane)
    - Electricity
    - Trash collection
    - Water
    - Homeowners' association fees (if any)
    - Any other recurring fees (ask what these are)

- **Do you have any pets?** Pets can cause damage you need to check for. If you're allergic to animals, it may take some effort to make the home comfortable for you, even after the current critters have moved out.

Disclosure Statements: What the Seller Must Tell You

More than two-thirds of all states require a seller to tell prospective home-buyers the condition and history of the house. (That means that some states *don't* impose this requirement—more on those in a moment.) A seller's disclosure spells out all of the home's known defects and problems (see this book's Missing CD at *http://www.missingmanuals.com/cds/* for sample forms for Indiana and Texas).

States that require disclosure statements use a standard form that details a property's legal, structural, and environmental condition. The forms vary from state to state. Some are only a couple of pages long; others go into a lot more detail and can run to 10 pages. Short or long, a disclosure typically touches on the following issues:

- Whether the seller has lived in the home (and if so, when)—some sellers inherited the home or bought it as an investment
- Roof condition
- Any known structural problems, such as a cracked foundation
- Water and sewage systems
- Electrical system
- Heating and air conditioning system
- Plumbing system
- Appliances included in the sale
- Environmental hazards, such as flooding, earthquake, or hurricane damage
- Hazardous substances within the home, such as lead paint or asbestos
- Mold growth
- Municipal violations against the property
- Legal disputes involving the property
- Zoned district

Not every form covers all these issues, and different regions have different requirements. For example, California requires earthquake hazard disclosure, but states in the middle and eastern parts of the country don't. In Alaska, a seller must disclose whether a home has ever been damaged by an avalanche—but you won't find that requirement in Georgia.

Federal law states that sellers of homes built before 1978 must provide buyers with a lead disclosure statement (as shown on the previous page; go to this book's Missing CD at *www.missingmanuals.com/cds/* to see the lead disclosure form). (The Consumer Products Safety Commission banned lead-based paint in 1978, which is the reason for the cut-off date.) If the seller knows that the house contains lead-based paint (or has contained it in the past), he must say so on this form. If he or a previous owner has taken steps to remediate the lead problem, the seller attaches proof to the form. But the seller also has the option of saying that he has no knowledge of whether the home contains lead-based paint. If that's what your disclosure form says, make sure you include a lead-based paint inspection contingency (page 252) in your purchase offer and have the home inspected for lead.

How do you know that you can trust a disclosure? States that require them impose serious penalties for not telling the truth. A seller who lies (or omits information) on a disclosure statement may face fines, responsibility for your legal costs, and reversal of the sale.

Ask for a copy of the disclosure statement *before* you make an offer. Some sellers prefer to hand it over after you sign the purchase agreement, but it's best to know the problems a house has when you calculate your offer.

Ask for a disclosure statement even if you live in a state that doesn't require one. In those states, the state Realtors Association probably has a voluntary standard form. An acceptable alternative would be a home inspection report paid for by the owner. (You'll still want your own inspection, though, to double-check what the seller reports.)

 Note Real estate agents must also disclose any flaws in the home that they know about. So if a seller confides to his agent that there's a problem with the foundation, for example, the agent must pass that information on to potential buyers.

Evaluate the Neighborhood

When you targeted areas for your search (page 72), you identified the features and amenities you want in a neighborhood. Whether you're looking only in neighborhoods you chose then or you're searching more broadly, pull out the list and use it to evaluate the environments of the homes you tour. For example, maybe one home is a few streets beyond the boundary of a neighborhood you want, but it's next door to a park or within walking distance of the library.

Spend time in the neighborhood. Take a walk, visit the café around the corner, drive through at night to see whether the atmosphere is quiet or lively. Talk to your potential neighbors and ask them what they like most and least about their homes' location. Even if you did some of this legwork earlier, it's a good exercise as you zero in on possible homes, rather than getting a feel for a wider area.

Compare Homes

As you look at homes, the more information you collect, the more data points you'll have when you sit down to compare properties. You probably won't buy a home based solely on your checklists—gut feelings and emotions will come into play. Most likely, you'll have a positive impression of a couple of homes that seem like good candidates. If you're buying a home with someone else—your spouse or a partner, for example—sit down and talk about your impressions. You may or may not be in sync. Pull out your notes, photos, and checklists to support your impressions as you try to reach consensus.

Use your checklists to compare features and amenities. Try this: Create a spreadsheet and label the far-left column Address. In that column, list the homes you're considering. Moving right, fill in the top row with amenities and features you identified as important in your wish list (page 77). For each house, type in a 2 for each "must have" feature the house possesses or a 1 for each "would like" feature. If the house is missing a feature, leave the cell blank. After you fill in the spreadsheet, add up the numbers for each house. The one with the highest sum comes closest to fulfilling your wish list. That doesn't mean it's the house you'll buy. There are other factors to weigh, such as price, location, and how the home feels to you, but the spreadsheet helps you sort through the information you collect and look at it objectively.

As you compare homes, consider this: Shopping for a home is a lot like dating. It can be fun, and you might fall in love. But buying a home is more like a marriage: After the honeymoon, you've got to settle down to the business of living with your choice. Keep that long-term commitment in mind as you visit, inspect, and compare homes.

6 Finance Your Down Payment

The variety and number of fees you have to pay when you buy a home can set your head spinning. They run the gamut from your lender's $35 credit-check fee to several hundred dollars for a home inspection to thousands of dollars in loan administration fees. But by far the biggest chunk of cash you need to come up with is the down payment, a percentage of your home's purchase price—usually in the range of 3.5 to 20 percent.

For many homebuyers, coming up with the down payment is the biggest obstacle to buying a home. Unless you're independently wealthy, you've had a recent windfall (an inheritance or a lucky horse, for example), or you're selling a home in which you've built up some equity, you probably don't have tens of thousands of dollars lying around to invest in a new home. This chapter helps you come up with your down payment. It starts off by explaining why lenders require such a hefty down payment in the first place, then moves on to strategies, both traditional and creative, for finding the money to put down on your new home.

Why a Down Payment?

You might wonder why lenders insist that you pour thousands of dollars of your own money into a home. After all, lenders make money from loans, so you'd think they'd want to give you as much cash as possible.

That's true, but lenders also need assurance that you'll repay the loan. To get that implied promise, they require you to have a personal financial stake in your house. From the lender's point of view, when you pay for part of the house with a pile of your own hard-earned cash, you're much more likely to pay back the loan. It shows you're committed to buying—and paying for—your new home.

As an extension of that assumption, the more money you invest in a down payment, the better you look to a lender. That's why borrowers who make higher down payments (20 percent or more) can get better terms and avoid paying private mortgage insurance (PMI, page 146).

Even if you don't fork over 20 percent of your home's purchase price, you need a down payment in almost all cases. Few lenders hand over the entire purchase price of a home. In the wake of the subprime mortgage crisis of the late 2000s, the once-ubiquitous no-money-down mortgage has gone the way of the dinosaurs. Today, lenders expect borrowers to reach deep into their pockets and come up with a sizable down payment.

Calculate Your Down Payment

How much money will you have to have to qualify for a mortgage? Ideally, 20 percent of the home's purchase price. That threshold offers several benefits:

- **Better chance of approval.** Starting in the late 2000s, and in response to the subprime mortgage meltdown, lenders ratcheted up the requirements for mortgages, requiring higher credit scores, bigger down payments, and proof that you're likely to keep your job. Some lenders eliminated so-called piggyback loans (page 187), which let homebuyers borrow part of their down payment as a second mortgage. If you can't pony up 20 percent of your home's purchase price, lenders may consider you at greater risk of *defaulting* on your mortgage, meaning you won't be able to make payments.

 For creative ways to finance your home purchase, see page 186.

- **Lower interest rates.** When you can afford a down payment of 20 percent or more, lenders see you as less of a risk, and your interest rate reflects this.

- **No PMI.** Lenders' confidence in 20-percenters excuses those buyers from paying for private mortgage insurance, too. If you get a mortgage with less than 20 percent down, lenders require that you get PMI, which protects the bank from loss if you fail to repay your loan (see the box on page 146). Depending on your credit score, which measures your creditworthiness based on your financial history (page 39 tells you more about credit scores), and other factors, PMI costs from 0.5 to 1 percent of your mortgage.

- **Lower payments.** When you make a higher down payment, you borrow less money. And that means you have less to pay back—each month and over the life of the loan. Take a look at the table to see the difference a bigger down payment makes to monthly and lifetime payments when you take out a 30-year, fixed-rate loan to buy a $250,000 home. Where the lender requires mortgage insurance, assume it's 0.5 percent. (For simplicity's sake, also assume that all the loans below have a 5 percent interest rate.)

Down payment %	Amount of down payment	Amount borrowed	Monthly payment	PMI	Total PMI paid	Total payments (including PMI) over 30 years
3.5	$8,750	$241,250	$1,395.60	Yes	$11,157.81	$502,417.08
5	$12,500	$237,500	$1,373.91	Yes	$10,390.63	$494,607.49
10	$25,000	$225,000	$1,301.60	Yes	$7,312.50	$468,575.51
15	$37,500	$212,500	$1,229.29	Yes	$3,895.83	$442,543.54
20	$50,000	$200,000	$1,073.64	No	$0	$386,511.57
25	$62,500	$187,500	$1,006.54	No	$0	$362,354.60

 Note Some lenders advertise "no mortgage insurance" loans, which let you start with a down payment of less than 20 percent and don't require you to buy PMI. In these cases, however, the lender usually buys the PMI itself—and you pick up the tab by paying a higher interest rate for the life of your loan. When you buy PMI outright, however, you can stop paying for that insurance once the equity in your home reaches 20 percent. So approach "no mortgage insurance" loans with caution. It may be cheaper in the long run to go for a loan that requires you to buy PMI you can cancel once you build up sufficient equity.

- **Instant equity.** One of the financial advantages of buying a home is building equity (see page 12), and a hefty down payment gives you a head start.

Private Mortgage Insurance

From a lender's perspective, a lower down payment indicates a higher risk of default. In other words, lenders see a buyer who can afford a down payment of only 5 percent as more likely to have trouble paying back his loan than a buyer who can put down 20 percent. To minimize their risk in writing such mortgages, most lenders require private mortgage insurance (PMI), which protects the lender in case you default on your loan. PMI ensures that the lender recovers a specific percentage of the loan amount if you stop paying.

Note that PMI protects the *lender*, not you. PMI won't step in to make payments for you if you run into financial trouble. Instead, it minimizes the lender's loss if he has to foreclose and ends up owning your house.

If your down payment is less than 20 percent, you'll almost certainly have to buy PMI. The amount is figured as a percentage of the loan and typically costs about $55 a month per each $100,000 you borrow. So if you borrowed $200,000, you'd pay $1,320 in PMI in the first year.

PMI isn't forever. You can request to end PMI payments when you accrue 20 percent equity in your home. (Your lender will probably require an appraisal of your home before canceling PMI.) And if you make your payments on time and are in good standing with your lender, the law requires cancellation of PMI when your equity in the home reaches 22 percent.

Coming Up with a Down Payment

For many first-time homebuyers, scraping together 20 percent of a home's purchase price can be daunting. If you find that the house of your dreams costs $300,000, for example, you need $60,000 in cash to make a 20 percent down payment. Not many people have that many greenbacks stuffed in their mattresses. It's clear that it's in your interest to pay 20 percent up front, but where can you get that kind of money? Here are some strategies.

Start saving

Many first-time homebuyers save for years to accumulate a down payment. If you take this route, deduct a set amount from each paycheck and put it into a dedicated bank account. And if you get an income tax refund, don't spend it—add it to your down payment account. Consider putting your savings into a money-market fund or a certificate of deposit (CD) to help it grow faster. Investment-grade bonds that mature in the year you want to buy are another good option (see Chapter 7 of *Personal Investing: The Missing Manual* for details on using bonds to achieve time-dependent financial goals).

 Tip Frugal living is another way to make your savings grow faster. You don't have to subsist on mac-and-cheese dinners, but when you get the urge to splurge, ask yourself whether you'd rather make that impulse purchase or buy a home. Then put the money you'd have spent toward the down payment.

Sell stuff

Look around. You may have items you can sell to put a few more dollars in your down-payment fund. Big-ticket items like an underused car, boat, or motorcycle can bring in a nice chunk of change. If you have investments like stocks and bonds, you might look into selling those (but don't forget about the capital gains taxes you may have to pay). Even a garage sale of tossed-aside household items can raise a few hundred dollars.

Convince mom and dad to help out

When you need a financial boost to come up with a down payment, family members might be willing to contribute to your cause. And although *you* wouldn't look that gift horse in the mouth, your lender certainly will—most banks require a copy of the gift check and a copy of your bank statement that shows you deposited the money into your account. Many also ask your donor to write a gift letter, an acknowledgement that the money was a gift and not a loan (the last thing your bank wants is a customer with two substantial outstanding loans). And sometimes the bank wants proof of the gift's provenance, such as a copy of the giver's bank statement showing that you benefactor deducted the amount from her checking account.

Borrow cash against your 401(k) plan

Ask your employer if you can borrow money against your 401(k) plan. As long as your payments stay on schedule, you won't have to pay any taxes or penalties. Here's a caveat, though: If you leave your job (whether you quit or get fired), the loan becomes due, usually within 60 days. If you borrowed a significant amount, you may find it a struggle to pay all that money back at once.

Tap your individual retirement account

If you haven't owned a home in the past two years, you can withdraw up to $10,000 from your IRA— without paying an early-withdrawal penalty— and use that money to help purchase a home. (That $10,000 is the lifetime maximum you can take out for this purpose.) Both conventional and Roth IRAs qualify, although you have to pay income tax if you use a conventional IRA or if your Roth IRA is less than 5 years old.

Alternatives to Paying 20 Percent Down

If you don't have 20 percent to pay up front, you're not necessarily condemned to a lifetime of renting. Although it's tougher now to qualify for a loan with less than 20 percent down, you still have options.

Low Down Payment Loans

During the housing boom of the mid-2000s, nearly a third of all first-time homebuyers paid little or nothing down to buy their homes. In the housing and financial crises that followed, these loans virtually disappeared. That's not surprising: When home values slid, so did the equity in those homes. Many homeowners who'd recently bought a house with little or no money down found that they owed more than their homes were worth (they had negative equity in the home, in other words). Defaults and foreclosures spiked, and lenders were saddled with properties worth less than what they had invested in them. A lower down payment means a riskier loan, and going into the second decade of the 21st century, lenders are less willing to take those kinds of risks. You can still find low down payment loans, but you'll probably have to look around to find one that works for you.

Your best bet is a loan insured by the Federal Housing Authority (the FHA, an agency of the U.S. Department of Housing and Urban Development). The FHA can help you get into a home if you don't have tons of money for a down payment. The agency doesn't *make* loans, it *insures* them. If you default on an FHA-insured loan, the FHA pays the entire amount you owe. That's why lenders who wouldn't accept a low down payment otherwise will make these loans when the FHA backs them. FHA-insured loans include a variety of fixed-rate and adjustable-rate mortgages (Chapter 7 tells you all about these kinds of loans).

If you qualify, you can get an FHA-insured loan for as little as 3.5 percent down. Income is the main determining factor—to qualify for an FHA loan, your mortgage payments can't be more than 31 percent of your gross income (that's before taxes). There are also limits on the size of the loan, determined by your geographic area; if your home is in a neighborhood of homes with a high median home price, the FHA bumps up your limit. As of this writing, FHA loan limits in most areas of the country are just over $271,000, although pricier areas, such as California, Hawaii, and parts of New York, can stretch that limit above $700,000.

 Tip To find the limit on FHA loans in your area, visit the FHA Mortgage Limits page at *http://tinyurl.com/2x4vsm* and search for the county where you want to buy.

There are a couple of caveats to an FHA-insured loan. You have to have mortgage insurance, which includes both an up-front fee of 1.5 percent to 2.5 percent of your loan, plus an annual premium of 0.5 percent, which your lender adds to your monthly payments. And if your credit score isn't so hot (if it's below 620, in other words), you'll probably have to make a bigger down payment—up to 10 percent instead of the rock-bottom 3.5 percent of most FHA loans. Finally, if you opt for a lower down payment, you're borrowing more money, and that means that both your monthly payments and the total amount of your loan will be higher than if you shelled out more money up front. Page 180 gives you more details.

What does an FHA loan look like in terms of cold, hard cash? Take a look at the following table, which shows you how much money you'd have to bring to close on a house with an FHA loan versus a conventional loan with 20 percent down; both loans have 30-year terms, with a fixed interest rate of 5 percent. (Keep in mind that the down payment and the initial mortgage insurance premium represent only part of a house's *closing costs*, the total amount you pay to complete the transactions involved in buying a home. Chapter 9 gives you a complete rundown of closing costs.)

	20 percent down	3.5 percent down FHA loan
Home value	$200,000	$200,000
Down payment	$40,000	$7,000
Loan amount	$160,000	$193,000
Initial mortgage insurance due at closing	N/A	$5,000
Cash required at closing for down payment and initial insurance premium	$40,000	$12,000

Of course, closing costs are only part of the story. Here's what those same loans look like in terms of monthly payments, total PMI, and total payments the life of the loan:

	20 percent down	3.5 percent down FHA loan
Monthly payment (principal and interest)	$925.58	$1,036.07
Monthly PMI payment	$0	$80.42
Total monthly payment (principal, interest, and PMI)	$925.58	$1,116.49
Months of PMI paid	0	111
Total PMI payments	$0	$8,926.25
Total payments over 30 years	$333,209.25	$401.933.66

80-10-10 Loans

If you have enough money for a 10 percent down payment, you may qualify for an 80-10-10 mortgage, sometimes called a piggyback loan—although these loans are rare nowadays. You come up with the equivalent of a 20 percent down payment by paying 10 percent in cash and borrowing the other 10 percent as a *second* mortgage—you take out two mortgages simultaneously, in other words. Because the first mortgage covers 80 percent of the home's purchase price, you avoid having to get (and pay for) private mortgage insurance. Page 187 gives you the details on 80-10-10 loans.

Seller-Financed Second Mortgages

Some sellers don't mind receiving a portion of a house's sale price over time and may agree to finance a second mortgage for you. Normally, you pay off a seller-financed second mortgage over a term of 5 or 10 years. If you go this route, make sure that your lender okays a seller-financed second mortgage and that the seller's interest rate is at least as good as what you'd pay a traditional lender. See page 189 for details.

7 Compare Mortgages and Other Financing Options

No matter how big your piggy bank, you aren't going to find enough pennies in it to buy your new home. Most people don't have the cash to buy a home outright, so they need help from a financial institution—a commercial bank, credit union, savings and loan company, or mortgage company.

Getting a mortgage is probably the most complex and confusing part of buying a home, but it doesn't have to be. You just need to understand your options and know what to look for as you read the fine print in a loan document. This chapter introduces you to the wonderful world of mortgages and real estate financing. You'll learn the basics of homeowner lending, including its relevant terms, and see how lenders process loan applications. You'll find out about many types of mortgages, and which may best fit your circumstances. And finally, you'll read about government programs for homebuyers and how to get creative with financing.

Mortgage Basics

Talking with a mortgage broker can feel like conversing in a language you studied for a year in high school. You might get the gist of what he's saying, but you might not fully understand what everything means. Don't get lost in translation. Before you apply for a mortgage, make sure you understand the basics.

What Is a Mortgage?

That's easy. A mortgage is money you borrow to buy a house and pay back over time, with interest. Even though that's how most people define the word *mortgage*, it isn't technically a loan at all. It's a document you give your lender so it can prove that it has a legal financial interest in your property. In other words, a mortgage secures a loan by creating a *lien*, or a financial claim, on your property. You're the property's legal owner, but you can't sell it to anyone else until you repay the loan in full, releasing the lien.

There are two parties involved in a mortgage:

- The *mortgagor* (that's you) borrows money from a lender and, in exchange, grants the lender a mortgage to ensure that you will repay the debt.

- The *mortgagee* (that's your lender) holds your mortgage until you pay off the debt.

People sometimes confuse these terms, because it seems like the lender is the one doing the giving. After all, the lender is handing over the cash you need to buy the home.

To keep the terms straight, remember that you're *giving* the lender the right to make a financial claim against your home if you fail to repay the money you borrowed (or if you sell the house). Your mortgage guarantees the loan.

A mortgage has two parts:

- **A pledge of collateral.** This means that you put up your house as security against the money you borrow.

- **A promise to repay the loan.** This means that you agree to pay back the loan in full.

It's important to understand both parts. When you put up your house as collateral, you grant the lender the right to seize the property if you go into default. That's what a foreclosure is.

But the promise to repay is equally important. Many homeowners don't realize that their mortgage allows the lender to sue for full repayment of the loan, even if the bank forecloses on the house or agrees to let you short-sell it (see page 124). The legally binding promise to repay is why it's so important to understand how much you can reasonably afford to pay toward your mortgage each month before you apply for a loan. (Chapter 2 tells you how to do just that.)

 Note Some states use a *deed of trust*, rather than a mortgage, as the document that secures a real estate loan. Like a mortgage, a deed of trust secures the loan by creating a lien on your property. Unlike a mortgage, it involves three parties: a trustor (you), a beneficiary (the lender), and a trustee (a neutral third party, often an attorney or title insurance company). The trustee holds temporary, limited title to your property until you pay the beneficiary in full. It's still your house, but if you default on the loan, the trustee can transfer the title to the lender. If you stay current with your payments, the trustee cannot confiscate the title from you.

Interest Rate vs. APR

When you borrow money, you have to pay it back—no surprise there. And it's also not surprising that the lender needs to make money on the transaction; otherwise, there'd be no reason to make loans. So lenders charge you a percentage of what you borrow, and that percentage is the loan's *interest rate*. You pay interest for the privilege of borrowing the money.

Although the interest rate tells you what you're paying to borrow the money, it doesn't reflect the whole cost of the loan. That's what the *annual percentage rate*, or APR, does. The APR bundles together all the costs associated with your loan—interest, upfront closing costs, and other costs and fees—and expresses the grand total as a yearly percentage. It's what your loan and its associated fees cost you on an annual basis. The APR will always be higher than the interest rate, because it adds all other costs to that rate.

The APR was designed to make it easier for borrowers to compare loans. If you're looking at loans with two slightly different *interest* rates, such as 5 percent and 5.125 percent, the 5 percent loan looks like a better deal. But that loan may actually cost you more when you add in all the fees and total the cost of the loan over its life—the higher interest-rate loan could end up being cheaper. The following table, which compares APRs for two 30-year, fixed-rate, $250,000 loans, shows how that works:

Cost	Loan 1	Loan 2
Interest rate	5.125%	5%
Monthly payment	$1,380.51	$1,342.05
Discount points	0 points	2 points (2% of $250,000) = $5,000
Origination fee	2 % = $5,000	2.5% = $6,250
Other closing costs	$800	$1,250
APR	5.3292%	5.4341%

As the table shows, even though Loan 2 has a slightly lower interest rate, its other costs are high enough that it's the more expensive of the two loans.

 Note The APR is less accurate for adjustable rate mortgages (ARMs, page 164) than it is for fixed-rate loans. That's because it's impossible to predict future interest rates. In 5 or 10 years, the 5 percent interest rate your ARM started out with may have increased to 6 or 7 percent (or it may have dropped to 4 percent).

A loan's APR is calculated over the life of the loan, usually 30 years. But most people sell their house and move on before those 30 years are up. So if you refinance or move within five years or so, a mortgage with high up-front costs may turn out to be even *more* expensive than the APR suggests. The longer you live in the home, the more your up-front costs are spread out over those years, and the less expensive they are in terms of the life of the loan.

 Tip Use APRs as a starting point for comparing mortgages. But be aware that not all lenders calculate APRs in precisely the same way. Page 215 tells you how to compare loans using the Good Faith Estimates that lenders must give you.

Term

The *term* of a loan is the length of time your lender allows you to pay it back. Along with the interest rate, lenders use the term of your loan to figure out how much you'll pay each month. Most loans *mature* (that is, come due) at the end of their terms. An exception is a balloon loan (page 173). For a 10-year balloon loan, for example, the term may be 30 years (thus giving you low per-month payments), but the loan matures at 10 years, when you must repay the balance in a lump sum.

Many homeowners take out loans with a 30-year term. Stretching your payments over 360 months helps keep those monthly payments smaller. But because you're borrowing the money for a longer period of time, you also pay more interest.

 Tip Page 176 has tips for choosing the right term for your loan.

Amortization

If you looked up *amortization* in a dictionary, you'd learn that it means the process of paying back a loan, including interest, in regular installments over time. That's a simple enough concept. But the way lenders calculate your payments isn't quite so simple.

To lenders, a mortgage is an investment. And lenders expect a good return on that investment. Because they know that most people stay in a home for five to seven years, they calculate your monthly payments so that you're paying a higher proportion of each payment toward interest than toward principal during the first half of the loan. For example, if you borrowed $250,000 at 5 percent interest over a 30-year term, you'd pay $1,342.05 each month for principal and interest. But those monthly payments aren't evenly split. For about the first half of the loan—15 years in this case—more of your monthly payment goes toward the interest than the principal. These amounts gradually flip-flop as you continue to pay.

The following amortization table shows how much of your monthly $1,342.05 goes toward principal and how much toward interest during the loan's first year.

Month	Principal	Interest	Total principal you've paid so far	Total interest you've paid so far	Principal balance
1	$300.38	$1,041.67	$300.38	$1,041.67	$249,699.62
2	$301.63	$1,040.42	$602.01	$2,082.09	$249,397.99
3	$302.89	$1,039.16	$904.90	$3,121.25	$249,095.10
4	$304.15	$1,037.90	$1,209.05	$4,159.15	$248,790.95
5	$305.42	$1,036.63	$1,514.47	$5,195.78	$248,485.53
6	$306.69	$1,035.36	$1,821.16	$6,231.14	$248,178.84
7	$307.97	$1,034.08	$2,129.13	$7,265.22	$247,870.87
8	$309.25	$1,032.80	$2,438.38	$8,298.02	$247,561.62
9	$310.54	$1,031.51	$2,748.92	$9,329.53	$247,251.08
10	$311.84	$1,030.21	$3,060.76	$10,359.74	$246,939.24
11	$313.14	$1,028.91	$3,373.90	$11,388.65	$246,626.10
12	$314.44	$1,027.61	$3,688.34	$12,416.26	$246,311.66

As the table shows, by the end of the first year, you've paid $12,416.26 in interest, and just $3,688.34 went toward the principal.

As the years go by, the amounts continue to adjust—each month, a little more of each payment goes toward principal and a little less toward interest. Somewhere around the 16th year, principal and interest payments become close to equal. Then, for the second half of the loan, you pay more in principal than in interest.

For a 30-year loan, the final year's payments break down like this:

Month	Principal	Interest	Total principal you've paid so far	Total interest you've paid so far	Principal balance
349	$1,276.72	$65.33	$235,596.81	$232,778.64	$14,403.19
350	$1,282.04	$60.01	$236,878.85	$232,838.65	$13,121.15
351	$1,287.38	$54.67	$238,166.23	$232,893.32	$11,833.77
352	$1,292.74	$49.31	$239,458.97	$232,942.63	$10,541.03
353	$1,298.13	$43.92	$240,757.10	$232,986.55	$9,242.90
354	$1,303.54	$38.51	$242,060.64	$233,025.06	$7,939.36
355	$1,308.97	$33.08	$243,369.61	$233,058.14	$6,630.39
356	$1,314.42	$27.63	$244,684.03	$233,085.77	$5,315.97
357	$1,319.90	$22.15	$246,003.93	$233,107.92	$3,996.07
358	$1,325.40	$16.65	$247,329.33	$233,124.57	$2,670.67
359	$1,330.92	$11.13	$248,660.25	$233,135.70	$1,339.75
360	$1,339.75	$5.58	$250,000.00	$233,141.28	$0.00

If you made all of your monthly payments for 30 years, you'd pay back the $250,000 you originally borrowed, plus an additional $233,141.28 in interest, for a grand total of $483,141.28. Although statistically it's likely that you'll sell your house, pay off the principal balance, and move on before you've made 360 monthly payments, it's instructive to see the total cost of borrowing money for 30-year term—it adds up.

 Tip For a simple-to-use amortization calculator, check out the one at Bankrate.com: *http://tinyurl.com/mda2hp*.

Points

When you shop for a mortgage, your broker or loan officer will talk about points. A *point* is equal to 1 percent of your loan. For a $250,000 loan, one point is $2,500.

You'll encounter two kinds of points when you go to a lender:

- **Origination points.** This kind of point is a fee you pay your mortgage broker or loan officer for processing your mortgage. This fee is negotiable, so discuss it with your lender. Unlike discount points, origination points aren't tax deductible.

- **Discount points.** You might decide to use this kind of point to reduce your loan's interest rate. Essentially, you pay part of your loan's interest up front, in one lump sum. The benefit? You pay a lower interest rate over the course of 30 years, and you can see from the following example how much interest adds up over time. One discount point typically reduces an interest rate between 0.125 and 0.25 percent. Because discount points are prepaid interest, you can deduct them from your taxes.

Over time, you can save a lot of money by paying a lower interest rate. Take a look at how much interest you'll pay if you borrow $250,000 using a fixed-rate, 30-year loan.

Interest rate (%)	Monthly payment (principal and interest)	Total interest paid over 30 years
4.75	$1,304.12	$219,481.80
4.875	$1,323.02	$226,287.90
5	$1,342.05	$233,141.28
5.125	$1,361.22	$240,037.32
5.25	$1,380.51	$246,982.96

Over 30 years, an extra one-half percentage point on the interest rate adds up to more than $27,500 in interest for this loan.

 Tip When your mortgage broker or loan officer talks about points, ask how much that means in dollars. Two points may not sound like much—until you realize that the loan officer is talking about $5,000 on a $250,000 loan. If you decide to prepay interest, be sure you know how much it'll cost you at the closing.

Given their impressive benefits, should you pay discount points to lower your interest rate? The answer depends on two factors:

- **Do you have the money?** If you're already stretching to come up with your down payment and closing costs, you may not have the cash to prepay interest.

- **How long do you plan to live in the home?** In general, the longer you live in a home, the more you can save by buying discount points. If you know you're going to move after a couple of years, buying discount points probably isn't worth it. On the other hand, if you plan to live in the same place for 10 years or longer, prepaying interest can save you a lot of money.

To make your decision easier, follow these steps:

1. Find out the monthly principal and interest payments for the full interest rate and for the discounted interest rate. Your loan originator can give you these amounts, or you can use an online calculator like the one at *www.mortgagecalculator.org*.

2. Subtract the lower, discounted payment from the full payment. That's how much you'll save each month.

3. Divide the amount you're paying for points by the monthly amount you'll save. The result tells you how many months it will take to reach the break-even point—the point at which the money you saved each month adds up to enough to repay what you paid for points at closing.

For example, say your interest rate on a 30-year, fixed-rate loan for $250,000 is 5 percent. Your monthly principal and interest payment would be $1,342.05. Your loan officer tells you that by paying one point ($2,500), you can get a discounted interest rate of 4.75 percent. At the discounted rate, your monthly payment would be $1,304.12. Each month, you'd pay $37.93 less at the lower rate.

Because you paid $2,500 to get that discounted rate, you'd have to live in the house for 66 months—5 1/2 years—to break even. If you plan to stay in your home longer than that, you'll start saving money. And the longer you live there, the more you save. If you lived in the home for 10 years, you'd save more than $6,100 in interest. If you stayed there for 30 years and paid off your mortgage on schedule, you'd save more than $13,600.

Escrow

When dealing with large amounts of money, it's smart to work with someone you trust until all the dust has cleared and the transaction is settled. That's what escrow is all about. *Escrow* means that a trusted, neutral third party holds money and legal documents for everyone involved in a house's sale until the transaction closes. That neutral third party, called the *escrow officer* or *escrow agent*, may be an attorney or someone who works for an escrow or title company. Some states allow an escrow officer to conduct real estate closings; others require an attorney to do that job. Chapter 13 explains the differences between how escrow states and non-escrow states conduct closings.

Depending on the terms of your loan, escrow may also come into play after closing. For most borrowers, the monthly payments include principal, interest, taxes, and insurance (PITI). Principal and interest go to the lender, and your taxes and insurance go into an escrow account. When these fees come due, the lender pays them from the escrow funds.

RESPA

Back in 1974, Congress passed the Real Estate Settlement Procedures Act (RESPA) to protect consumers from unscrupulous goings-on in the real estate industry, including kickbacks and undisclosed fees. For example, a loan officer might steer you toward a particular title company without telling you that he got a commission for each new customer he referred. In that context, hidden costs and improper referral fees made it difficult for borrowers to compare loans. RESPA prohibits kickbacks and requires lenders to provide certain information about the loan at different times during the loan process.

Thanks to RESPA, when you apply for a mortgage, the lender must give you these documents within three days:

- **Special Information Booklet.** This booklet describes the steps involved in buying a home and contains consumer information about the costs associated, including an explanation of the detailed HUD-1 form you get on closing day (see page 325).

- **Good Faith Estimate (GFE).** This three-page document lists the terms of a loan and the charges you're likely to pay at the closing (when you formally transfer the property). Because it's an estimate, the actual charges may differ, but not by much, and that's what the GFE was designed for. To prevent nasty surprises at the closing, lender fees may not change from what's stated in the GFE, and third-party fees may change, but by no more than 10 percent.

  The GFE also includes a handy table that compares the loan as quoted with one that offers lower up-front costs (but a higher interest rate) and one that offers a lower interest rate (and higher up-front costs). Page 215 tells you more about how to read your GFE.

- **Mortgage Servicing Disclosure Statement.** This document tells you whether the lender intends to service your loan itself or transfer (sell) the loan to another lender.

You'll get these disclosures between the time you apply for a loan and the closing:

- **Controlled Business Arrangement.** Lenders sometimes make referrals to other service providers—they may recommend a title insurance company, for example. If the lender owns or has any kind of interest in the service provider, this document informs you of that interest.

- **HUD-1 Settlement Statement.** You'll get a copy of this at closing, but the law says you're entitled to get it 24 hours before your closing takes place. Ask for it in advance so you'll have ample time to look it over. This form itemizes who pays for what—and how much—at the closing. It lists all the charges and credits for both you and the seller. It includes the home's purchase price, the amount of money you are borrowing, how much you've already put down on the house (such as earnest money), and how much you'll bring to the closing. Review your HUD-1 carefully to make sure it's accurate. Page 325 shows you what's in each section of this form.

 Tip Compare your HUD-1 statement to your Good Faith Estimate to make sure that estimated costs haven't risen past their legal limit.

Whether or not you get your HUD-1 a day in advance, you'll get the final copy at the closing. If part of your monthly payment will go into escrow to pay for recurring costs like taxes and insurance, you'll also get an **Initial Escrow Statement**, which tells you how much you're paying into escrow and for what. This statement breaks down estimated taxes, insurance premiums, and any other costs the lender collects, holds in escrow, and pays on your behalf for the first year of your loan.

After the closing, RESPA wants your lender to stay in touch. So your lender must send you these documents (as applicable):

- **Annual Escrow Statement.** Your Initial Escrow Statement itemizes how much your lender sets aside for the first year of your loan to pay taxes, insurance, and other charges. But these costs tend to increase over time. Each year your lender must send you a new statement, so you can see how much you'll pay and where that money is going.

- **Servicing Transfer Statement.** If the lender sells your loan (and you know whether this is likely from the mortgage servicing disclosure statement described above), this statement notifies you that he's done so.

The Mortgage Process

Before you take the mortgage plunge, know what you're getting into. This section takes you behind the scenes to show you what happens to your mortgage application from the time you submit it to the time you're clear to close.

Applying for a Loan

The journey to getting a mortgage begins with a single step—and you're the one who has to take it. The mortgage process begins when you submit a loan application. Of course, preparing to take that initial step requires some work on your part. That's why Chapter 8 tells you all about the process of applying for a loan.

After you've completed your application, you give it (along with supporting documentation, described below) to your mortgage broker or loan officer, who passes it on to the loan processor for the next phase.

Processing Your Application

When you submit your loan application, a *loan processor* checks it over and verifies the information in it. She checks your credit history; orders an appraisal of the property; requests the title search; and contacts your employer, your landlord (if you currently rent), and financial institutions where you have accounts. Basically, assume that the loan processor checks every piece of information you supply.

Loan processing often takes a week or two. But delays can happen, especially as the loan processor waits to hear back from various sources. If the house appraiser has a backlog, for example, or if your vacationing boss is off climbing the Himalayas and can't verify your employment, this phase might take longer.

After the loan processor collects and verifies all the necessary information, she packages up your loan application with the appraisal and the preliminary title report and sends it on to a mortgage underwriter, who specializes in analyzing risk.

Analyzing Risk

Before your lender hands over the very large sum of money that enables you to buy your new home, it needs to assess whether the benefits of lending you that money outweigh the risk. Lenders make a profit from good loans, but they stand to lose a great deal from bad loans. They take the decision to make a loan—or not—very seriously. That's where an underwriter comes in.

The *mortgage underwriter*, who may work for the lender or a company that does business with the lender, evaluates the information in your loan application and decides whether you're an acceptable risk. Expect another round of checking and verifications: The underwriter may double- or triple-check with the same people the loan processor contacted. It's common for him to ask some pointed questions about recent account activity, like why you deposited an unusually large amount in your checking account on a particular date. Ultimately, the underwriter is the person who approves or denies your loan.

 Note To speed up the application-review process, many lenders use automated underwriting. That means a computer program, not a person, analyzes your application and approves or denies it. Afterward, a human underwriter reviews the supporting documentation to confirm that decision. Automated underwriting can shave several days off the underwriting phase of processing a loan.

The underwriting phase usually takes a week or less, longer in a hot market with lots of loan applications. The underwriter will probably send your loan officer a list of "conditions to close." Usually, these are requests for further or updated documentation, such as recent bank statements. After you supply the documentation, the underwriter gives the clear to close.

When your loan originator gets word that your loan is clear to close, she lets you know, coordinates among the parties to set up the closing, and draws up the documents you need to sign.

 Note Chapter 13 tells you what to expect at the closing.

Types of Mortgages

If you're the kind of person who has trouble deciding what to watch on TV or choosing an ice cream flavor, you might feel intimidated by the variety of mortgages you can choose from. Never fear. This section explains your options.

Fixed Rate Mortgage

A *fixed-rate loan* has an interest rate that doesn't change over the life of the loan. If you get a 30-year fixed-rate loan with a 5.25 percent interest rate, for example, your interest rate remains 5.25 percent from the day you sign the loan papers until the day you pay off the mortgage.

With a fixed-rate loan, your monthly principal and interest payments remain the same, year in and year out, for as long as you have the loan. (Of course, if you make payments into escrow toward taxes and insurance, that portion of your monthly payment changes from one year to the next.) Fixed-rate loans are appealing because they're stable and predictable, making it easier to budget for them.

Fixed-rate loans are a good choice if you plan to stay in your new home for several years. They're a great choice when interest rates are low; if interest rates rise in the future, you're unaffected. Of course, the reverse is also true: If interest rates are high when you get your loan, you'll watch with envy if the rates drop. You still have an option at that point, though—you can refinance the loan at a lower rate.

Fixed-rate loans are available in different terms—that is, for the amount of time you have to pay them back—such as 15 or 30 years. Page 176 has tips for choosing the term of your loan.

Adjustable Rate Mortgage

Adjustable-rate mortgages (ARMs) have a variable interest rate—it's tied to a specific financial index. The interest you pay fluctuates with the index; as the index goes up and down, so does your interest rate. Usually, an ARM has an initial, fixed interest rate for a set period of time, anywhere from a few months to several years. After that, the initial rate expires, and the index-tied adjustable rate takes over. Adjustment periods vary, but you'll commonly find the rate set every six months or a year.

 An ARM that has an initial fixed-rate period of 3 to 10 years, followed by an adjustable-rate period, is sometimes called a *hybrid loan*.

You may see lenders refer to ARMs by number, which represents the initial fixed-rate period followed by the frequency of adjustments, so you might see a bank advertise a "5/1 ARM," for example. The following table shows some common rate-adjustment schedules for ARMs.

ARM type	How it works
3/1	Fixed for three years (36 months), then adjusts annually for the rest of the loan's term
3/3	Fixed for three years (36 months), then adjusts every three years for the rest of the loan's term
5/1	Fixed for five years (60 months), then adjusts annually for the rest of the loan's term
5/5	Fixed for five years (60 months), then adjusts every five years for the rest of the loan's term
7/1	Fixed for seven years (84 months), then adjusts annually for the rest of the loan's term
10/1	Fixed for ten years (120 months), then adjusts annually for the rest of the loan's term

Here's an example of how ARMs work: Say you borrow $250,000 for a 30-year term with a 3/1 ARM that has an initial interest rate of 5 percent. The principal and interest portion of your monthly payment is $1,342.05. Three years down the road, that initial rate expires, and you get a new rate that applies to the money you still owe. So say your rate goes up a point, to 6 percent. At the new rate, your monthly principal and interest payments become $1,498.88, an increase of $156.83 a month. If the interest rate takes a bigger jump, so would your payment. If your new rate is 7.5 percent, for example, your new principal and interest payment would be $1,748.04—over $400 more each month than what you paid during the first three years.

Interest rates also go down, of course. When that happens, your monthly principal and interest payments drop, too. If the first adjustment lowers your interest rate from 5 percent to 4 percent, for example, your new monthly principal and interest payment is $1,193.54, saving you $148.51 a month.

How your lender determines your rate

Two factors work together to determine the adjustable part of an ARM rate:

- The *index*, which is a measure of interest rates in general.

- The *margin*, which is the amount your lender adds to the index rate to come up with your rate.

To set your rate, the lender starts with the current rate of a particular index and then adds some percentage points (the margin). Although ARM margins can vary from one lender to another, the margin usually doesn't change for the life of your loan. When your lender adds the margin to the current index rate, the result is called the *fully indexed rate*, which is the adjusted rate on your loan. If the index your lender uses is currently at 2 percent and your loan's margin is 3 percent, your fully indexed rate is 5 percent.

Your lender can tie your ARM's rate to one of many different indexes. Mostly likely, however, the lender will use one of the three below, which together account for about 80 percent of ARM indexes:

- **London Inter Bank Offered Rates (LIBOR).** This international index averages the interest rate on dollar-denominated deposits, also known as Eurodollars, traded between banks in London. Most lenders use the LIBOR rate that was current 45 days before your scheduled interest rate change date.

- **11th District Cost of Funds Index (COFI).** This index reflects the interest rate paid by savings institutions in the 11th federal district (institutions headquartered in Arizona, California, or Nevada).

- **Constant Maturity Treasury (CMT).** This index is based on the average yield of different U.S. Treasury securities adjusted to a one-year maturity.

 Note The LIBOR and CMT indexes both respond quickly to economic changes, which means rates tied to these indexes move up and down faster than COFI. COFI lags behind market interest rates, so ARMs tied to this index rise (and fall) more slowly than rates in general. This lag is good for you when rates are rising (your rate rises more slowly than those tied to other indexes), but not so good when rates are falling.

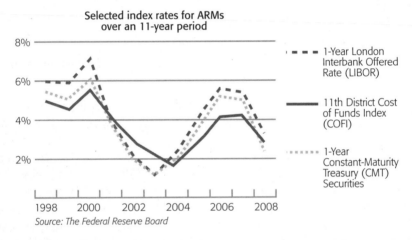

Selected index rates for ARMs over an 11-year period

1-Year London Interbank Offered Rate (LIBOR)

11th District Cost of Funds Index (COFI)

1-Year Constant-Maturity Treasury (CMT) Securities

Source: The Federal Reserve Board

Rate caps

When you start paying back an ARM, you know what your interest rate is (along with its associated monthly principal and interest payments), now and for the initial, fixed-rate term of the loan. So if you take out a 5/1 ARM with an initial interest rate of 5 percent, you know that your rate will stay at 5 percent for 60 months' worth of mortgage payments. But what happens when month 61 rolls around? No one can predict what interest rates will be so far in the future—what if they've soared into double digits?

Most ARMs have rate caps that prevent your rate from rising (or falling) too far, too fast. This *rate cap* restricts the interest-rate change either from one adjustment period to the next or over the life of the loan:

- **Periodic cap.** This cap limits how much your rate can go up or down from one adjustment period to the next. A typical periodic cap is 2 to 3 percent.

- **Lifetime cap.** This cap limits how high your interest rate can go over the life of the loan. For example, if you start off with a rate of 5.25 percent and your lifetime loan cap is 6 percent, the highest rate you will ever pay is 11.25 percent.

 Tip Before you take out an ARM, figure out what your monthly principal and interest payments would be at the maximum rate. (Use an ARM calculator like the one at Interest.com: *http://tinyurl.com/yjzloge*.) If you can't afford payments that high, don't go with the ARM.

Caps work both ways, slowing or limiting changes to your interest rate when the index rate drops—not just when it rises.

It's even possible for the index to drop or stay the same, while your interest rate rises. This is thanks to a practice called *carryover*. If your loan is subject to carryover, here's what happens: Say the interest rate takes a jump, but your periodic cap keeps your rate from jumping quite so high. Then, at the next adjustment, index rates have declined slightly. But when you get your adjusted rate, it didn't drop as far as you expected—it may even have increased. When rates went up, your cap held your rate below what it would have been if your rate had increased to the fully indexed rate. Because the cap held down your interest rate, your lender carries over whatever increase it couldn't apply during the earlier adjustment to the next adjustment.

Here's an example. Say your initial interest rate is 5 percent, with a 2 percent periodic cap—that means your rate can't rise more than 2 percent from one adjustment period to the next. When it's time to calculate your new rate, interest rates have risen 3 percent. Because of your 2 percent cap, your rate rises only 2 points, to 7 percent. So far, so good. At the next adjustment, however, interest rates stay the same—but your rate goes up. That's because the *current* index rate is now within your loan's 2 percent cap; your rate can rise another percentage point, all the way to 8 percent, because it didn't rise the full amount the previous year. That's carryover.

Some ARMs have a payment cap, but that's *not* the same as a rate cap. A *payment cap* limits the dollar amount that your monthly payment can increase at each adjustment (as opposed to limiting your interest rate). For example, if your loan has a payment cap of 10 percent, your monthly payment won't increase more than 10 percent over your previous payment, no matter how much interest rates have increased. So if your payment is $1,300 a month, you won't pay more than $1,430 a month after the next adjustment.

Payment caps may sound like a good thing, but they're not. Stay away from them. If your ARM has a payment cap, it may not come with a periodic rate cap—and when interest rates increase, your payments aren't keeping up with them, and that can lead to negative amortization. Negative amortization is a bad thing, as you can read later in this section.

Convertible ARMs

Some people start out with an ARM and later decide that they prefer the comfort of knowing what their principal and interest payments will be from one year to the next. When that happens, you have a couple of options: You can refinance, or, if you have a *convertible ARM*, you can convert your loan from a variable-rate to a fixed-rate loan without having to go through the whole refinancing process.

Your agreement with your lender may include a clause that lets you convert your ARM to a fixed-rate loan at designated times. If you decide to convert, your lender sets the fixed rate using a formula spelled out in your loan documents. If you opt for a convertible ARM, be aware that you might spend more money up front than for a regular ARM. You may also have to pay a fee to convert the loan.

Things to watch out for

If you're shopping for an ARM, you'll encounter a bewildering variety of options. There are some things you definitely *don't* want your loan to have; this section tells you what they are.

Negative amortization

You make your 3required payment each month, so it's reasonable to assume that, over time, the amount you owe the lender is decreasing, right? Usually, yes, even though you initially pay far more toward interest than toward your principal (page 155 explains how that works). But in some cases, even though you make those payments faithfully, your balance actually *increases*. You can end up owing the bank more at the end of the year than you did at the beginning, even though you made every required payment on time.

The culprit is something called *negative amortization*. As page 155 explains, when you pay your principal and interest each month, you amortize your loan—that is, you gradually pay it off according to a set schedule. Negative amortization means that the balance increases rather than decreases as you make your payments. This can happen when your ARM has a payment cap (page 168) but no periodic rate cap (page 203).

Say your loan has a payment cap of 10 percent but no rate cap. At a 4 percent interest rate, you pay $1,200 a month for principal and interest. At the next adjustment period, your interest rate jumps to 6 percent, which increases what you owe each month to about $1,500. But thanks to the rate cap, what you owe is *not* what you pay. Your 10 percent payment cap holds your adjusted payment to $1,320 (the $1,200 you were paying plus 10 percent, or $120). Looks like you're saving money, right? You're not. The $180 you're not paying each month gets added to your principal. Instead of decreasing, your principal balance is increasing. In other words, the unpaid interest gets rolled into the balance of your loan—and you end up paying interest on the interest you haven't yet paid. That makes your loan balance shoot up, along with the total interest you owe.

Some ARMs include a cap on negative amortization, which limits the total amount you can owe—usually topping out at 110 to 125 percent of the amount you originally borrowed. If your balance increases to that point, the lender recalculates your monthly payment amount so that you fully repay the loan over the remaining term. Expect your payments to take a big jump, because now you're paying back an amount of up to 25 percent more than you borrowed.

 Tip To limit negative amortization, increase your monthly payments beyond your payment cap, if you have one. Ask your lender what the fully amortized monthly payment is—the full amount you need to pay to keep up with the interest you owe—and pay that.

Teaser rates

Some ARMs advertise super-low, super-attractive initial interest rates. But these low starter rates, called *teaser* or *discounted rates*, may come at a high price. A teaser rate is lower than the lender's current fully indexed rate (page 165) and looks like a terrific deal. But look closely: To get the teaser rate, you may have to pay a hefty fee (in the form of discount points, page 157), and after the teaser rate expires, your interest rate (along with your monthly payments) will probably take a big jump.

If you're thinking about a discounted ARM with a teaser rate, make sure you know:

- When the discounted rate expires
- What the fully indexed rate is
- How much you'd pay each month at the fully indexed rate

Depending on how the loan will change after the teaser rate expires, you may find that the discount points you pay up front don't reduce the overall cost of the loan enough to make it worthwhile.

Prepayment penalties

Some ARMs make you pay special fees or penalties if you pay off your loan early, say within the first 3 to 5 years of the loan. Lenders impose two kinds of prepayment penalties:

- *Soft prepayment penalties* mean that you pay fees if you refinance your loan (thereby paying off your current loan), but not if you sell your home.

- *Hard prepayment penalties* charge you fees if you pay off the loan early for any reason: either through refinancing, by selling the property, or because of a windfall (such as an inheritance).

Prepayment penalties exist because lenders don't want you signing up for an ARM with a low teaser rate, only to turn around and refinance when your rate is about to adjust upward. So the penalties can be hefty, such as six months' worth of interest on your remaining balance (in some cases, it's 80 percent of the loan's balance). For example, say you borrow $250,000 using a 5/1 ARM with an initial rate of 5 percent. After 32 months, you decide to refinance. At that point, your balance is $239,740. On that balance, six months' worth of interest would cost you just under $6,000!

 Note Prepayment penalties are legal under federal law, but some states don't allow them. Talk to your lender or a real estate attorney to get the scoop for your state.

Who's a good candidate for an ARM?

If you plan to stay in your new home for just a few years, an ARM can be a good choice. Their initial rates are lower than fixed-rate mortgages, so if you're likely to move in a few years, you benefit from the ARM's lower rate. (Find out if there's a prepayment penalty and, if so, how much.)

ARMs can also be a good choice for first-time homebuyers who plan to buy a starter home and trade up to a larger home later. Their lower initial rates can make ARMs a good way to enter the housing market. You get a good rate, and your initial monthly payments are low.

Questions to ask

If you're considering an ARM, make sure you get the answers to these questions:

- **How long does the initial interest rate last?** It's important to know this, because it tells you when your rate will start to change. You don't want to be caught by surprise with a rate that jumps unexpectedly.

- **To what index is the interest rate tied?** When you know which index your lender uses to determine the loan's rate, you can check how the index has performed over the past year and what its current rate is. You can also get a sense of whether the index moves quickly with market rates or lags behind them.

 To track the major indexes that the banking industry uses, visit Bankrate.com's RateWatch (*http://tinyurl.com/y87jaqa*).

- **What's the interest rate's margin?** When you know this number, you can look at current index rates and get a sense of what your interest rate would be if your initial rate expired today.

Tip Loan officers sometimes increase their commission by padding the index margin. If the margin is higher than about 2.5 percent, ask the lender to decrease it.

- **Does the loan have a periodic interest rate cap? What is it?** As page 167 explains, periodic caps protect you from too-sharp increases in your interest rate from one adjustment period to the next. The lower the cap, the more restricted the increase.

- **Can rate increases carry over from one adjustment period to the next?** Page 167 tells you what carryover is and why you should avoid it if you can.

- **How much can the rate increase in the first adjustment period?** Some loans allow the first adjustment to ignore the periodic cap—which means you could be facing a huge increase in your monthly principal and interest payments if the rate has increased.

- **What is the lifetime cap for the loan's interest rate?** Use the lifetime cap to figure out what your maximum monthly principal and interest payments would be to make sure you can afford to continue paying if rates skyrocket.

- **Can this loan be subject to negative amortization?** Don't get into any situation where meeting your monthly payment obligations can increase your balance.

- **Is there a penalty for prepaying the loan?** Many ARMs come with some kind of penalty for paying off the loan early. Know how long the penalty is in effect, whether the penalty is hard or soft, and how much it would cost to pay off the loan ahead of time.

Option ARM

Everyone likes to have choices. And, on the surface, that's what an option ARM appears to offer. With an option ARM, you can choose to pay any of four amounts each month. But beware: These loans can lead to negative amortization (page 169).

The list of your payment options appears below. It shows what your monthly payment options are on a 30-year option ARM, from the smallest payment to the highest:

1. **Minimum payment.** This amount is less than the interest you owe for the month. Choosing it increases your loan's balance (see negative amortization, page 169). Avoid it.

2. **Interest-only payment.** This amount keeps you up to date on your interest but doesn't pay anything toward your principal, so your loan's balance stays the same. (Page 174 explains why interest-only payments are a bad idea for most borrowers.)

3. **Fully amortized.** This amount pays both principal and interest according to the loan's amortization schedule, so you're on track to pay off the loan fully in 30 years. It decreases the loan's balance.

4. **Accelerated payment.** This amount pays the principal and interest you currently owe plus some extra money that helps you pay off the loan faster—for example, on a 15-year schedule instead of a 30-year schedule. It decreases your loan's balance faster than option 3.

If you always take option 3 or 4—if you make payments high enough to cover both principal and interest each and every month—then an option ARM isn't a problem. It's the first two options that get homeowners in trouble. Neither lets you build any equity in your home, and option 1 can leave you owing more than what you initially borrowed, even after years of payments!

For most borrowers, option ARMs are bad news. If you can handle options 3 and 4, you don't need an option ARM—take out a regular ARM or a fixed-rate loan. If options 1 and 2 look like the only way you can buy the home, you're probably trying to buy a home you can't afford. Turn back to Chapter 2 and figure out whether you need to scale back your expectations.

Balloon Loan

A *balloon loan* is fixed-rate loan whose payments are calculated for a 30-year term, but whose true term is far less. After a set period of time (often 3, 5, 7, or 10 years), the loan matures, and you owe the entire balance in one lump sum. To pay, you have to sell the home, refinance, or win the Lotto.

Balloon loans offer a low interest rate, so they can sometimes be a good alternative to an ARM. If you're confident you can sell or refinance when the balance comes due, you may find that a balloon loan's lower rate saves you money over fixed-rate and ARM options.

Two-Step Loan

A two-step loan is an ARM that starts off with a fixed rate for a specified period of time, usually 5 or 7 years (that's step 1). Then the lender applies a new interest rate, based on current market rates, to the remaining balance (that's step 2). You might see these mortgages referred to as 5/25 and 7/23 loans. The first number reflects the number of years in step 1, and the second shows the number of years in step 2.

Two-step mortgages typically have a cap on how much the interest rate can go up at the end of the initial period. Even with a cap, however, it's possible that your rate could skyrocket if interest rates climb sharply during the first step. For example, if you borrowed $250,000 in a 5/25 two-step mortgage with an interest rate of 5 percent in step 1 and a 5 percent cap, your principal and interest payments would be about $1,342 a month for the first 60 months. If interest rates climb steadily during those five years, and your rate adjusts to reach its full 5 percent cap, your new interest rate jumps to 10 percent. After five years of payments at 5 percent interest, your loan's balance would now be $229,572. At the new interest rate of 10 percent, your monthly principal and interest payment would shoot up to $2,015. You'd have to come up with an additional $673 each and every month to keep repaying the loan.

 Note With a two-step loan, the lender sometimes has the option to call the loan due after 7 or 10 years with 30 days notice. Read your contract carefully and make sure you understand its terms.

So why do people go for two-step mortgage loans? For several reasons:

- Interest rates are high, and you expect them to drop in time for step 2.
- In step 1, a two-step loan tends to have a lower rate than a fixed-rate loan. So if you expect to sell your home before step 2 kicks in, you get the benefit of the lower initial rate.
- A two-step loan can be a stepping-stone for people who don't currently meet the income level lenders require for a fixed-rate loan. If you're sure that your income will increase enough in the next 5 to 7 years that you can make the higher payments in step 2, a two-step loan may get you into the home you want.

 Tip It's always risky to count on future income when you're making plans now. Don't use a two-step mortgage to buy a more expensive house than you can afford.

Interest-Only Loan

During the housing boom of the mid-2000s, interest-only loans were all the rage. As the name suggests, you pay only your loan's interest—but not its principal—for a specified period of time (usually 5, 10, or 15 years). When interest-only loans were popular, house prices were rising quickly, so it seemed like all a homeowner had to do was buy a home and wait for the price to go up, and voilà—instant equity. You didn't have to worry about reducing the principal, the reasoning went, because the house would increase in value so quickly that the loan-to-value ratio worked in the homeowner's favor, without the homeowner's having to pay for it.

In that super-hot housing market, interest-only loans seemed like a great way to buy a home. With prices rising so fast, it was difficult for many homebuyers—especially first-time buyers—to come up with the money to buy a home. Enter the interest-only loan. Because borrowers paid only interest for a set period (such as 5 or 10 years), payments were lower than they would have been for a traditional loan. Those lower payments meant homebuyers could buy more expensive houses. And increasing housing prices, everyone trusted, would work in their favor, reducing the amount borrowed in relation to the home's value.

It was fun while it lasted, but when the housing boom did an abrupt U-turn and became the housing slump, interest-only loans became a problem for many homeowners. Instead of gaining equity through rising prices, homes *lost* equity as the market cooled off. Homeowners with interest-only loans had done nothing to reduce the principal of their loans, so even those who'd been making regular monthly payments for years owed their lenders the same amount they borrowed. As prices continued to slide, many of these homeowners found themselves with negative equity and couldn't afford to sell their homes—they were worth less than they owed on the mortgage.

Here's how an interest-only loan works: If you borrow $250,000 with an interest rate of 5 percent and a term of 30 years, your initial monthly payments are $1,041.67—about $300 less each month than a fully amortized 30-year fixed-rate loan at 5 percent. (**Fully amortized** means that you're paying both principal and interest in an amount that will repay the loan plus interest over the life of the loan.) Saving $300 a month looks good, right? The problem is, you have to pay back the principal at some point.

When your interest-only period is up, the lender amortizes the loan for whatever term is left on it. If your interest rate remained at 5 percent, your payments would increase sharply, depending on how long you'd been paying just interest. Instead of $1,041.67 in interest-only payments, you'd be paying one of these amounts:

Years remaining	Monthly payment
25	$1,461.48
20	$1,649.89
15	$1,976.98

But most interest-only loans aren't fixed rate; they're ARMs. The interest rate may vary during the interest-only period (on some loans, the rate adjusts every month), or the loan switches to an annual variable rate after the interest-only period. If your initial interest rate of 5 percent has jumped to 7.5 percent when you start making fully amortized payments, for example, you'll be in for some serious payment shock: After 10 years of interest-only payments of $1,041.67 each month, you suddenly have to start paying nearly **three times** that—just over $2,967. Ouch.

If you borrowed $250,000 with a 5 percent interest rate and a 30-year term, the following table gives a snapshot what your financial picture would look like after 10 years, comparing an interest-only loan with a fixed-rate loan:

	Interest-only loan	30 year fixed-rate loan
Monthly payment	$1,041.67	$1,342.05
Total principal paid	$0.00	$46,644.84
Total interest paid	$125,000.00	$114,401.65
Payoff amount after 10 years	$251,041.67	$203,355.16

When you're thinking about making payments from one month to the next, that $300 savings on the interest-only loan looks good. When you look at the bigger picture, though, you can see how an interest-only loan costs you money—a lot of it. After 10 years, you've paid more than $10,500 more in interest than with a fixed-rate loan—and you haven't gained a penny in equity. Compare that to the more than $46,000 you gained in equity making by making fully amortized payments on the fixed-rate loan.

Bottom line: Interest-only loans are expensive and risky. You'll write a smaller number on your monthly checks, but over time you'll pay a lot more. And if home values decline, as it did in many cities in 2008, you could have paid all that extra interest only to end up with negative equity.

Bridge Loan

If you're selling your current house because you want to buy your dream home, it would be ideal if you could hold the two closings in quick succession: sell the house you own now, and then use the money you made in the sale to help pay for your new home. But with all the variables in any given real estate transaction, things often don't line up that smoothly. What if you have to close on the home you're buying before you can sell your current home? That's what bridge loans are for.

A *bridge loan* is a short-term loan—six months is common—that bridges the time between when you purchase a new home and when you sell your current one. If you already have a firm purchase-and-sale agreement on the house you're selling, you can probably get an unsecured bridge loan. If you don't have an agreement for your current home, you can get a secured bridge loan in the form of a second mortgage on that home.

Bridge loans are often interest-only loans with high rates, so make sure that you're not going to get into financial trouble trying to pay your old mortgage, your new mortgage, and a bridge loan for an extended period of time. You may have to make arrangements to rent out your old place—or you may decide to wait until you've got an offer on your current home before you go house hunting.

Choose the Term of Your Mortgage

Although it may feel like you'll be paying back your mortgage forever, the loan does have a definite lifetime, its *term*. Lenders use a loan's term to amortize the mortgage (page 155), figuring out how much you need to pay each month in order to repay the loan, plus interest, over that term. In general, the longer the term, the lower your monthly payments. However, a longer term means that you're borrowing the lender's money for a longer period of time—and that means you end up paying more interest.

Shorter Term or Longer Term?

Mortgages commonly come in terms of 15, 20, 30, 40, 45, and even 50 years. Fifteen- and 30-year terms are among the most popular, although in markets where homes are more expensive than the national average, up to a quarter of loans may have terms of 40 years or longer, thanks to the way these loans lower borrowers' monthly principal and interest payments.

In general, shorter-term loans have lower interest rates, and rates increase as the terms do. The following table compares the cost of different terms—monthly and over the life of the loan—for principal and interest on a fixed-rate loan of $250,000.

Term	Interest rate	Monthly payment (principal & interest)	Total interest paid over full term	Total interest plus principal
15 years	4.5%	$1,912.48	$94,247.15	$344,247.15
20 years	4.75%	$1,615.56	$137,734.12	$387,734.12
30 years	5%	$1,342.05	$233,141.28	$483,141.28
40 years	5.25%	$1,247.18	$348,639.84	$598,639.84
45 years	5.375%	$1,229.88	$414,146.34	$664,146.34
50 years	5.5%	$1,224.61	$484,778.16	$734,778.16

 Note Although the table shows fixed-rate loans for the purposes of comparison, most longer-term loans (those for more than 30 years) are ARMs. For example, many loans with 50-year terms are 5/1 ARMs; you pay a steady, fixed interest rate for the first five years of the loan, and after that the rate adjusts annually—and you can count on a lot of interest rate ups and downs over 45 years.

In general, a shorter term lets you build equity faster. With each payment, more money goes toward the principal, so over the term of the loan you pay less interest and reduce the principal balance faster. For example, here's what you've paid at the end of five years for the 15- and 30-year fixed-rate loans in the previous table:

Term	Interest rate	Interest paid after 5 years	Principal balance after 5 years
15 years	4.5%	$49,283.23	$184,534.43
30 years	5%	$60,095.11	$229,572.11

If the home's value remains the same over those five years, you'll have gained just over $65,465 in equity with the 15-year loan. That's $45,037 more than the $20,428 in equity you'd accumulate with the 30-year loan.

Of course, to accumulate that extra equity, you have to be able to afford a higher monthly payment—about $570 more each month in this example. Lower, more affordable monthly payments are the main reason borrowers choose a longer-term loan. But as the tables show, interest adds up quickly with longer-term loans, even over a relatively short period of time.

If you're trying to decide between a 15-year and a 30-year loan, your first consideration will probably be how much you can afford to pay each month. Many people choose 30-year loans because they're willing to make the trade-off of paying more money in the long run for lower monthly payments now. They'll sell or refinance long before the loan's term is up, they figure, so they won't pay the full interest of the 30-year term.

On the other hand, if your goal is to build equity faster or to pay off the loan and own your home outright as quickly as possible—and you can swing the higher monthly payments—you should consider a 15-year mortgage.

 Tip If you'd like a 15-year loan but are nervous about making the higher monthly payments, look for a lower-priced home. Because looking only at monthly payments can make a 30-year loan seem more attractive, some homebuyers are tempted to overspend, thinking they can get more house for less money. If a 15-year loan looks too expensive, you may be home-shopping in a higher price range than you can really afford.

Reducing Your Loan's Term

Many homeowners choose a 30-year mortgage, thinking that they want the lower payments so they can free up extra money for day-to-day expenses. After a few years in the home, however, your priorities may change; instead of lower monthly payments, you want to build equity faster or pay off your loan earlier to save on interest charges.

You can do that by making extra payments toward the amount you borrowed, called *paying down the principal*. These extra payments reduce the term of your loan, which means you build equity faster. Each time you make an extra payment to reduce the principal, you also reduce the balance on which you're paying interest—and that means you pay less interest over the life of the loan. In fact, by paying one extra month's worth of principal and interest each year, you can shave years off your loan—and save tens of thousands of dollars in interest. For example, say you took out a 30-year, fixed rate loan to borrow $250,000 at 5 percent interest. By making the equivalent of one extra monthly payment each year, you pay off your mortgage nearly five years early and save more than $42,000 in interest:

Monthly payment	Months before loan is paid off	Total interest paid
$1,342.05	360	$233,141.28
$1,453.89	304	$190,722.07

You can make this extra monthly payment by mailing in an extra check once a year (include a letter saying that the entire amount is to go toward your loan's principal), or you can divide your monthly payment by 12 and add that amount to your principal and interest payment each month. That's where the second monthly payment amount in the table came from: When you divide $1,342.05 by 12, you get $111.84 (rounded up to the nearest penny). Adding $111.84 to each monthly payment makes the new monthly payment $1,453.89. So over the course of a year, you made the equivalent of 13 payments, not the usual 12.

Making extra payments toward the principal can help you build equity faster while allowing you some flexibility. During times when you have extra money, you can use it to pay down the principal and build equity faster. But if you need to do some belt-tightening, you can go back to your regular payment schedule. Before you start sending in extra payments, though, check with your lender to make sure there's no prepayment penalty.

 Tip You may see ads for "biweekly loans." These are loans that you pay every other week instead of once a month. Over the course of a year, you make 26 biweekly payments (each at half the amount of your full monthly payment) instead of 12 monthly payments. This adds up to the equivalent of one extra monthly payment each year, helping you pay off the loan faster. Paying off the loan faster is a good idea, but you don't need to convert to a biweekly loan to do it. These programs charge a conversion fee and, sometimes, additional administrative fees. There's no reason to pay them when you can do the same thing yourself for free.

Government Financing Programs

Uncle Sam can help you buy your home if you meet certain qualifications. There are government-sponsored financing programs for first-time home-buyers, people in service professions, and those who need extra help to qualify for financing. This section gives you a brief overview.

FHA-Insured Loans

Since 1934, the Federal Housing Authority, part of the U.S. Department of Housing and Urban Development, has been helping Americans achieve their dreams of home ownership. The FHA doesn't make the loans itself; it insures loans offered by financial institutions, like banks and mortgage companies. FHA-insured loans offer homebuyers these benefits:

- **Lower down payments.** Unlike loans that aren't insured by the FHA, which require an initial down payment of 10 or even 20 percent of the purchase price, if you qualify for an FHA-insured loan, you can buy a home with as little as 3.5 percent down. Instead of having to come up with a down payment of $20,000 or $40,000 to buy a $200,000 home, for example, you can qualify for a loan with a down payment as low as $7,000.

- **Lower closing costs.** As Chapter 9 outlines, the costs associated with closing, especially from fees associated with your loan, can run to thousands of dollars—and that's on top of the down payment. With an FHA-insured loan, you can roll many of the closing costs into the loan and pay them back over time, so you need less cash in hand at closing.

- **Easier loan qualification.** Because the FHA insures your loan, lenders are more confident about lending to you. You don't need a stellar credit history to qualify.

- **Better interest rates.** If your credit score isn't great, you may get a better rate through an FHA-insured loan than you could otherwise.

To qualify for an FHA-insured loan, you have to meet these conditions:

- **You meet the residence and age criteria.** You must be a legal resident of the United States with a valid Social Security number and be of legal age to obtain a mortgage in your state.

- **You'll live in the home you're buying.** These loans aren't for investors or second-home buyers. You have to be buying a primary residence, but it can have up to four units (you can rent out the others as long as you live in one).

For the home to be considered a primary residence, you must live there for at least 12 months after you buy it.

- **You meet standard credit guidelines.** This is what the FHA looks for in an applicant:

  — Steady employment for the past two years or longer, preferably with the same employer

  — Stable or increasing income during those two years

  — A monthly payment amount that's no more than 30 percent of your household's pre-tax income

  — No bankruptcies during the past two years or foreclosures during the past three years

  — A credit score that's acceptable to the lender

 HUD doesn't impose a minimum credit score to qualify for an FHA-insured loan, but individual lenders may look for a credit score of 620 or higher to minimize their risk. If you have no credit history at all, you may still qualify for an FHA-insured loan. The lender will look at your past rent payments, utility bills, auto insurance payments, and so on to see whether you pay them reliably.

  — The ability to qualify for the loan you're applying for and pay private mortgage insurance (PMI, page 146)

- **Your loan amount falls within FHA limits.** There's a cap on how much you can borrow with an FHA-insured loan. That cap varies by area, but for most regions it's currently $271,050 for a single-family home. To find out what the cap is for your area, go to *http://tinyurl.com/2x4vsm*.

Most lenders who work with FHA-insured loans offer terms of 15 or 30 years, and you can choose from fixed-rate loans or ARMs. The interest rate varies by lender and with your credit history and other financial information. To find a lender who'll work with you to get an FHA-insured loan, go to *www.hud.gov/buying/localbuying.cfm*.

Buying a fixer-upper

If you're thinking about buying an older house and fixing it up to make it your home, the FHA has a program for you. HUD's 203(k) program lets you take out a loan that covers the cost of both buying a primary residence and fixing it up.

Here's how the 203(k) program for fixer-uppers works:

1. When you find a home you want to buy, make your purchase offer contingent on getting a 203(k) loan.

2. Find a lender approved by the FHA to make this sort of loan and submit a proposal that details the scope of the repairs and improvements, along with cost estimates.

3. Arrange to have an appraisal done. The appraiser estimates what the home's value will be after you complete renovations.

4. The lender processes your loan application. If you qualify, the loan covers the purchase price, the remodeling costs, you submitted, and some of your closing costs, plus a contingency reserve of 10 to 20 percent of the total remodeling costs (to cover unanticipated work that comes up during the renovations).

5. At the closing, the seller gets the home's purchase price, and the funds for renovating the house go into an escrow account. The lender releases those funds to pay for renovations as you have them done.

To find an FHA-approved lender in your area who works with 203(k) loans, visit *http://tinyurl.com/7yfwfa*.

 Tip If the 203(k) program sounds like too much paperwork, there's a Streamlined 203(k) Program that lets you borrow up to $35,000 over the home's purchase price for approved repairs and improvements. The streamlined program *doesn't* cover major remodeling, repairing structural damage, moving a load-bearing wall, building an addition, or landscaping. But it does cover many of the most common upgrades, including painting, flooring, energy-efficiency improvements, minor kitchen and bath remodels, new appliances, and more. Ask your FHA-approved lender for details.

Buying a manufactured home

If you're thinking about buying a manufactured home (page 62), you'll be pleased to know that these homes are also eligible for FHA-insured loans. To qualify, the manufactured home must meet these conditions:

- The home's living area is 400 square feet or larger.

- The home was built after June 15, 1976 and is certified to meet federal manufactured home construction and safety standards (page 63). Certified homes have a label to attest that they meet these standards.

- The home must meet the definition of a manufactured home (which means it has a permanent chassis) and must be attached to a permanent foundation that meets FHA standards.

- The home must be your primary residence.
- The home must be taxed as real estate, not personal property.
- The home cannot be in a flood zone.

Veteran's Administration Loans

If you're an armed services veteran, on active duty, serving in the reserves or National Guard, or you're a military spouse, you may be eligible for a Veteran's Administration loan. You get your loan through a private lender, and the Veterans Administration guarantees a portion of it. If you want to buy a home, condominium, or manufactured home, the VA guarantees up to $417,000 of the total loan. With a VA-guaranteed loan, you don't have to worry about financing a down payment, but you do have to pay some financing fees and closing costs.

Here's how a VA loan guarantee works: When you borrow money thought a commercial lender, the VA protects the lender against loss if you fail to repay the loan. This makes VA loans very attractive to lenders, and you can get a good interest rate through the program.

Eligibility is based on your military service and typically falls into one of these categories:

- **Wartime.** This category covers service during the following periods:
  — World War II: September 16,1940 to July 25, 1947.
  — Korean War: June 27, 1950 to January 31, 1955.
  — Vietnam War: August 5, 1964 to May 7, 1975.

 Note You must have been on active duty for at least 90 days, and you cannot have been discharged under dishonorable conditions. If you served less than 90 days, you may be eligible if you were discharged for a service-related disability.

- **Peacetime.** This category includes service during these periods:
  — July 26, 1947 to June 26, 1950.
  — February 1, 1955 to August 4, 1964.
  — May 8, 1975 to September 7, 1980 for enlisted personnel; May 8, 1975 to October 16, 1981 for officers.

Note You must have served at least 181 days of continuous active duty, and you cannot have been discharged under dishonorable conditions. If you served less than 181 days, you may be eligible if discharged for a service-related disability.

- **Service after 9/7/1980 (enlisted personnel) or 10/16/1981 (officers).** If your service began after these dates, you must meet these one of these criteria:

  — You completed 24 months of continuous active duty or the full period (at least 181 days) for which you were ordered or called to active duty, and you were not discharged under dishonorable conditions.

  — You completed at least 181 days of active duty and were discharged under the specific authority of 10 USC 1173 (Hardship), or 10 USC 1171 (Early Out), or you were determined to have a compensable service-related disability.

  — You were discharged with less than 181 days of service for a service-related disability. You may also be eligible if you were released from active duty due to an involuntary reduction in force or certain medical conditions.

- **Gulf War.** This category covers service from August 2, 1990 to a date that's yet to be determined. If you served on active duty during the Gulf War, you must meet one of these criteria:

  — You completed 24 months of continuous active duty or the full period (at least 181 days) for which you were ordered or called to active duty, and you were not discharged under dishonorable conditions.

  — You completed at least 90 days of active duty and were discharged under the specific authority of 10 USC 1173 (Hardship), or 10 USC 1171 (Early Out), or you were determined to have a compensable service-related disability.

  — You were discharged with less than 90 days of service for a service-related disability. You may also be eligible if you were released from active duty due to an involuntary reduction in force or certain medical conditions.

- **Active duty service personnel.** If you are now on regular duty (not active duty for training), you are eligible after you've served 181 days (90 days during the Gulf War), unless you were discharged or separated from a previous qualifying period of active duty service.

- **Selected Reserves or National Guard.** If you are not otherwise eligible, you may qualify if you completed a total of 6 years in the Selected Reserves or National Guard (as member of an active unit who attended required weekend drills and two-week active duty for training) and meet one of these criteria:

  — You were honorably discharged.

  — You were placed on the retired list.

  — You were transferred to the Standby Reserve or an element of the Ready Reserve other than the Selected Reserve after honorable service.

  — You continue to serve in the Selected Reserves.

 Note If you completed fewer than 6 years of service, you may be eligible if you were discharged for a service-related disability.

Under certain conditions, military spouses may also qualify for VA-guaranteed loans:

- If your spouse was a serviceperson who died in action or of a service-related injury, and you haven't remarried.

- If your spouse is a serviceperson who's missing in action or a prisoner of war.

To apply for a VA-guaranteed loan, you first need to obtain a Certificate of Eligibility, which requires a copy of your service record. Then you work with a commercial lender to get the loan. The VA requires an appraisal of the property to confirm the home's value.

If you think you may qualify for a VA home loan, go to *www.military.com/ Finance/HomeBuying* to learn more about the process and to apply for your Certificate of Eligibility.

HUD Special Home-buying Programs

HUD offers several home-buying programs for people in special situations:

- **The Good Neighbor Next Door program.** If you're a teacher (pre-K through grade 12), firefighter, law enforcement officer, or emergency medical technician, you may be able buy a HUD home at a 50 percent discount. You have to meet two conditions: The home must be in a revitalization area, and you must agree to live there for 36 months after you buy the home.

- **Public housing home ownership programs.** Local Public Housing Authorities (PHAs) may make public housing units available for low-income families to buy as their primary residence. PHAs may also offer financial assistance.

- **Home ownership vouchers.** Some PHAs offer voucher programs that help new homeowners pay their monthly home ownership expenses. These vouchers can go toward PITI payments, utilities, routine maintenance, repairs, and handicap access.

 Tip To find a local PHA home-buying assistance program, go to *www.hud.gov/buying/localbuying.cfm* and click the name of your state.

- **Section 184 Indian Home Loan Guarantee program.** Designed for Native American and Alaskan Native home buyers, this program requires a loan down payment (1.25 percent for loans under $50,000, 2.25 percent for loans over that amount), no monthly mortgage insurance payments, and special underwriting requirements designed to make it easier for Native Americans to buy a home. There's a 1 percent loan guarantee fee, which you can roll into the loan.

Tip To search for specific government programs that offer assistance with housing, visit *www.govbenefits.gov*. In the Quick Benefits section, select Housing, and then click Go for a list of programs.

Creative Financing Options

Some homebuyers look beyond the traditional options offered by commercial lenders and government programs. This section describes other kinds of financing that may help you buy your new home. Before you head down the road less taken, though, be aware that these options may be riskier than traditional financing. Always consult a real estate attorney to make sure you know what you're getting into.

Getting Help with the Down Payment

One of the biggest obstacles to buying a home is finding the money for the down payment. Today, many lenders want 20 percent down before they'll approve a loan.

80/20 loan

You may have heard about "no money down" or "zero down payment" loans that let you buy a home now, without spending years scraping together a down payment. These loans were popular in the 1990s through the mid-2000s, before the housing bubble burst. Now, they're practically extinct. That's not a bad thing. By skipping the down payment, many homeowners borrowed more than they could afford and got into trouble when housing prices slumped.

A "no money down" loan, also called a *piggyback* loan, is really two loans:

- A primary mortgage that lends you 80 percent of the home's purchase price.

- A second mortgage that lends you the other 20 percent at a higher rate.

You still have to pay closing costs and fees. Because the primary mortgage is for 80 percent of the home's value, you don't have to buy private mortgage insurance (PMI—see the box on page 146).

Because the second mortgage is at a higher rate than the first, 80/20 loans can be expensive. In addition, you build equity slowly because you're paying off two loans simultaneously, and both are front-loaded with interest payments. And if housing prices fall, you could end up with negative equity (page 23), making it difficult to sell or refinance the home.

80/10/10 loan

Another kind of piggyback loan lets you make a smaller down payment and take out a second mortgage to make up the difference between the amount you're able to pay in cash and the amount you need to avoid PMI. Here's how an 80/10/10 loan breaks down:

- A primary mortgage lends you 80 percent of the home's purchase price.

- A second mortgage lends you 10 percent at a higher rate.

- You pay a 10 percent down payment (instead of the traditional 20 percent).

80/10/10 loans are less risky than 80/20 loans because the down payment starts you off with some equity in your house. Lenders also have more confidence in a borrower who can invest money up front in their home.

If you're considering an 80/10/10 loan, look into FHA-insured loans (page 180) as an alternative. If you qualify, you may be able to buy a house with as little as 3.5 percent down and saving money on interest. Even though you'll pay PMI, it may be worth it to avoid the higher interest rate on the second mortgage of the piggyback loan. Ask your mortgage broker or loan officer to compare the costs of an 80/10/10 loan with your other options.

Seller Financing

Some sellers are willing to help you buy their house. You'll see this option more often in a buyer's market. Sellers may try to grab buyers' attention by offering to help with closing costs or make arrangements to finance all or part of the purchase. Seller financing is relatively rare, though, and there are a couple of good reasons why:

- **The seller has to pay off his existing mortgage.** In most situations, a homeowner can't transfer title to a new owner without paying off the property's current mortgage. A seller who had to take out his own mortgage probably can't afford to finance your mortgage.

- **The seller wants the money from the sale all at once.** Even if the seller owns his home free and clear (because he paid off the mortgage, perhaps, or inherited a paid-off property), most sellers expect a big infusion of cash when they sell a home. Often, they need that cash as a down payment on their next home. Many sellers don't want to bother with incremental payments from buyers, even if they'd make more money from them in the long run.

In some cases, however, sellers have both the means and the motive to help with financing. This section explains seller-financing arrangements you might encounter.

 Sellers who offer financing sometimes do so because they're desperate to sell a property. There may be problems with the home they hope you don't discover before you finalize the sale. Others try to take advantage of buyers unfamiliar with conventional financing arrangements. If you consider seller financing, you *must* consult a real estate attorney to check all documents related to the sale and financing before you sign anything.

Seller mortgage

The seller may agree to hold a mortgage so that you can purchase the home by paying installments over time, just as you would with a commercial loan. Sellers who do this may require a higher interest rate or a shorter term than you'd get from a commercial lender.

If you're considering a seller mortgage, you need to hire a real estate attorney to help you draft the paperwork and to make sure you're not signing anything that would work to your disadvantage.

Second mortgage from seller

Sometimes the seller may not be in immediate need of all the cash from the sale of his house. This usually happens when he's built up lot of equity in the house—for example, when retired empty-nesters sell the family home to downsize to a smaller place. A seller in this situation may offer you a second mortgage on the property (in addition to the one you get from a commercial lender to finance most of the purchase price) to help you buy it. This kind of seller financing usually has a 5- or 10-year term, after which the loan is due in full.

A second mortgage from the seller can help you avoid paying PMI. Since most lenders require PMI for financing above 80 percent of the purchase price, seller financing can make up the difference between your down payment and the amount you need to put up to avoid PMI or to meet loan-program requirements. Some sellers let you defer payments on the second mortgage for up to a year (though the amount you borrow still accrues interest during that time).

During the term of the second mortgage, your equity will grow, and you can combine that equity with savings to refinance your loan and get a single, conventional, PMI-free 80 percent loan—and pay off the seller's second mortgage.

 Tip If you plan to get a second mortgage from the seller, tell your primary-mortgage lender up front, before you apply for a mortgage. The lender will want to see documentation about the proposed second mortgage, so have that ready.

Rent-to-own

At one time or another, most renters have pondered the fact that they pay money each month just to live in their homes—instead of building equity or putting the money toward a place of their own, they simply pay for the right to live in a house or apartment from one month or one year to the next. Wouldn't it be great if some of that rent money could go toward buying a home? That's what rent-to-own financing does.

There are two common kinds of rent-to-own arrangements:

- **Lease option.** In this arrangement, you buy an *option* to buy the home. That is, you give your landlord some money in exchange for the exclusive right to buy the property for an agreed-upon price within a specified period of time, usually one to three years. You also sign a lease agreeing to pay a certain amount of rent each month, some of which goes toward your purchase of the home. During the option period, your landlord agrees not to sell the house to anyone else. You can exercise the option to buy any time the option is in effect. If you decide not to buy, you can let the option expire, but you probably won't get back the money you paid for the option.

- **Lease purchase.** This works similarly to a lease option, except instead of saying that "maybe" you'll buy the home, you agree to buy it after a specified period of time. During the lease, part of your rent payments go toward the purchase. After that, you apply for a bank loan to complete the purchase. During the lease, you'll probably be responsible for costs associated with the home, including maintenance, repairs, taxes, and insurance.

The purchase price is, of course, negotiable. With a lease option, you might agree on a specific, set price or agree to pay market value when you exercise the option. With a lease purchase, it's common to agree on a price that's slightly above the current market value. Remember that, in either case, your lender will require an appraisal to confirm the home's worth what you're paying for it.

 Tip Laws governing lease options and lease purchases vary from state to state, so consult a real estate attorney before you enter into a rent-to-own agreement.

Assuming the Seller's Loan

Most mortgages have a "due on sale" clause that says that the mortgagor must repay the loan in full when he sells the home. But some loans are *assumable*, which means that you can take over the seller's loan, paying off the current balance with the same terms the seller got. This can be a good deal when interest rates are high and the loan you're assuming has a low one.

When you assume a loan, you pay the seller cash for the equity in the house. The amount of cash is the difference between the purchase price and the balance on the loan you're assuming. (You can also get a second mortgage to help pay that difference.) Assumable loans are almost always ARMs, so be aware that the loan's rate can rise after you assume it.

To assume the loan, you have to qualify, just as you would if you were taking out a new loan. You'll pay an assumption fee of several hundred dollars and other processing fees, but these should be lower than the fees for a new loan. Some loans are subject to a rate adjustment at assumption—so make sure you're not losing the benefit of a lower interest rate when you assume the seller's loan.

Paying with Cash

Sounds great, doesn't it? Cut out all the hassle of dealing with lenders and just fork over the cash to pay for you new house. For most of us, that's a daydream—most homebuyers don't have the spare cash to buy a home. But sometimes people get a chunk of money through a windfall, such as an inheritance, and find themselves in a position to buy a house without going through a lender.

If the seller is in a hurry, a cash sale is a good thing. You eliminate weeks of waiting if you don't have to apply for financing. In a slow real estate market, or when a seller is eager to move on, this makes your cash offer very appealing. Under other conditions, though, a cash offer may not stand out as much as you think. As long as the seller gets paid, he doesn't care all that much whether the money comes from a commercial lender or out of your bank account. A cash offer is better than an offer where the financing is in doubt, but if the seller is reasonably confident that a competing bidder will get financing, there's no strong reason to prefer cash.

Also, if you pay cash for a home, you lose the tax benefit of deducting mortgage interest from your income taxes. You may find that it makes more financial sense to invest your windfall, take out a mortgage, and claim the tax break. Talk with an accountant to see what's best for you.

8 Choose and Apply for a Mortgage

What you pay for your mortgage depends on a number of factors: the current interest rates, the amount you want to borrow, your credit history and financial profile (income, debt, employment), the kind of loan you choose, the size of your down payment—the list goes on and on. Some of these factors you control; others you don't.

Before you apply for a mortgage, educating yourself is key. When you understand how mortgage loans work, you can identify which kind is best for you. So if you haven't yet read Chapter 7, now is a good time to do so.

This chapter takes you through the next stage of getting a mortgage—choosing and applying for a loan. It shows you how to find the right lender and compare the full costs of their mortgages. Then it guides you through the maze of applying for a loan—from gathering the documents you need to filling out the application and understanding the forms the lender gives you in return. Knowing what to expect when you apply will make the process smoother and easier—and will get you into your new home faster.

Find the Right Lender

Google the phrase *mortgage lender* and you'll be inundated with results—local and national lenders all crying out for you to take a look at their loans. How do you wade through all of them to find the best one? This section steers you in the right direction.

Decide the Kind of Loan Originator You Want

You can set up a mortgage loan through one of two people: a mortgage broker or a loan officer, both described below. Collectively, these people are known as *loan originators*.

You might prefer to work with a mortgage broker, an independent third party who searches the different mortgage products lenders offer regionally or nationwide to find the best one for you. Or you might work with a loan officer, an employee at a specific financial institution who represents that institution only. If you want to select from a wide variety of lenders and loans, go with a mortgage broker. If you prefer to work with a local institution, you'll probably be working with a loan officer.

 Tip Before you decide to work with a particular loan originator, have at least one conversation with them. You need to find someone you can trust and feel comfortable with, someone you can ask questions and rely on to explain things clearly. Page 97 has questions you can ask mortgage brokers and loan officers to find the best one.

Ask for Referrals

Friends, family members, neighbors, coworkers—anyone you know who owns their home almost certainly has experience with a mortgage lender. Ask if they're happy with their lender and their loan. Would they work with the same lender again? Why or why not?

Your real estate agent is another good source of referrals. Agents work with mortgage professionals on a regular basis and can recommend those they've had good experiences with.

Visit Your Local Bank

The bank, savings and loan, or credit union where you have your checking and savings accounts knows you. You know them, too, and probably feel comfortable with them. Almost every local bank has a loan officer who can tell you what kinds of mortgages the bank offers (15- and 30-year fixed, ARMs, and so on). When you keep it local, you work with a lender who knows you, your finances, and the value of real estate in your area. Local lenders may be a bit more flexible in granting loans to people they know than large mortgage companies that make loans nationwide.

Check Out Online Lenders

The Internet lets you apply for a mortgage from lenders across the country, expanding your options for finding the best loan. At the same time, you might feel uncomfortable going online and filling out a form with detailed personal and financial information—your full name, Social Security number, current address, employer, salary, and more—exactly the kind of information that scammers and identity thieves would love to get their hands on.

To find a trustworthy online lender, follow these tips:

- **Stick with companies you've heard of.** When you're looking online, get recommendations from friends and acquaintances, just as you would when looking for a local lender.

- **Know what's a realistic rate.** Before you go loan shopping online, check interest rates locally (call a couple of banks or look in the newspaper) to get an idea of what they are in your area. Reputable online lenders' rates will be in the same ballpark.

- **Be wary of big loans.** An online lender may say you qualify for a much larger loan than other lenders offer. Some predatory lenders dangle a loan that's more than you can reasonably afford so you'll have to take out subsequent loans at a much higher interest rate to keep up with your first loan's payments. Every lender determines its loan amounts differently, but there shouldn't be a huge difference between the highest and lowest loans they offer you.

- **Check the lender's "About Us" page.** See how long the lender has been in business (the longer its track record, the better).

- **Check the lender's track record.** Federal agencies have websites where you can check to see whether a lender has gotten in trouble with the feds:

  - **Federal Trade Commission** (*www.ftc.gov*). The FTC, a consumer protection agency, collects complaints about companies, business practices, and identity theft.

  - **Federal Deposit Insurance Corporation** (*www.fdic.gov*). If the lender is federally insured, search for it on the FDIC's website to get more information.

  - **National Credit Union Administration** (*www.ncua.gov*). Some credit unions have online loan forms. Before you apply, check out the credit union with the NCUA.

- **Look for complaints at consumer review sites.** To read about problems consumers have run into with online lenders, check out *www.consumeraffairs.com* and *complaints.com*.

- **Don't get hooked by a phishing scam.** When scammers go *phishing*, they send out official-looking emails promising a great interest rate or no credit check. The email includes a link that takes you to a website with a form for you to fill out. But instead of giving you a rate quote, the scammer steals your personal information. If a too-good-to-be-true mortgage offer lands in your email inbox, don't fall for it. Never click a link in an unsolicited email offer.

Here are some online lenders that have been in business for a while:

- **Ditech** (*www.ditech.com*). Owned by GMAC, this company has been around since 1995.

- **EverBank** (*www.everbank.com*). Based in Jacksonville, Florida, this company offers mortgage loans nationwide.

- **LendingTree** (*www.lendingtree.com*). This site lets you compare loans from up to four different lenders to find the best rate.

- **Quicken Loans** (*www.quickenloans.com*). *National Mortgage News* named Quicken Loans the largest online lender in the U.S.

Most online lenders show you current interest rates and provide calculators that let you compare loans. If you have any questions, you can contact the lender several ways: fill out an online form, chat in real time, or call them.

Get the Best Mortgage

Nobody wants to pay more for a loan than they have to. But with so many loan products available (see Chapter 7), it can be hard to know whether you're getting the best possible deal. Should you find the cash to pay up-front discount points and lower your interest rate? Is a shorter term (and the resulting higher monthly payments) worth the lower interest rate and faster repayment? Whether you're looking at a fixed-rate loan or an ARM, this section helps you find the best all-around mortgage loan.

Researching Rates

When you shop for a mortgage, your goal is clear: You want to find the least expensive loan possible. But that *doesn't* always mean the loan with the lowest interest rate.

You might open the newspaper or go to Bankrate.com to check available loans and compare rates. Or you might pick up the phone and start calling local lenders to ask for their rates. And although these methods can give you a ballpark, they're not the best way to shop for a loan, for several reasons:

- **There are too many variables among loans.** Interest rates vary according to the type of loan you get. ARMs, for example, have lower initial rates than fixed-rate loans. Different terms also mean different rates: A 15-year loan will have a lower interest rate (but higher monthly payments) than a 30-year loan. And prepaying interest in the form of discount points (page 157) gets you a lower interest rate but costs you more up front. With all these variables, simply comparing interest rates is like comparing apples to oranges to bananas to mangoes. Looking at a single number—the interest rate—won't show you the least expensive loan.

- **The interest rate doesn't give you the total cost of a loan.** Your mortgage costs more than the interest rate and principal you pay. You also have to pay up-front costs, including processing and origination fees, an appraisal fee, a credit check fee, and more (Chapter 9 details typical closing costs). To make it easier for borrowers to compare mortgage costs, the annual percentage rate (APR, page 153) calculates the *total* cost of a mortgage loan, including all these fees. Comparing APRs gives you a better basis for evaluating loans—but even they don't tell the whole story, as the next point explains.

- **Lenders calculate APRs differently.** APRs are supposed to create a standard so consumers can easily compare loans. But there *is* no standard way to calculate APRs. Some unscrupulous lenders may exclude charges from the calculation to make their APR look lower than it actually is—which makes the loan look less expensive than it actually is.

- **Without figuring in information specific to you, a rate quote is meaningless.** If you see or hear that Bank X offers 30-year fixed-rate loans at 4.875 percent, it doesn't mean that you'll qualify for that rate. A lender assesses the amount of your down payment, your ability to pay back the loan, and your financial history before offering you a specific interest rate. The better your credit score, for example, the better the rate you can qualify for. In addition, a rate quoted over the phone represents a ballpark figure; to actually get that rate, you have to lock it in (page 204).

- **Rates change daily.** When you see interest rates published in the newspaper, they're already old news (by at least a day or two). And interest rates change daily, so the great-looking rate you see in the paper or online on Monday may no longer be the best deal by the time you submit your loan application on Wednesday.

If the information you get about interest rates through published sources or over the phone represents only part of the mortgage loan story, how do you shop for a loan? Easy. Use these sources to get good ballpark figures for your loan, but then get full estimates in writing. Follow these steps:

1. **Get your documentation together.**

   Start by gathering all the documents you'll need to apply for a loan (page 206 lists those for you). This puts your financial information at your fingertips for the interview you're about to conduct and tells the mortgage broker or loan officer you're serious about getting a loan. And it allows you to act quickly when you decide to apply.

2. Choose three mortgage brokers to ask for a quote.

You can find them through several sources. The best is to get a recommendation: Ask friends, family, coworkers, and your real estate agent, for example. You can also check the local Yellow Pages or use an online directory like the one at the National Association of Mortgage Brokers website (go to *www.namb.org* and click Find a NAMB Broker).

 Tip As you learned above, a mortgage broker (as opposed to a bank's loan officer) has access to information about loans from many lenders, so you get a wider variety of quotes. On the other hand, local banks and credit unions know the local real-estate market and often have good rates for local purchases. So you might want to consult two mortgage brokers and one local loan officer instead of three brokers, especially if you want to keep your transaction local.

3. Call the loan originators you chose.

Tell each the basics of your financial situation and the kind of loan you want, and then ask for a Good Faith Estimate (GFE) for that loan. Say that you need the Good Faith Estimate by the next day because you want to make an accurate comparison of what three brokers can find for you. Also mention that you're prepared to move quickly to apply.

 Tip Page 221 shows you how to read your Good Faith Estimate to compare the total costs of different loans.

Tell the broker or loan officer your current credit score (see page 45 for details on how to get that), the purchase price of the home, the amount of your down payment, and the amount you want to borrow. For the type of loan, mention the term you want (15- or 30-year, for example), whether you want a fixed-rate loan or an ARM (and if the latter, the ARM type, such as 5/1 or 7/1), and any special considerations you want, such as no prepayment penalty.

If the broker is reluctant to supply a GFE (it takes some work to fill one out), explain that you understand it's an estimate and that rates are subject to change.

You want a GFE and not just a quote because the GFE gives you the clearest picture of the total cost of a loan. Some brokers may be reluctant to fill out an actual GFE because of recent changes to regulations governing this form. In that case, ask the broker to prepare an estimate using the same calculations and information as a GFE but without using the form itself. Or ask the broker to fill out a column of the "shopping chart" section of the form (page 215 shows an example of a GFE shopping chart).

4. **Compare GFEs.**

It's important that you get your three GFEs on the same day, because if the forms are even a day apart, rates may have changed and you're no longer comparing similar loans. Page 215 takes you through a GFE section by section, so you know how to read it.

 Tip When requesting GFEs to compare, make sure you get the same information from each broker: The type of loan, the term, and the number of points should be the same for each quote. You want to compare apples to apples.

Comparing fixed-rate loans

Homeowners choose fixed-rate loans because they're the most stable, predictable ones on the market: For the term of your loan (or until you sell or refinance), your principal and interest payments remain the same. These loans should be easy to compare, but look at the following table, which show actual rates for 30-year fixed-rate loans at the time of writing:

Loan	Interest rate	APR	Points	Fees
1	4.750%	4.876%	1.000	$884
2	4.500%	4.757%	2.500	$884
3	4.875%	5.013%	0.750	$1,217
4	4.875%	5.034%	1.000	$1,600
5	4.625%	4.828%	2.250	$0
6	5.125%	5.220%	0.000	$2,121
7	4.500%	4.704%	2.000	$695
8	5.000%	5.072%	0.000	$1,217
9	4.875%	4.905%	0.000	$695
10	4.750%	4.870%	1.000	$749
11	4.625%	4.983%	1.375	$950
12	4.625%	4.790%	0.898	$1,995

A table of numbers like this can make your eyes cross. Loan 6 is clearly the most expensive, with the highest interest rate, the highest APR and the highest up-front fees. Even though it doesn't require any points at closing, you'll pay the most for this loan in the long run.

Loan 7 looks like the least expensive loan: It has the lowest interest rate and the lowest APR. But it'll cost you more up front than some of the other options, with 2 points and $695 in lender fees. Loan 2 is comparable in terms of interest rate and APR, although it costs a few hundred dollars more at closing, with its extra half-point and higher fees.

Which of these loans is best? Unfortunately, there is no single answer. Every borrower has different needs. If you can afford the cost of prepaid interest and you expect to live in your new home long enough to see its benefit (page 158 tells you how to calculate the break-even point), you might decide to pay some points to get a lower interest rate. If you don't have much spare cash or if you expect to move in a few years, you might accept a slightly higher interest rate for lower up-front fees. There's simply no such thing as a one-size-fits-all loan.

That said, here's how you decide what works for *you*. First up, here's what to look for in fixed-interest loans, followed by the variables you'll find if you shop for an ARM.

When you shop for a fixed-rate loan, pay attention to these components:

- **Interest rate.** In general, the lower your interest rate, the better. But a low interest rate is never the whole story. A lower rate may be tied to something you don't want or can't afford right now, such as a shorter term (15 years) or prepaid interest points. On the other hand, you may prefer to pay more now for those things precisely because they'll save you money on interest in the long run.

- **Term.** If you want lower monthly payments, choose a longer-term loan, such as 30 years—but be aware that the longer term costs you more in interest as the years go by. If you want to build equity faster, choose a shorter-term loan, such as 15 years. But shorter terms mean higher monthly payments. Read about loan terms on page 177.

- **Number of points.** By prepaying some of the loan's interest at the closing, you can reduce your loan's interest rate. This prepaid interest is referred to as *points* or *discount points*. Each point equals 1 percent of the loan amount, and each point lowers the interest rate a little. (How much depends on a variety of factors, but it's usually between 0.125 and 0.25 percent of the interest rate.) Most lenders let you prepay interest in the range of 0 to 4 points.

To find out whether you'll save money by prepaying interest, find the *break-even* point: the number of months it takes for the lower interest rate to pay for the cost of the points. If, for example, you paid 1 point to get the interest rate on a 30-year fixed-rate loan down from 5.25 percent to 5 percent, that prepaid interest would cost $2,500. The lower interest rate means lower monthly payments, and after 65 months (about 5 1/2 years), you'd have saved that $2,500. From that point on, you'd reap the financial benefits of the lower interest rate. Page 158 shows you how to calculate a loan's break-even point.

 Tip When you shop for a loan, ask to see the same loan with 0, 1, and 2 discount points. You can compare monthly payments, find the different break-even points, and see which combination of points and interest rate works best for you.

When you decide what you're looking for in a fixed-rate loan and shop around for loans with those characteristics, you'll be able to compare apples to apples to find the best option.

Comparing ARMs

ARM interest rates look attractive because they're lower than the interest rates on fixed-rate loans. But remember, what you see is the *initial* interest rate, and that rate will change. For some ARMs, the initial rate remains steady for a year or longer. For others, your rate can change as quickly as a month after you sign the loan papers.

No one can predict what interest rates will do. If you shop for an ARM when interest rates are low, it's a good guess that rates will increase in the future. And that means that your index-tied interest payments will increase, too (see page 164 to learn how lenders tie ARM interest rates to an index).

When you compare ARMs, keep these factors in mind:

- **Index.** This is what your lender uses as the base for your interest rate. Page 165 goes over the indexes most commonly used to determine ARM interest rates. If you shop for a loan when rates are low, look for an ARM whose index lags a bit behind market rates, such as a COFI-based ARM (page 166), because your rate will rise more slowly.

- **Margin.** This is the markup on the index that determines your interest rate (index rate + margin = the rate you pay). For loans linked to the same index, a lower margin means a better interest rate.

- **Adjustment period.** This tells you how often the loan's rate can change. More frequent adjustments make the loan less predictable, subjecting your monthly principal and interest payments to wider swings up and down. Hybrid loans (page 164) have two adjustment periods: the one that marks the end of the initial fixed-rate period and the periodic adjustment after that. So, for example, a 5/1 ARM keeps its initial rate for 5 years and then it adjusts annually after that.

 If you look for a mortgage when rates are low, a longer initial adjustment period (such as 5 or 7 years) will keep your interest rate low if rates start to creep up. But that first adjustment could cause a big jump in your payments—up to the full periodic cap (see below).

- **Caps.** ARMs usually come with a periodic cap, which limits the amount your interest rate can increase from one adjustment period to the next, and a lifetime cap, which sets the maximum interest rate your loan will ever have. Typical periodic caps are 1 percent for a loan that adjusts every six months and 2 percent for a loan that adjusts annually. A typical lifetime cap is 5 or 6 percent above your initial interest rate. Avoid loans that have a payment cap—which limits the amount your monthly payments can rise in terms of dollars, not interest rate—because this can lead to negative amortization (page 168). Even though your payments are capped, the interest you owe can keep increasing to the point where you owe more than the house is worth.

If you're considering a hybrid loan (page 164) and there's a chance you'll stay in your home beyond the initial, fixed-rate period, figure out how much your monthly payments would jump in the worst-case scenario. If your rate were to go up by the maximum amount allowed by each periodic cap until it hit its lifetime cap, how much would that cost you each month? Before you sign the loan papers, you need to assess whether you could make the required payments if that happens. Use the ARM calculator at Interest.com (*http://tinyurl.com/yjzloge*) to get a sense of the highest your payments could rise.

 Many people go with an ARM thinking that, if rates start to rise too sharply, they can refinance to a fixed-rate loan. That is true, but keep in mind that, to refinance, you have to pay closing costs—and perhaps a prepayment penalty (page 170).

Prepaying Interest

You can reduce the interest rate on your loan by paying some interest in advance, using discount points (page 157). If you plan to stay in your home for many years to come, paying points on a fixed-rate loan can save you a substantial amount of money—tens of thousands of dollars—by reducing the interest you pay over the long term. But you have to stick around long enough to get to your loan's break-even point, where the money you save on interest payments becomes greater than the cost of the points (page 158 shows you how to find your loan's break-even point).

What about ARMs? Those usually start out with a lower interest rate than a fixed-rate loan that has the same term. Is it worth it to reduce the rate further by paying points up front? To answer that question, consider these factors:

- **When would you reach the break-even point at your loan's initial rate?** Using the formula on page 158, figure out how long it would take to reach the break-even point if your initial rate never changed.

- **When does the initial rate adjust?** If your rate will change after only a few months or a year, that's not enough time to reach the break-even point, and paying points up front makes no sense. If the loan is a hybrid ARM, however, with an initial fixed rate period of 5 years or longer, you may be able to save some money by prepaying interest if you'd reach the break-even point before the loan adjusts.

Whether you're considering a fixed-rate loan or an ARM, discount points are all about the break-even point: Will you stay in your home long enough to realize the savings you get by prepaying interest? For an ARM, make sure that your initial fixed-rate period stretches past that break-even point. You're more likely to save money if you pay points on a 5/1 or 7/1 ARM than on an ARM with a shorter initial rate.

Locking In Your Rate

The interest rate shown in your Good Faith Estimate can expire and is subject to change—right up until you sign the loan papers—unless you lock in that rate. A *rate lock* is just what it sounds like: a set-in-stone guarantee that your interest rate won't change between the time you lock in that rate and lock's expiration date, usually 30 days.

When you lock in your rate is partly up to the lender and partly up to you. Some lenders won't let you lock in a rate until after you get your loan approved; others let you do it earlier, usually after they've appraised the house. And some automatically lock in the rate when they approve a loan.

Ask your mortgage broker or loan officer when you can lock in the rate. After that, the time you lock in the rate is up to you. Watch rates using a site like Bankrate.com (go to *www.bankrate.com* and then click Mortgage). If rates seem to be going down, you might wait to lock in the rate. When you see a rate that looks good—in other words, a rate at which you'd be comfortable paying the monthly principal and interest on your loan—call your mortgage broker to lock it in and be assured that that's the rate you'll pay. Rate locks work both ways: Your loan's interest rate won't increase if rates go up, but it won't decrease if it goes down, either.

 Tip Don't gamble on your loan's interest rate. Even when rates are decreasing, something can cause them to spike suddenly. If you're happy with a rate, lock it in.

Many lenders don't charge you to lock in your rate for 30 days (some loans come with 45- or even 60-day locks). If it looks like you might need more time than that to get to closing, you can buy a longer rate lock. How much that costs depends on the lender and on how long you want the rate lock to last—you may pay up to a point (due at closing) for the lock to last another 60 days. You may also have the option to pay for the lock over time, by locking in at a slightly higher interest rate.

 Note Your rate isn't locked in until your mortgage broker or loan officer sends you a letter confirming it. Don't trust a phone confirmation. If your loan officer is late filing the paperwork to lock in the rate, you may find that it's higher than what the loan officer told you it would be.

Your rate-lock confirmation letter has four parts:

- The type of loan (30-year fixed-rate, 5/1 ARM, and so on)
- The interest rate
- The points you're paying for the loan, including origination and discount points
- The rate-lock period, including its expiration date

If any of that information is missing, contact your mortgage broker or loan officer immediately. You need all of it to make sure that your loan is correct at the closing.

If something delays your closing and your rate lock will expire before you can close, you may be able to buy a rate-lock extension. But for some lenders, an expiration date is an expiration date, and they won't honor the rate lock after it expires. Know your lender's policy on extensions before you lock in a rate.

 Tip You're not stuck with a particular lender if you lock in a rate. If rates go down, you can walk away from your loan application and go to a different lender, although you'll give up any fees you've already paid. If you work with a mortgage broker, who has access to loans offered by many lenders, the broker may be able to switch to a different lender to get you locked in at a better rate.

Gather Documents and Information

Applying for a mortgage can sometimes feel like you're scaling—or maybe being buried under—a mountain of paperwork. Not only do you need to fill out forms that can run to several pages long, you have to provide back-up documentation to support just about everything on those forms. Before you fill out your loan application, gather the documents you need. And watch out for paper cuts.

 Tip If you got preapproved for a loan (page 34), you've already done the groundwork for your formal mortgage application. You may need to update your documentation, but you won't have to supply everything all over again.

Here's a list of the documents and information your lender may require (not all items apply to everyone):

- Your purchase agreement
- Original pay stubs from the last 30 days. These need to have your name, Social Security number, and year-to-date earnings on them
- Tax returns for the past two years
- Original W2 forms for the past two years

Note If you're self-employed, you won't have any W2s. Instead, you'll need your complete income tax returns, including all schedules, from the past two years, along with any business tax returns. If you file estimated income taxes each quarter, bring along two years' worth of your 1040-ES forms as well.

- Proof of any other income you have (such as alimony)
- Proof of other assets (including stocks, IRAs, and pension funds)
- Most recent statements for all loans and credit card accounts
- Three months' worth of bank statements for all your accounts (checking, savings, and so on)
- The source of your down payment, such as personal savings or a gift from a relative
- Your residential history for the past two years (addresses and dates)
- Names, addresses, and phone numbers of any landlords from the past two years
- Names, addresses, and phone numbers of your employers from the past two years
- Driver's license or state ID and Social Security card (for FHA loans)
- Certificate of Eligibility (for VA loans)

Your loan originator should give you a list of the documents you'll need for your specific situation. If not, ask for one. It'll save everyone time for you to have the necessary papers in hand.

Do the Paperwork

When it's time to apply for your loan, you may meet with your loan originator and fill out the application together, or you may give the originator your information over the phone or via an online form. Some borrowers fill out the application themselves and bring it in. It's best if you can do the paperwork with your loan originator in case you have any questions.

However you fill out the paperwork, though, there's a lot of it, and it shines a bright light into all areas of your financial life. The information flows both ways: You tell the bank about your employment, your assets and liabilities, and your finances, and the bank gives you information about the loan and how much it will cost you. Read on to learn about the paperwork involved in a typical loan application.

Uniform Residential Loan Application

Although different lenders use different application forms, many work with the Uniform Residential Loan Application, often called Form 1003. Whether or not your lender uses this form, it shows the typical information that a mortgage application collects (you can follow along with the discussion below by going to this book's Missing CD at *www.missingmanuals. com/cds/* to get a copy of the form). Going through the application form section by section helps you prepare to apply for your loan, so you'll have all the information you need ready when you need it.

Section I: Type of Mortgage and Terms of Loan

In this section, you specify the kind of loan you're applying for:

- The type of loan (FHA, VA, conventional, and so on)

- The amount of money you want to borrow

- The interest rate of the loan you're applying for

- The loan's term (in months)

- The amortization type (fixed rate, ARM, and so on)

You've already worked with your mortgage broker or loan officer to get the answers to these questions. Make sure this part of the application matches your understanding of the loan.

Section II: Property Information and Purpose of Loan

In this section, you describe the property and how you intend to use it. Here's what it asks for:

- **Details of the property.** Give the property's address and a legal description of it. The legal description appears on the deed or property tax records; you can get it from the seller.

- **The purpose of the loan.** Are you buying or refinancing the house? Will the property be your primary residence, a second home, or an investment?

- **Information about title.** In this section, give the name (or names) of the title holder and indicate what type of title you'll hold (see page 270 for a description of the different ways you can hold title).

- **Where you'll get the down payment and closing costs.** Explain where your down payment is coming from—personal savings, for example, or a gift from a family member. If you'll get a second mortgage, to help pay for your down payment or closing costs, explain that here.

Section III: Borrower Information

This part's all about you. It's where you—and your co-borrower, if you have one—provide your name, Social Security number, date of birth, and how many years of school you've completed. You also must give your marital status and the number (and ages) of dependents. Finally, you provide your home phone number, current address, and previous address if you've lived in your current home for less than two years.

Section IV: Employment Information

To make sure you've got a stable job and can pay back your loan, the lender needs to know about your current and past employment. This section collects the name, address, and phone number of your current employer. It also asks you to specify its type of business, your position there, how long you've been at this job, and how long you've worked in the same industry. Fill in all this information for yourself and your co-borrower if you've got one. And if you work at more than one job, give the information for all your employment.

If you've held your current job for less than two years, you must also give the same information about the previous job (or jobs) you held during those two years.

 Note If you're self-employed, check the "Self Employed" box in this section and supply the other information (type of business, how long you've been self-employed, and so on) as relevant.

Section V: Monthly Income and Combined Housing Expense Information

This part of the form comprises two sections: one for your household's total monthly income, the other for your expenses:

- **Gross monthly income.** Here, write down how much money comes into your household each month from employment (salary or base wages), overtime, bonuses, commissions, dividends and interest, rental income, and anything else that regularly brings in money. If you're self-employed, be prepared to attach business-related tax returns and financial statements as supporting documents.

You don't have to disclose money received for alimony or child support if you don't want that money included in the lender's calculations of whether you can repay the loan. If you want them included, you need to supply a copy of the court order that mandates the payments and proof that you're getting them, such as bank statements showing regular deposits.

- **Combined monthly housing expense.** In this part, write down your current housing costs, including rent (if you don't currently own your home), any mortgages, insurance, taxes, homeowners' association dues, and any other monthly charges related to housing. Then estimate how much you expect to pay for those same costs in your new home.

 Page 26 shows you how to create a household budget. Use that budget to get your current monthly housing expenses.

Section VI: Assets and Liabilities

This section presents your financial profile beyond month-to-month income and expenses. Assets, the things you own that have value, may be liquid (cash or quickly convertible to cash, like CDs) or other property. List these assets:

- Your earnest money deposit
- Checking and savings accounts
- Certificates of deposit
- Stocks and bonds
- Life insurance
- Any real estate you currently own
- Retirement accounts
- The net worth of any businesses you own
- Automobiles
- Other assets (list what they are)

Next come your liabilities—the money you owe. Common liabilities include car loans, student loans, credit card debt, mortgages on other properties, stocks you've pledged to secure a debt, alimony, child support, and recurring job-related expenses that you pay (such as union dues or child-care costs), and so on.

Although it's up to you whether you want to include alimony and child support payments as part of your monthly income if you receive such payments, if you *pay* alimony or child support, you *must* include the amount you pay as a liability.

For each debt, list the name and address of the creditor, your account number, how much you pay each month, how much time remains on the loan, and your current balance. If you're selling your current home, mark any debts that the sale will pay off with an asterisk (*).

 If you apply for a loan with a co-borrower, the two of you can fill out this section jointly if you've got significant joint assets and liabilities—such as joint bank accounts or a loan you've taken out together. (This is true whether or not you and the co-borrower are married.) Otherwise, each of you must fill out your own Assets and Liabilities section and provide supporting documentation separately.

Section VII: Details of Transaction

This section details the total cost to buy the house. In the first part, add up all the costs related to the transaction:

- Purchase price
- Alterations, improvements, repairs
- Land (if you're buying the land separately—otherwise, it's included in the purchase price)
- Refinance (if you're refinancing your current home rather than purchasing a new one, this is the amount you're refinancing, including any liens that must be paid off)
- Estimated prepaid items
- Estimated closing costs
- PMI
- Discount (any points you're paying)

From the total of those costs, subtract the loan amount, any secondary financing (such as a second mortgage), any of your closing costs that the seller will pay, and other credits. The result shows an estimate of how much cash you need to come up with for your down payment and closing costs.

 Read Chapter 9 to get an overview of typical closing costs.

Section VIII: Declarations

The first part of this section asks you and your co-borrower to check a box to answer yes or no to a series of questions about your legal and financial situation. If either of you answers yes to any of these questions, you must supply more information about what's going on—such as your alimony agreement (along with a copy of your divorce papers) or the circumstances of a recent bankruptcy (along the schedule you used to repay creditors and the discharge papers).

Here are the questions:

- **Are there any outstanding judgments against you?** If you've lost a lawsuit and haven't yet paid what you owe, note that here.

- **Have you been declared bankrupt within the past 7 years?** A recent bankruptcy will make it harder for you to get a loan.

- **Have you had property foreclosed upon or given title or deed in lieu thereof in the past 7 years?** The lender wants to know if you've been unable to honor the obligations of a mortgage in the recent past.

- **Are you a party to a lawsuit?** If you're suing someone or being sued, you must give the details of the lawsuit.

- **Have you directly or indirectly been obligated on any loan that resulted in foreclosure, transfer of title in lieu of foreclosure, or judgment?** This applies to all kinds of loans, not just mortgages, whether you were the primary borrower or a co-signer.

- **Are you presently delinquent or in default on any federal debt or any other loan, mortgage, financial obligation, bond, or loan guarantee?** If you are, it's not a good time to apply for a mortgage.

- **Are you obligated to pay alimony, child support, or separate maintenance?** The lender requires details of any divorce or separation agreement under which you must pay money to the other person.

- **Are you a co-maker or endorser on a note?** A *note* is a promise to pay a specified amount on demand or at a certain time. If you have such an obligation, the lender wants details.

The second part of this section has two yes-or-no questions, and one question that, if you answer yes, requires further information:

- **Are you a U.S. citizen?**

- **Are you a permanent resident alien?**

- **Do you intend to occupy the property as your primary residence?** If yes, you must indicate whether you've owned or partially owned a property in the past three years. If you have, you need to give information about the type of property (primary residence, second home, or investment property) and how you held title (by yourself, jointly with your spouse, or with someone who's not your spouse).

Section IX: Acknowledgment and Agreement

In this section, you promise that all the information in your application is true and you understand that anything you said that's false could result in penalties, such as a lawsuit or even criminal charges. The rest of the fine print says that you agree to these conditions:

- Everything you state in the application is for the purpose of getting a loan to buy residential property, and if you get the loan you're applying for, it will be secured by a mortgage or a deed of trust.

- You won't use the property you buy with this loan for any illegal purpose, and you'll occupy the property as you state in the application (primary residence, second home, and so on).

- Whether or not your application gets approved, the lender can keep a copy for its records.

- If information you provided on the application changes, you'll update the lender about the change.

- If you get the loan and fall behind in your payments, the lender can report that information to the credit bureaus.

- The lender can sell your loan to someone else.

- The lender isn't responsible for the condition of the property you're buying.

- If you submit the application electronically, your electronic signature is as legally binding as your pen-and-ink signature.

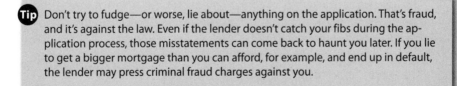

Tip Don't try to fudge—or worse, lie about—anything on the application. That's fraud, and it's against the law. Even if the lender doesn't catch your fibs during the application process, those misstatements can come back to haunt you later. If you lie to get a bigger mortgage than you can afford, for example, and end up in default, the lender may press criminal fraud charges against you.

Section X: Information for Government Monitoring Purposes

The government checks up on lenders to make sure that they're following federal laws about fair housing and equal credit opportunity for certain kinds of loans. That's what this optional section is for. It collects information about your sex, race, and ethnicity that the government uses to check lenders' compliance with those laws. If you prefer not to provide this information, check the box that says, "I do not wish to furnish this information."

 If you choose not to give the information requested in this section and you applied for the loan in person, the lender is required by law to look you over, check out your last name—and make a guess about your sex, race, and ethnicity.

Authorization to Verify Your Information

After you fill out the mortgage application, the lender will probably ask you to sign another form, giving the lender permission to check your information. By signing this form, you agree to give the lender access to information related to your application, including your credit history, employment history, bank accounts, and information about past mortgages.

HUD Settlement Cost Booklet

By law, your lender must give you a copy of the booklet titled, *Shopping for Your Home Loan*. It contains information about the home-buying and financing process: deciding to buy a home, finding the home you want, shopping and applying for a loan, understanding what your loan will cost you, and how closing works. If you don't get a copy of this booklet, ask for it.

Truth-in-Lending Disclosure Statement

After you apply for a loan, the lender must give you a Truth-in-Lending (TIL) disclosure statement. The TIL statement spells out the costs associated with your loan:

- **Annual percentage rate (APR).** This expresses the totality of your loan costs: its interest rate plus various lender fees and closing costs. Page 153 tells you more about APRs.

- **Finance charge.** This tells you, in dollars and cents, how much the loan will cost you if you pay it off over its full term.

- **Amount financed.** Confirm that this is the amount that you're borrowing.

- **Total payments.** This amount shows you how much you'll pay in principal and interest over the full term of the loan.

- **Other information about your loan.** Your TIL statement notes other information about this loan, such as whether it has a variable rate (if so, you get a separate ARM disclosure), whether there's a prepayment penalty, whether the loan is assumable, whether the lender can demand payment in full on a certain date (for a balloon loan, page 173), and what filing fees and late charges are.

Because some of the information on your TIL statement can change between the time you apply and the time you close (or lock in your rate), the lender must give you a revised TIL statement before closing.

ARM Disclosure Statement

If your loan has an adjustable rate (page 164), you'll also get an ARM disclosure statement to make sure you understand how these loans work. This disclosure, which you should receive with the application form, is a written summary of the terms and costs of your loan. The ARM disclosure also includes an overview of the past performance of the index to which your loan is tied (page 215 explains how that works), and a copy of the Federal Reserve Board's *Consumer Handbook on Adjustable-Rate Mortgages*.

Good Faith Estimate

The Good Faith Estimate (GFE) describes your loan and how much it costs (to get a copy of the form so you can follow along with the discussion below, see this book's Missing CD at *www.missingmanuals.com/cds/*). In 2009, HUD revised the form to make it easier to understand and easier to compare the costs listed here with the HUD-1 form you receive at the closing (see page 325 for information on the HUD-1 form). Another improvement: Lenders must stick by this estimate. The fees the lender charges to originate and process your loan cannot change between the time you receive the GFE and the closing. (Some third-party costs, over which the lender has no control, can change.) Holding lenders to their estimated loan origination fees prevents those fees from increasing and junk fees from creeping in. HUD estimates that the new GFE rules will save the average borrower $700 in closing costs.

Your GFE won't do you much good, though, if you don't understand what's on it. This section takes you through the three-page form and explains each part.

Purpose

This section simply tells you what this GFE is for: to set out the loan's terms and estimate the closing costs you'll pay if the lender approves your loan.

Shopping for your loan

Here, you're advised that you can use GFEs to compare loans and find the one that works best for you. The section directs your attention to the shopping chart on page 3, which helps you do a straightforward comparison of the loans you're considering. (More on how to use the shopping chart in a moment.)

Important dates

Your GFE doesn't last indefinitely, so pay attention to this section, because it lists expiration and other important dates:

- When the quoted interest rate expires. After the date listed here, the interest rate and other charges may change until you lock in the rate.

- When the other quoted closing costs expire

- If you lock in your rate, how long the rate lock lasts

- The number of days before closing at which you must lock in your rate

 Tip To make sure that you get the rate listed on your GFE, lock in that rate as soon as possible.

Summary of your loan

Here's the meat and potatoes of your loan, the basics spelled out clearly for you. Read it carefully, paying attention to the following:

- **Your initial loan amount.** This is how much you're borrowing.

- **The term of your loan.** This states how many years you have to pay back the loan.

- **Your initial interest rate.** This line says "initial" even for fixed-rate loans. A couple of lines later, the form spells out whether the interest rate is fixed or adjustable.

- **Your initial monthly payment, including principal, interest, and mortgage insurance (if required).** Again, this line talks about "initial" payments for all loans; the next line identifies whether your loan is fixed-rate or an ARM.

- **Can your interest rate rise?** If No is checked, you have a fixed-rate loan. If Yes is checked, the lender must specify the highest possible interest rate and the date of the first rate change.

- **Can your loan balance rise?** If No is checked, your monthly payments will chip away at the loan's balance. If Yes, your loan is subject to negative amortization (page 168) and the lender must specify how high the balance can get—it may be as high as 125% of the amount you originally borrowed, so pay attention to any number that appears here.

- **Can your monthly amount for principal, interest, and mortgage insurance rise?** Again, fixed-rate loans will have No checked here. If your loan is an ARM, you'll see a checkmark in the Yes box and a dollar amount for how much your monthly principal and interest payments can rise—both for the first adjustment period and if interest rates hit the maximum allowed by your loan.

- **Prepayment penalty.** If your lender doesn't impose one, you'll see the No box checked. If there is a penalty, Yes is checked and you'll see the maximum amount it would cost you to pay off the loan early.

 Tip If your loan has a prepayment penalty, ask whether that penalty is hard (you'll pay it whether you sell the house or refinance) or soft (you'll pay it only if you refinance the loan).

- **Balloon payment.** If you take out a balloon loan (page 173), which becomes due in full after a certain period of time, this section tells you how much you have to pay and when it's due.

The information in this section should match what's on your Truth-in-Lending statement. Compare them to make sure, and ask about any discrepancies.

Escrow account information

As you saw in Chapter 1, PITI—your monthly payment—stands for principal, interest, taxes, and insurance. All lenders collect principal, interest, and any required PMI via your monthly payments. Some lenders leave property taxes and other insurance up to you. Many lenders, however, want to protect their financial interest in your home by making sure that your tax and insurance payments stay up to date. These lenders estimate what your annual tax and insurance charges will be and collect 1/12 of these charges with your monthly payment. That money goes into an escrow account; when the charges are due, the lender pays them on your behalf from that escrow account.

This section of the GFE tells you whether or not this lender requires you to pay taxes and insurance fees into escrow. If so, you get an estimate of how much tax and interest payments will add to your monthly principal and interest payments for the first year of your loan.

Understanding your estimated settlement charges

At the bottom of page 1, you see an overview of what your closing costs will be:

- **A: Origination charges.** This amount shows the administrative fees your lender charges for making the loan (see page 227 for an explanation of the fees).

- **B: All other settlement services.** This amount is an estimate of the charges and fees due at the closing that don't go to the lender.

Page 2 breaks down these amounts, so you can see exactly what goes into them. For the origination fees, which cannot change at the closing, the lender spells out these charges:

- **Origination charge.** This gives the dollar amount that the lender charges to make your loan.

- **Adjustments.** This section details how origination charges affect your interest rate. You may be paying a slightly higher interest rate and lower up-front closing costs or higher closing costs to get a lower rate.

The rest of page 2 explains other required settlement charges and estimates how much these will cost you at closing. Some of these charges may vary from what's estimated here (you'll find out which ones in a minute). Here's how these charges break down:

- **Required services that we select.** These charges may include an appraisal fee, credit check fee, and other services that the lender needs to process your loan. The lender lists the service and how much it costs.

- **Title services and lender's title insurance.** Here the lender estimates the cost of the title search and the lender's title insurance policy you must buy.

- **Owner's title insurance.** It's up to you whether you want to buy title insurance to protect yourself if someone challenges the title after closing. (Page 269 tells you more about owner's title insurance.)

- **Required services that you can shop for.** The lender may require certain services, such as a home inspection, but not dictate who must perform that service. Such services are outlined here, along with an estimated cost for each.

- **Government recording charges.** As page 232 explains, the government charges a fee to record documents related to your home purchase.

- **Transfer taxes.** These state and local taxes (page 232) vary widely; this line tells you how much you'll pay in your area.

- **Initial deposit for your escrow account.** If the lender collects money for taxes and insurance and holds the funds in escrow, this section tells you how much and what it's for.

- **Daily interest charges.** You start owing the bank interest from the moment you sign the loan documents—that means each day between the day you close and the day your first payment is due. The lender calculates the total of these daily interest charges based on an estimated closing date. (If the closing date changes, so will the amount.)

- **Homeowner's insurance.** Here, the lender lists the kinds of homeowner's insurance you must get (hazard, flood, and earthquake insurance, for example) and estimates its cost.

Understanding which charges can change at settlement

At the top of page 3, the GFE makes clear which settlement charges may increase between now and the closing and which must stay the same, as you see noted on this form:

- **Charges that may not increase.** Fixed charges include the lender's origination fee listed on page 2, the number of points you agree to pay (after you lock in your rate), the adjusted origination charges at the bottom of page 1 (after you lock in your rate), and transfer taxes.

- **Charges that may increase by a maximum of 10 percent.** If you use any service that the lender requires or identifies, you won't pay more than 10 percent above the amount estimated. (This keeps lenders from underestimating third-party charges from providers they require or recommend.) Government recording charges are also limited to no more than a 10 percent increase above the lender's estimate.

- **Charges that may change.** Some charges are beyond the lender's ability to estimate. If you use a third-party service, such as a home inspector, that you shopped for and choose yourself—without any input from the lender—the charge for that service may be higher than what the lender thinks it should cost. Homeowner's insurance rates and your initial escrow deposit (if required) are other charges that may be higher than the lender's best guess. Finally, the lender bases the estimate of the daily interest charge on a hypothetical closing date—you may end up closing on a different date, which will increase or decrease that daily interest charge, depending on whether it's closer to or further away from the date of your first scheduled payment.

Using the tradeoff table

One question that makes homebuyers scratch their heads is, "Should I pay points to get a lower interest rate, or should I go for lower closing costs?" To help you see the difference between paying points to get a lower interest rate (which means higher up-front closing costs) and minimizing closing costs with a higher interest rate (which means you spread out the higher rate over the life of the loan, paying more interest in the long run), your GFE includes a tradeoff table. It gives you three versions of the loan side by side, so you can compare interest rates, monthly principal and interest payments, and total closing costs for three variations of the loan:

- The loan as quoted in this GFE
- The loan with a higher interest rate and lower closing costs
- The loan with higher closing costs (discount points) and a lower interest rate

The table is well-named. It clearly shows the tradeoff you make when:

- You opt for a lower interest rate by prepaying some interest at the closing.
- You opt for a higher interest rate to minimize closing costs.

Putting the amounts side by side lets you see what you'll pay in one lump sum up front and then each month thereafter. Using this table and knowing how long you plan to stay in your house, you can decide between the three options.

	The loan in this GFE	The same loan with lower settlement charges	The same loan with a lower interest rate
Your initial loan amount	$250,000	$250,000	$250,000
Your initial interest rate	5%	5.625%	4.5%
Your initial monthly amount owed	$1,342.05	$1,439.14	$1,266.71
Change in the monthly amount owed from this GFE	No change	You will pay $97.09 **more** every month.	You will pay $75.34 **less** every month.
Change in the amount you will pay at settlement with this interest rate	No change	Your settlement charges will be **reduced** by $750.00.	Your settlement charges will **increase** by $5,000.00.
How much your total estimated settlement charges will be	$3,415	$2,665	$8,415

Note If you choose an ARM, the tradeoff table shows only your interest rate and monthly payments for the initial, fixed-rate period of the loan. It cannot predict what your rate or monthly payments will be when your rate adjusts in the future.

Using the shopping chart

You may request GFEs from several lenders to compare the loans they offer. If you do, the shopping chart, which appears on page 3 of the GFE, lets you lay out the main points of each loan for an easy, at-a-glance comparison. Here's what the shopping chart might look like if you're in the market for a fixed-rate, 30-year loan of $250,000:

	This loan	Loan 2	Loan 3	Loan 4
Loan originator name	Lender #1	Lender #2	Lender #3	Lender #4
Initial loan amount	$250,000	$250,000	$250,000	$250,000
Loan term	30	30	30	30
Initial interest rate	5%	4.875%	5.125%	4.625%
Initial monthly amount owed	$1,342.05	$1,323.02	$1,361.22	$1,285.35
Rate lock period	30 days	30 days	45 days	30 days
Can interest rate rise?	No	No	No	No
Can loan balance rise?	No	No	No	No
Can monthly amount owed rise?	No	No	No	No
Prepayment penalty?	No	No	No	No
Balloon payment?	No	No	No	No
Total Estimated Settlement Charges	$3,415	$3,384	$3,089	$4,240

As you compare loans, you may notice that Loan 4 costs $56.70 less a month than Loan 1, but it requires an extra $825 at closing. If you have the $825, it would take about 15 months for the lower monthly payments of Loan 4 to recoup that up-front investment. After those 15 months, Loan 4 would be cheaper thanks to the lower interest rate. If you don't have that extra money now, one of the other options might look more attractive.

The point of the shopping chart is to let you compare different loans to see which best meets your needs. Only you can balance affordable payments with affordable closing costs to choose the loan that's right for you.

If your loan is sold in the future

The last section of your GFE is a notification that the lender may sell your loan after closing. (If that happens, the company that buys your loan cannot change its terms.)

 Tip Keep your GFE and bring it with you to the closing. If there are any discrepancies between it and the HUD-1 form that shows your final closing costs, you'll have the GFE right there to help you set things right.

Mortgage Servicing Disclosure Statement

Federal law requires lenders to give you a mortgage servicing disclosure statement. This document tells you whether your lender intends to keep your loan after closing, servicing the loan itself, or sell it to an investor. As your GFE emphasizes, if another institution buys your loan, it must honor the loan's terms.

What to Do If the Lender Rejects Your Application

I applied for a loan—and got turned down. What can I do now?

In the mid-2000s, it seemed like anyone and his dog could get a mortgage. But thanks to the credit crunch that began in late 2008, lenders have made it much harder to qualify for a loan. According to the Mortgage Bankers Association, by mid-2009 about half of all mortgage loan applicants were being turned down. If it happens to you, there are steps you can take that may help you get the loan you want.

First, find out why the lender rejected your application. If you submitted a formal application (as opposed to having an informal conversation with a loan officer), the lender must give you an *adverse action notice* explaining why you were turned down. Common reasons include an appraisal that came in too low, problems with your credit history, too much other debt, or an employment history that the lender sees as unstable.

Depending on the lender's reason (or reasons) for turning you down, you may be able to take action to turn the tide:

- **If the lender's appraisal was too low, request that the lender consider a second appraisal.** Back up your request with information about recent sales of comparable homes. If the original appraiser wasn't local to your area, the lender may listen to a local appraiser.

- **Check your credit report for errors.** If the lender rejected you based on a credit report, it must tell you which bureau's report it used. You can then get a copy of your credit report from that bureau and correct any errors. If there aren't any mistakes, work to improve your credit score (page 39) to reduce the chances that you'll be disappointed the next time you apply.

- **Negotiate with the lender.** If you get turned down for loan with, say, a 4.5 percent interest rate, you may qualify to borrow the same amount at a higher rate. Or you may qualify if you can find the funds for a higher down payment (which means you borrow less). Work with your loan originator to see if you can tweak the loan so you'll qualify.

- **Try another lender.** Many homebuyers find that smaller, community-based institutions, such as savings and loans or credit unions, are more flexible than big commercial lenders.

Getting preapproved for a loan (page 34) makes your chances of getting final approval more likely. The lender may still reject the loan based on problems with the property or title or changes in your financial picture (such as taking on a big new debt or changing your job). But getting preapproved gives you a degree of certainty that the lender will approve your formal application up to a certain amount.

9 Know Your Closing Costs

It's as certain as death and taxes: Whenever a piece of real estate changes hands, money changes hands, too. The swap takes place at an event called the *closing*, a meeting of all the parties involved in the sale of a house (the lender's attorney, the owner's representative, and you and/or your representative). There, you sign a dauntingly large stack of papers that bind you to the terms of your mortgage and make the property transfer official. Then you review the closing costs (sometimes called settlement costs), the fees and charges involved in the sale. There's quite a list of them; you pay some and the seller pays others. (Chapter 13 gives you a step-by-step tour of a real estate closing so you know what to expect.)

Closing costs can add up fast, but lenders provide you with an estimate of them beforehand. So you'll have an accurate list of the costs you can use to plan ahead. In this chapter, you'll get an overview of the different kinds of closing costs: those related to your mortgage, those related to the property transfer, and those that go to the government. You'll also see how these costs add up at a typical closing—and get tips for keeping them to a minimum.

Kinds of Closing Costs

Closing costs fall into three categories:

- Costs related to getting your mortgage
- Costs related to transferring ownership of the property
- Government taxes and fees

 Tip Take closing costs into account when you decide what to offer for a home. And remember that many of these fees are negotiable; a seller eager to close a deal may kick in some money toward closing costs. It never hurts to ask. See "Reduce Your Closing Costs" on page 236.

Costs Related to Your Mortgage

After you fork over the down payment on your new house (see Chapter 6), the bulk of your one-time costs come down to the fees required to get your mortgage approved. You'll find a list of the fees below, but keep in mind that every mortgage is different—you won't always pay all of these costs, and as time goes on, lenders will probably add new ones, not listed here:

- **Application fee.** This is the fee you pay for the lender to consider your mortgage application. If you don't pay an application fee when you apply for a mortgage, you'll pay it as part of some other fee. Application fees average $250 but vary by lender and region.

 Note When you see an ad for a no-application-fee loan, be skeptical. There's no such thing as a free lunch—or a free loan. When you apply for a loan that advertises "no application fees," you may find yourself reaching for your checkbook to pay a document processing fee, an appraisal fee, or a credit-check fee. Sounds a lot like an application fee, doesn't it? By the way, you pay these fees whether or not the lender approves your loan.

- **Credit check.** Lenders pass along the cost of checking your credit to you. Sometimes, they include this charge in the mortgage application fee. If not, expect to pay $30 to $35. On the bright side, your lender has to give you a copy of the report, so you get something tangible in return.

- **Appraisal fee.** To make sure your house is worth what you're paying for it, lenders require you to hire an independent third party to determine its fair market value. The lender chooses the appraiser, but you pay the fee, which can run anywhere from $200 to $400.

 Some lenders bundle together the application fee, credit check, and appraisal fee into one charge, calling it a document processing fee (or something similar).

- **Loan origination fee.** This nebulously named fee covers administrative aspects of the mortgage process: setting up the file for your loan, entering the loan into the lender's books, and preparing the documents necessary to offer and execute your mortgage (the bank's estimate of closing costs, for example, and the terms of your mortgage).

  It also covers the underwriter's fee. The underwriter certifies, based on the numbers presented to him, that both you and the property you're buying are an acceptable risk for the bank. In other words, he determines whether it's likely that you'll pay back your mortgage and certifies that if you don't, the property in question equals the value of the bank's investment. Page 162 tells you more about the underwriter's role in evaluating your mortgage application.

  And finally, the origination fee pays the commission of the loan officer or broker who initiated and completed the loan transaction.

  Expect to pay a loan origination fee of between 1 and 2 percent of the amount you're borrowing. If you're borrowing $275,000, you'll pay in the range of $2,750 to $5,500.

 Like an undercover spy, the loan origination fee has several different aliases. Your lender may call it a processing fee, an administrative fee, an underwriting fee, an origination fee, or something similar.

- **Points.** Points, too, can be a murky concept because lenders use the word in a couple of ways. But no matter how they apply it, the definition remains constant: One point equals 1 percent of your loan. If your loan is $250,000, 1 point is $2,500.

  Lenders use points a couple of ways:

  — To express the "price" of your loan origination fee ("Acme Bank charges a loan origination fee of 2 points", for example)

— To boost the financial interest you have in your house. If your down payment is less than 20 percent and your credit score is below 640 or so (the number varies with different lenders), your lender may require you to pay a point or two up front. In this case, points are interest that you're paying in advance. Your lender wants some assurance that he'll get a good return on the investment he's making in your home. If you're unable to provide that assurance with a sizable down payment, the lender may insist on collecting some interest in advance in the form of points.

On the other hand, you may volunteer to pay some points up front to reduce the interest rate of your mortgage (lenders call these points *discount points*). Discount points are also prepaid interest. In this case, paying extra interest in advance lowers your loan's interest rate, which in turn lowers your monthly payments and the total amount of your loan. If you have the money to pay points, as the practice is called, you can substantially reduce the amount of interest you pay over the life of your loan. For example, if you're borrowing $275,000 with a 30-year fixed-rate loan, you might have a choice between paying no points and getting an interest rate of 5 percent or paying 1 point and lowering your interest rate to 4.75 percent. The following table shows how paying $2,750 up front can save you more than $15,000 over the life of the loan:

	Number of points	Interest rate	Up-front cost of points	Monthly payment (principal & interest)	Total P&I paid over 30 years
Loan 1	0	5%	$0	$1,476.26	$531,453.41
Loan 2	1	4.75%	$2,750	$1,434.53	$516,430.86

 Tip The trick to knowing whether it's worthwhile to pay points is to find the ***break-even point***, where the money you save in interest payments pays back the discount points you paid at the start of the loan. If you plan to stay in your home past the break-even point, you'll save money on interest. Page 158 shows you how to calculate a loan's break-even point.

- **Prorated interest.** Although you won't have to make your first mortgage payment until four to six weeks after you close on your house, you start owing interest as soon as you sign your name on the dotted line. The lender figures out the interest between the date of your closing and your first mortgage payment, and you pay that at the closing.

- **Private mortgage insurance.** If your down payment is less than 20 percent of your home's purchase price, you have to buy private mortgage insurance (see page 146) and pay for it annually until you accrue 20 percent equity in your house. You'll most likely pay the first year's PMI in a lump sum at the closing; after that, the lender takes the annual premium out of an escrow account it sets up and that your mortgage payments fund (see "Escrow fund" on the next page). The cost of PMI depends on several factors, including your credit score and the amount of your mortgage, but it most often falls in the range of 0.5 to 1 percent of your loan.

 Federal law requires that your lender automatically cancel your PMI when the equity in your house reaches 22 percent. You can request cancellation of PMI at 20 percent equity; if you do, the bank will probably require you to pay for an appraisal to prove the home's value.

- **Government agency fees.** If the FHA insures your mortgage or if the Veterans Administration guarantees it (see Chapter 7 for details on government-assisted loans), you need to pay the associated premium or fee at the closing. The FHA premium is about 1.5 percent of your loan. VA guarantee fees range from 1.25 percent to 2 percent of your loan and depend on the size of your down payment—the bigger it is, the lower your percentage.

- **Survey.** The lender may want to *survey* your property to verify the property lines and the locations of the house and any other buildings on it. The survey also checks for encroachments, such as a neighbor's fence that strays onto your property or a corner of your garage that juts onto the neighbor's property (you have to resolve any encroachment issues before the closing). The survey should cost $150 to $400.

- **Home inspection fee.** Your lender wants to be sure that the home you're buying is in good shape—that you're not buying a ready-to-collapse nightmare, in other words. You'll probably have to pay a professional home inspector to check the home's structure and central systems (electric, heating, septic, and so on). Of course, it's in your best interest to give the home a thorough going-over, too, so you'll probably find this fee easy to swallow. Costs vary depending on where you live and the size of your house, but expect to pay $200 to $400. Chapter 12 walks you through a typical home inspection.

- **Pest inspection fee.** In addition to the home inspection, your lender may require a separate pest inspection that checks for wood-boring insects like termites and powder-post beetles. Usually, you have to get this inspection done within 30 days before the closing. Depending on the size and age of the house, this inspection typically costs from $75 to $200.

- **Insurance costs.** A homeowner's insurance policy protects you from the costs of vandalism, fire, wind, and other damage to your property. It also covers the *contents* of your home in cases of theft and damage. And it protects you if someone gets injured on your property. In flood-prone areas of the country, such as many coastal regions, your lender requires you to get a separate flood insurance policy.

   At the closing, you must prove you have a homeowner's policy in effect (condo and co-op buyers, see the Note below). The cost of the insurance depends on the value of your home and its location (high-crime areas or places with extreme weather mean a more costly policy), but the national average is $760 a year.

 If you buy a condo or co-op, part of your monthly common charges (condo) or maintenance fees (co-op) goes toward hazard insurance for the building. You're covered for structural damage but not for the contents of your home; be sure to buy your own homeowner's policy to protect the latter.

- **Escrow fund.** Some lenders require you to set aside money to pay recurring fees associated with your mortgage—homeowner's insurance, hazard insurance, PMI (if any), and property taxes. The lender holds this money in an escrow account, a separate account set up on your behalf to hold funds that pay these fees when they're due. You may have to deposit seed money into your escrow account at the closing. After that, the lender takes the fee payments out of your monthly mortgage payment.

- **Miscellaneous charges.** You may have to pay for various other fees at the closing, including courier fees to shuttle papers between the lender and the lawyers; brokerage fees (if you use a mortgage broker to find your lender); prorated fees for utilities, condo fees, and homeowners' association dues; an assumption fee (if you're taking over the seller's mortgage; page 190 tells you about assumable mortgages); flood certification (to check whether the home requires flood insurance); wire transfer fees; and so on.

Costs Related to Transferring Ownership

You want to make sure that the home you're buying is all yours, and to do that, you have to be sure that the seller actually owns the property he's selling and that he has the right to transfer ownership to you. So expect to pay these costs:

- **Title search.** Someone has to go through public records to prove that the seller has the legal right to sell you her home—they have to show that no one has an outstanding claim of ownership against the prop-erty and that no one has placed a lien (a financial claim) against it. Any one of several parties may conduct the title search: the insurance company, a title company, an escrow company, or a lawyer. Whoever does it looks through local government records, including those for the county courts, tax assessor, surveyors, and the recorder of deeds. In addition, the person conducting the search needs to look for and examine records related to liens, divorces, deaths, and contested wills that might affect ownership.

- **Lender's title insurance.** Even with a vetted title, most lenders want a guarantee that no errors were made during the search. That guarantee comes in the form of title insurance. If someone later makes a claim against the property, title insurance protects the lender's investment (the money it loaned you). This insurance is a one-time fee based on the amount you borrow; it's usually 0.5 percent of your home's pur-chase price. And the lender doesn't pay for it—you do. Like many clos-ing costs, however, you may be able to negotiate with the seller to pay this fee.

 If the seller has owned her house for just a few years, contact the seller's title insur-ance company and ask them to reissue the seller's title insurance policy in your name. If the property changed hands fairly recently and no claims have surfaced against the title, the current title insurance company may consider the property a low risk and give you a favorable rate.

- **Owner's title insurance (optional).** The title insurance you buy to protect the lender's interests doesn't protect yours. Some home buyers buy title insurance for themselves as well. Usually, this is a percentage of the lender's insurance policy. And in some areas, it's customary for the seller to buy title insurance for the new owner.

 Tip If you buy a home in California, use the California Land Title Association's free Title Wizard to compare title insurance companies and rates. You can find it at *http://clta.titlewizard.com*.

- **Settlement fees.** Someone has to prepare the paperwork and conduct the closing proceedings, making sure all those legal t's and i's are crossed and dotted. The settlement agent may be a lawyer, a real estate broker, a representative of the lender, or an escrow company, and it may be your responsibility to pay his services. In addition, you may want to hire your own attorney to keep an eye on your interests at the closing (page 99 explains why this is a good idea).

Government Taxes and Fees

The seller isn't the only one who wants proceeds from the sale of her house—so does the government. The taxes and fees you pay to city, county, and state agencies depend on where you buy. In some parts of the country, the amount is negligible. In others, it represents a big chunk of your closing costs, sometimes in the thousands of dollars. Here are some typical taxes and fees:

- **Property tax.** As soon as you own a home, you're liable for its property taxes. The amount you owe at closing depends on when your community collects its property taxes. You might owe the seller a prorated amount for property taxes she's already paid, for example.

- **Transfer and recording tax.** This is a transaction fee the government charges to transfer the property's title from the seller to you. It's a percentage of the property's selling price. Usually, this is a local tax, paid to your new city or county (or both), but some states charge this tax, too.

- **Mansion tax.** Some states levy a luxury tax on homes worth more than a certain amount of money. New York state, for example, adds 1 percent to the recording tax of homes valued at more than a million dollars.

A tax by any other name is just as hard on your wallet. Other names for transfer and recording taxes include mortgage tax, deed recording tax, documentary transfer tax, and stamp tax.

- **Recording fee.** This fee pays for recording your house's deed and mortgage in local records. The amount often depends on the number of pages in the deed.

 You can't deduct mortgage transfer and recording taxes from your federal tax return, but ask your accountant or tax preparer if you can deduct them from state and local returns.

Add It All Up

Take a look at the following table to see how closing costs add up. It compares closing costs for a $250,000 home with two different down payments, one of 10 percent (second column), the other of 20 percent (third column).

Cost	10 percent down payment	20 percent down payment
Mortgage amount	$225,000	$200,000
Down payment	$25,000	$50,000
Application fee (may include credit report fee)	$150–$350	$150–$350
Credit report fee (if not part of application fee)	$25–$35	$25–$35
Loan origination fee (1 to 2 points)	$2,250–$4,500	$2,000–$4,000
Points (0 to 3)	$0–$6,750	$0–$6,000
Appraisal fee	$200–$400	$200–$400
Home inspection fee	$200–$400	$200–$400
Pest inspection fee	$75–$200	$75–$200
Prepaid interest (assumes a 6 percent interest rate and 15 days left in the month)	$550	$490
Homeowner's insurance	Varies	Varies
Private mortgage insurance (one month)	$95–$280	N/A
Title search and lender's title insurance	$700–$900	$700–$900
Prorated property taxes	Varies	Varies
Survey	$150–$400	$150–$400
Recording and transfer fees	$50–$4,500	$50–$4,000
Attorney fees	$500–$1,500	$500–$1,500

As you can see, closing costs vary widely. Your down payment and the size of your mortgage affect the fees. Other factors include the home's location, your credit score, your mortgage interest rate, whether you buy points to reduce that rate, and the lender's policies. As a rule of thumb, most buyers pay closing costs of 3 to 6 percent of the loan amount.

 According to a 2009 survey by BankRate.com, the average closing costs nationally were $2,732 (based on a $200,000 loan). Texas homebuyers shelled out the highest fees at $3,855, and Nevada buyers spent the least at $2,276. Find average closing costs for your state by visiting *www.bankrate.com* and type *closing costs* into the search box in the upper-right corner of the page.

How Much Will You Pay?

Even setting aside 3 to 6 percent of the loan amount for closing costs you might worry whether you'll have enough cash at the closing. Fear not. When you apply for a loan, federal law requires that, within three days, your lender give you a written estimate of those costs. To do this, the lender uses a form called the Good Faith Estimate (GFE), developed by the Department of Housing and Urban Development (HUD) for just this purpose. This recently revised, three-page document helps you compare loans from the same or different lenders and understand the total closing costs you'll pay. Chapter 8 goes through a GFE section by section. Here, you get an overview of how the GFE estimates your closing costs.

The Good Faith Estimate isn't just the lender's best guess at your closing costs—it's a realistic estimate that comes surprisingly close to the true figures. That's because federal regulations dictate the degree to which closing costs can increase. For example, the following costs cannot be higher at the closing than they are on your GFE:

- The loan origination fee
- The points required for the given interest rate (after you lock in your interest rate—see page 204 to learn how to do that)
- Transfer taxes

The following third-party charges may increase before closing, but not by more than 10 percent:

- Required services, such as an appraisal (your bank selects the provider)
- The title search
- Title insurance
- Government recording fees

 Note The 10 percent cap on third-party charges applies only to third parties that the lender specifically requires or recommends. For some services, such as an appraiser or home inspector, the lender may let you shop around—but if you choose a provider that's not on the lender's recommended list, the amount you pay for the service could exceed the amount shown on the Good Faith Estimate by more than 10 percent.

Other charges in the GFE may change by more than 10 percent:

- Homeowner's insurance, which is between you and your insurance company
- The amount of the initial deposit into your escrow account (that's because the date of the closing may change between the time the lender creates the GFE and the day you actually close)
- Daily interest charges (ditto)

The GFE also lets you compare the trade-offs you make when you choose lower closing costs now (which result in paying more over the life of the loan) over a lower interest rate (which results in higher closing costs but a lower overall cost).

To compare loans, use the worksheet on page 3 of the GFE, called the "shopping chart." Fill in the figures from different lenders and compare them. You'll get a clear picture of the closing costs with a quick, accurate comparison.

 Tip A couple of days before the closing, check with your lawyer or closing agent to get the actual amount you'll need to bring with you on the big day. Chapter 13 gives you a blow-by-blow description of a typical closing.

luce Your Closing Costs

ou add up all the closing costs, you might be shocked by the total. f these costs are negotiable, however. Try the tips below to see if you can rein in your spending. Whether you save a few bucks or a few hundred, that's money in your pocket.

- **Compare lenders.** Lenders aren't required to give you a Good Faith Estimate until after you apply for a loan, but ask for an informal estimate beforehand. Some lenders may refuse, but many will give you a ballpark figure. Compare them to get the best deal. Just remember that any estimate a lender gives you as you shop for a mortgage is just that—an early estimate—and it may change.

- **Ask for a seller's concession.** If the seller agrees, you may be able to bundle some or all of your closing costs into your loan by getting a seller's concession. Here's how that works: Say you and the seller agree on a price of $175,000 for the house and you request a seller's concession of 3 percent, or $5,250. If the seller agrees (and your lender approves), you add that $5,250 to the price of the house, and the lender determines the mortgage based on a sale price $180,250. (For this to work, the property appraisal must match or exceed the actual sale price—$175,000 in the example—plus the concession amount.) At closing, the seller gets her $175,000 and gives you back the $5,250 concession—and you use that money to pay some or all of your closing costs.

 Note Most lenders won't let you profit from a seller's concession. Although you can use that borrowed money to pay closing costs, you can't take the cash, say, "Hey, thanks!" and head off to St. Bart's.

- **Negotiate with the seller.** When a seller is eager to sell—you may be shopping in a buyer's market, for example, or the seller may be in a hurry to move—you can often get help with closing costs. It's in the seller's best interest to complete the sale, after all, and many sellers won't quibble over a few hundred (or even a few thousand) dollars if the alternative is a house that stays on the market. For example, the seller may offer a credit of a few hundred dollars to replace the family room carpet or agree to a clause in your purchase agreement that says, "The seller agrees to pay up to $2,000 of the buyer's closing costs." Your real estate agent will help with these negotiations.

- **Negotiate with the lender.** You may find that a lender has some wiggle room with its charges. Ask if there's anything your lender can do to pare down your overall closing costs.

- **Don't pay for two attorneys.** You need a lawyer to represent your interests when you buy a home. If you choose one from the lender's list of approved real estate attorneys, that attorney can work for both you *and* the lender and save you several hundred dollars in the process. If you prefer to use your own attorney because you're worried about a potential conflict of interest, you can request that the lender remove its attorney's fee from the closing costs you pay (the lender may or may not agree, but it doesn't hurt to ask).

- **Question individual fees.** Mortgage closing costs are infamous for "junk fees," additional processing and documentation charges that do little for you besides remove money from your wallet. For example, if you notice an application fee, processing fee, and underwriting fee all listed as closing costs, you may be paying twice for the same service. If a fee seems redundant or you don't understand it, ask about it—and see whether you can get it waived.

- **Compare third-party services.** A lender may give you a list of approved third-party service providers—appraisers, home inspectors, title insurance companies, and so on. Don't pick the first name on the list. Take some time and do your research; call several providers and ask for estimates, then compare costs.

- **Time your closing to save money.** One of the costs you pay at the closing is interest on your loan (page 228). Mortgage loans are due on the first of each month, so at the closing you prepay interest from the date of the closing until the end of the current month. If you close on (or near) the last day of the month, you'll owe little or no prepaid interest—a strategy that can reduce your closing costs by hundreds of dollars.

- **Scrutinize your settlement statement in advance.** The settlement statement, called a HUD-1 form (see page 325), itemizes all the costs associated with your mortgage. By law, your lender has to give you this form at least one day before the closing—although it's not unusual for the various parties to tweak the statement until the moment everything is signed. Grab your HUD-1 in advance, sit down, and compare it to your Good Faith Estimate. Take the time to check for discrepancies and bring any to your lender's attention.

10 Make an Offer

t's an exciting moment—you found a home you love, and you're ready to make an offer. You're ready to take the next step—and it's a big one—on your journey from househunter to homeowner. Even in the midst of all the excitement, though, it's easy to worry whether you're doing things right. If you offer too much, the bank might not approve your loan. If you offer too little, the seller might reject the offer without a counteroffer from which you can negotiate. In addition, you need to think carefully about how to protect yourself if something goes wrong between now and closing.

Although you may make a verbal offer to the seller, nothing is binding until you put it in writing. And a formal offer is a *promise to buy*. When you write up an offer with your real estate agent, you're not simply feeling out whether the seller *might* sell at a certain price—you're making a commitment to buy the home. If you and the seller can work out all the details, the home will be yours. It's important that you craft your offer carefully to make sure it reflects your desires *and* protects your interests. This chapter takes you through the process: figuring out how much you want to offer, deciding on the contingencies and other conditions you want to include in your offer, and negotiating with the seller to come to an agreement that both of you can live with.

Figure Out What the Home Is Worth

The central part of any purchase offer is the proposed purchase price. You already know how much the seller wants for the home, but it's called the "asking price" for a reason. The amount of money that the seller would like to get for her home is not necessarily the price at which the home will sell. Prices are always negotiable. Even a seller who sets a firm price and refuses to consider other offers may have to think again if the house sits on the market for a few months.

 Note It's part of the human psyche—homeowners often have an inflated sense of how much their home is worth, so it's common for them to set an initial asking price that's too high. A seller working with a real estate agent may simply decide to work with the agent who suggests the highest list price—and some agents may inflate the asking price in order to get the listing, figuring that they can convince the seller to set a more reasonable price later. And a FSBO seller may not do the research needed to set a realistic price.

It's up to you to evaluate the price the seller has set and decide whether the home is worth it. The asking price is only one part of the equation, however. You need to look at that price in the context of similar homes (both those on the market now and those that have recently sold), how long the home has been for sale, and how hot—or cold—the local real estate market is.

Look at Recent Sales of Comparable Homes

Ask your real estate agent to pull up information on similar homes that have recently sold in the same neighborhood. (Real estate insiders call these sales *comparables*, or comps.) Limit your search to houses sold within the past six months that are similar in age, size, and number of bedrooms to the home you're considering. That's exactly what the lender's appraiser will look at when he determines the house's value.

Comps give you a price range for similar homes in the local real estate market. Your home should be worth somewhere between the lowest-priced and highest-price comparable. Figure out the average price of comps, and compare that to the seller's asking price. That'll give you an idea of whether the seller's asking price is too high or a bargain.

Compare Asking Prices to Selling Prices

How have the list prices of homes compared to their actual selling price? Your agent can help you spot trends in pricing. Ask for a trend report that covers the past six months, comparing what properties were listed for with what they sold for. Are the two numbers pretty much in line, or do selling prices tend to be higher or lower than asking prices? How wide is the gap? These comparisons tell you the state of the market and help you determine an offer for the house you want. If buyers are snapping up homes for prices consistently higher than list prices, you may have a hard time convincing a seller to accept an offer below the asking price. (Individual circumstances vary, of course, and you may find a motivated seller who's happy to consider your offer.) If, on the other hand, you notice that selling prices trend below list prices, you may be able to buy a house at a comparable discount. For example, say that, on average, houses have sold for 3 percent below their list prices. That trend could indicate what's considered a reasonable offer in the current market: 3 percent below the asking price.

 Tip Ask your agent to look at the track record of the agent who listed the house you want. She may be able to spot an agent-specific trend in the gap between asking and selling price. For example, maybe the homes listed by this agent tend to sell for 5 percent below the asking price. This information could give you a ballpark for your offer.

Use Online Home Appraisal Tools

To get an idea of how much other homes in your prospective neighborhood are worth, check out some online appraisal tools. These websites ask you for the address of the home you're interested in and estimate the value of neighboring homes, giving you a quick overview of comparable prices and even estimating the current value of the home you're interested in. Several sites provide this service for free, including Domania (*www.domania.com*), RealEstateABC (*www.realestateabc.com*), and Zillow (*www.zillow.com*). Others, such as Electronic Appraiser (*www.electronicappraiser.com*), Homesmart (*www.homesmartreports.com*), and RealtyTrac (*www.realtytrac.com/value-trac*) offer to sell you a property valuation report; these reports range in price from $20 to $30. If you're working with a real estate agent, you probably don't need to pay for a valuation report. Although your agent won't tell you how much to offer, she can use her comps to work with you to interpret numbers and trends. Your agent's information is probably more up to date than what you'll find online, as well.

Get the Home's Sales History

Before you make an offer on a house, get as much backstory as you can—it'll help you make a more informed offer. Find out:

- **How much the seller paid.** If the seller has lived in the home for years and years, this figure probably won't say much about the property's current value. But if he's lived in the house for only a few years, you can get a good idea of how realistic his pricing is. If home prices in the neighborhood have remained flat or lost ground, for example, the home's current price should be fairly close to what the seller paid.

- **How much the seller owes.** You can ask; the seller may or may not tell you. But knowing this amount can keep you from making a lowball offer that the seller is sure to reject. Unless the seller is in default on her mortgage, she's unlikely to accept an offer that's lower than the amount she owes the bank (called a short sale; page 124 tells you all about them). Here's another hint you can get from this information: If the seller's mortgage balance is low, she may not be in any big hurry to sell and will hold out for her asking price.

 If you make an offer that's close to the amount the seller owes on his mortgage, don't expect the seller to chip in much for repairs or closing costs.

- **How long the home has been on the market.** Newly listed homes get a lot of attention, raising sellers' hopes that they'll get an offer that meets or beats the asking price. If the home hasn't sold after a month to six weeks, cooling interest from buyers and an eagerness to move may make the seller more amenable to an offer below the initial list price.

- **Whether the home has been relisted.** Listing agreements expire after a set time, which may be 90 days, 180 days, or even a year. When they do, many sellers switch agents to try and find one who does a better job of selling the home. Sometimes, a listing that looks brand new is a relisting of a house that's been on the market before and failed to sell. And behind the relisting, there's probably a frustrated seller who wants to get the house sold. Such sellers are often willing to consider more aggressive offers. Your real estate agent can tell you whether a home has been relisted.

Take the Market's Temperature

Is your local real estate market hot—or not? Real estate agents measure market "temperatures" from the seller's point of view. If homes sell quickly at market price or better, the market is hot; if *inventory* (the number of unsold homes) piles up, the market is as cold as a glacier creeping down a mountainside.

Agents define three kinds of housing market, one of which benefits you:

- **Neutral market.** Neither the buyer nor the seller has an advantage.
- **Seller's market.** "Hot" markets favor sellers.
- **Buyer's market.** "Cold" markets favor buyers.

Read on to learn more about these markets and how to make an offer suited to each.

Neutral market

In a *neutral market*, the number of buyers looking for homes balances the number of homes for sale. Prices are stable, and both buyer and seller are on an equal footing in negotiations. You're in a neutral market when inventory remains stable at about six months (see page 248 to find out how real estate agents calculate inventory), median prices stay stable from month to month, and houses sell within four to six weeks of their listing.

 Note The median price marks the dividing line between higher-priced and lower-priced houses; half of listings are above the median price and half are below it. Your real estate agent can tell you what the median price is in your area.

When you go house-hunting in a neutral market, you're not at any particular advantage or disadvantage in negotiations. Sellers have confidence that new listings will sell within a couple of months, so they're less likely to lower the price or make concessions. You can bide your time, as well—although desirable homes will have interested buyers, it's unlikely you'll get caught up in the bidding frenzies that can roil a seller's market. If you shop for a home in a neutral market, take the time you need to make a decision and arrive at a comfortable offer—once you're sure, act quickly.

Seller's market

In a *seller's market*, more buyers are hunting for homes than there are homes to buy. As economists put it, demand exceeds supply. Active listings quickly disappear from the market, and prices rise as more buyers compete for fewer homes.

Here how to tell if you're in a seller's market (your agent can get the numbers you need):

- **Low inventory.** Inventory—the number of houses on the market—is much lower than in previous months or years. Real estate agents consider inventory low if there's less than six months' worth of listings on the market (meaning that it would take six months to sell off all currently listed homes; see the sidebar "Determining Housing Inventory" on page 248 for more details).

- **Increasing prices.** Steadily increasing median prices over several months and list prices that are higher than comps for homes sold a few months ago both suggest a seller's market.

- **Fast-moving homes.** When listings stay active for just days or a week, it's a good sign for sellers, but makes things much harder for buyers. If you notice a new For Sale sign in your target neighborhood, only to see a Sale Pending sign attached to it the next time you drive by or if a home sells before your agent can set up a showing, be prepared to move fast when you decide on a home.

- **Upward-tracking sales.** When buyers are eager to buy (instead of browsing or feeling like they have the luxury of many homes to choose from), the number of completed sales increases. Homes that have been lingering on the market start to sell. You'll see an upward trend in sales volume due to more than simple seasonal buying patterns.

- **Limited-time bidding.** In a very hot market, some agents limit how long a home stays on the market by taking bids for only a specified period, such as a week. These listings say something like "Accepting bids until 5 p.m. Saturday, April 24." At that time, the seller reviews the bids and makes a decision. Agents do this to create a sense of urgency among prospective buyers, in hopes that many bids will come in and that several will exceed the asking price.

Buying during a seller's market is more challenging than at other times, but you *can* get the home you want even in a hot market (after all, sales are what make the market hot). These tips give you an edge:

- **Get preapproved for a mortgage.** You've already done this, right? The box on page 34 explains how preapproval helps you set a price range for your home and how it speeds up the home-buying process. In a seller's market, submitting a preapproval letter with your offer shows you can close the sale fast. This may impress a seller more than a higher offer without preapproval letter—the seller may decide your offer is more solid because you already have a commitment from a lender.

- **Don't be demanding.** Although you need to include some contingencies (page 251) in your offer (such as a home inspection contingency), don't go overboard . For example, don't try to get the seller to pay for closing costs that the buyer normally covers in your area. If the seller has several offers to choose from, the one with the most demands may go straight to the bottom of the pile.

- **Don't expect a counteroffer.** Many buyers expect to haggle before agreeing on a price. They bid low, figuring that the seller will counter with a different, somewhat higher price. Often, that's a smart strategy. But in a seller's market, the current owner has no motivation to haggle. If your offer is too low, he'll simply reject it. And if there are multiple offers on the home, you won't get a second chance.

- **Offer to close quickly.** If you can be ready to close in, say, three weeks instead of 30 days, you might give yourself a leg up on the competition. You can speed up closing, for example, by getting preapproved for a mortgage and scheduling the home inspection was early as possible. Before you promise a speedy closing, though, read Chapter 11 to find out everything you need to do between signing a purchase agreement and closing the sale. Don't underestimate how much time you'll need.

 You might be tempted to speed things up by waiving contingencies like a home inspection. Don't. If you waive your right to an inspection, you may end up owning a house with serious structural or other problems—with no one to blame but yourself. Instead of waiving the home inspection, see if you can shorten the window for the inspection. A standard time frame for an inspection is 17 days— two weeks to arrange the inspection and three days to interpret the results. If you've got an inspector who's ready to go, you can shorten that window to 10 days (or less) and close at least a week earlier, while still protecting yourself against a substandard house.

- **Get earnest about earnest money.** Earnest money (page 250) shows that you're serious about buying the house. If you put down a sizable deposit—more than is customary in your area—you signal to the seller that you can afford the home and that you're not going to run away from the deal on freezing cold feet.

- **Add a personal touch.** When you make an offer to purchase real estate, you're making an offer to buy someone's home—the place they decorated and cared for, and lived, laughed, and loved in. Many homeowners have mixed feelings about selling their homes and moving on.

Consider writing a personal letter to submit with your offer to let the seller know what you love about the house. Don't focus on the changes you'll make; focus on your appreciation for the place that has been the seller's home. A short, heartfelt letter can set you apart from other buyers.

 Tip Always communicate with the seller through your agent. It's her job to act as an intermediary between you and the seller.

If you're shopping for a home during a seller's market, don't get discouraged. When the market is hot, you may have to make offers on several homes before a seller accepts one. (Avoid making multiple offer simultaneously, though—you could end up losing your earnest money on one of them if two different sellers accept your offer.) When the competition to buy is fierce, try not to get too emotionally attached to a particular home, because there's a good chance someone else will beat your offer. Keep your wish-list priorities in mind and know that many properties out there would make a terrific home.

A hot market can also put pressure on buyers to jump in with offers before they're ready. Don't rush. A home is too large a purchase to make simply because you're feeling pressured. And don't overbid or stretch your budget to its breaking point. You may be happy to get the home, but once the excitement dies down, you'll regret overspending. Remember that you'll be living in your new home for years, and you want your budget to be as comfortable as your living room.

Buyer's market

A *buyer's market* is the flip side of a seller's market; there are more homes available than buyers looking for them. Supply exceeds demand—and buyers benefit. Sellers may be more willing to drop prices, consider below-asking-price offers, and make concessions like helping you pay closing costs.

These are all signs that you're in a buyer's market:

- **Lots of active listings.** There are more homes for sale on the market than there were in previous months or at this time in previous years.

- **High inventory.** There's currently more than six months' worth of inventory on the market (see the box on page 248 to learn what this means).

If sales continue to slow, inventory increases as homes come on the market at a faster rate than listings sell.

- **Dropping prices.** Median home prices are declining and active list prices are consistently lower than those of recent comps.

- **Slow-moving listings.** Houses remain on the market for six weeks or longer before they sell. You may notice the same listings week after week and For Sale signs that stay in place for a long time. As time passes, you may notice that some For Sale signs add enticements like "Price Reduced" or "New Price."

If you're shopping during a buyer's market, you're in luck. The longer a house stays on the market, the more anxious the seller is to sell. And that may give you some leeway in crafting your offer. You may be able to buy the house at a discount or get seller's concessions to help pay closing costs or put toward upgrades or repairs.

Use these tips to get the most out of a buyer's market:

- **Tour homes that have been on the market for six weeks or longer.** When a seller first lists a home, there's usually a flurry of interest. Even in a buyer's market, the seller hopes to get the home's asking price— and is less willing to negotiate. As time passes, most sellers start to wonder what they can do to unload the home and are more willing to negotiate.

- **Justify a low offer.** Nobody likes to be seen as desperate, and the seller may be insulted by a lowball offer. Do your homework, and attach information about comps to show they justify the price you're suggesting. The seller is more likely to listen.

- **Request contingencies and concessions.** A buyer's market gives you the chance to attach conditions to your purchase. Think about what would make your purchase easier and smoother—such as extra help with closing costs—and then put your wish list into your purchase offer. Even if the seller doesn't agree to everything, you'll have opened negotiations.

 Page 236 suggests some ways a seller may help you pay closing costs.

- **Negotiate.** If the seller comes back with a counteroffer, don't throw up your hands and walk away. A counteroffer isn't a rejection—it's an indication of the seller's willingness to negotiate. The seller didn't accept your offer but did leave the door ajar. Counter the counteroffer with a new one of your own—and realize that the back-and-forth could go on for a while before you reach an agreement.

 Note A seller's counteroffer may be the full listing price. The seller's signal? It's hard to say. He may be testing the waters to see whether you'll pay the full price. Or he may be firm about the price but willing to negotiate elsewhere, like giving you a credit toward closing costs or making repairs or upgrades. The only way to find out what the seller is thinking is to ask. Make a counteroffer of your own, and see how the seller responds.

Determining Housing Inventory

My agent told me that it's a good time to buy because there are eight months of inventory on the market. What does that mean, and how did she come up with this number?

Agents calculate a market's housing inventory by figuring out how long it would take to sell all the houses listed within a specific price range at the rate homes are selling right now. This number, sometimes called the *absorption rate*, gives you an idea of how quickly or slowly homes are selling over time.

To figure out the absorption rate, pick the price range you're interested in, and then look at the total number of active listings in that range last month. Next, get the number of listings sold (your agent calls these "closed listings") during that month. Then get out your calculator and divide the total inventory by the number of closed listings. The result tells you how many months it would take to sell all listings if sales continued at last month's rate.

Here's an example: The total number of listings in your area last month was 2,459, with 302 closings. When you divide 2,459 by 302, the result is just over 8. So your agent would tell you that there's eight months' worth of inventory currently on the market. (And since you're a buyer, that's good news.)

When taking the market's temperature, agents use these guidelines:

- Six months of inventory is a neutral market, favoring neither buyers nor sellers.
- More than six months of inventory (as in the example above) represents a buyer's market; properties may languish for weeks or months before they sell.
- Less than six months of inventory is a seller's market, and homes are selling quickly.

Tip Page 257 lists tips for negotiating with a seller.

- **A strategy for rejected offers.** Even if a seller rejects your offer outright and shows no inclination to bargain, keep an eye on the listing as you look at other homes. If the house is still on the market a month or two later, have your agent resubmit the offer. By then, the seller may be happy to reconsider.

How Much Should You Offer?

There's no set formula for deciding how much money to offer for the home you want to buy. Too bad, because the issue is one of the knottiest ones you'll encounter in your quest to buy a home. You don't want to offer too much—nobody likes to overpay, and the bank's appraiser may disagree that the home is worth what you offered, delaying or nixing the sale. You might even end up with negative equity if home values drop. But if your offer is too low, you may anger the seller or lose out to another buyer.

Like all tough questions, this one doesn't have an easy answer. You have to do your homework and weigh numerous factors to determine the price that *you* should offer for *this* home. If necessary, revisit your budget (page 26) to make sure you don't overspend. Then look at all the factors discussed in this section—comparable home prices, price trends, how much the seller owes her lender, how long the home has been on the market, and whether the market is hot or cold—and weigh them to come up with a price that's fair for the property. And if that price is below the asking price, be prepared to negotiate (page 257).

 Tip It's your responsibility to determine how much a house is worth and whether you can afford it, so don't ask your real estate agent how much you should pay. Instead, ask your agent about current market trends and whether the price you're considering seems reasonable.

What Goes Into an Offer

After you settle on a price—and maybe you and the seller have agreed verbally on that price—you're ready to write up an offer to present to the seller. But you need to include more than just a price in your purchase offer. You also want to include conditions, called *contingencies*, that you're attaching to the offer, along with earnest money to show that you're serious about buying the home.

Purchase offers work differently in different parts of the country. In some states, your purchase offer is exactly that—an offer to purchase a home. In these states, you submit a purchase offer as a first step and then, if the seller accepts your offer, you write and sign a purchase-and-sale agreement (often called just a purchase agreement) that spells out your and the seller's conditions and expectations in greater detail. In other states, your purchase offer *is* the purchase-and-sale agreement, as long as the seller agrees to its terms, so you need to make sure it's complete. This section discusses everything you might need in a purchase-and-sale agreement. (If some of the sections listed here would be overkill for a purchase offer in your area, your agent will let you know.)

 Tip Purchase offers and purchase-and-sale agreements are legally binding documents. In some states, a qualified attorney has to draw up these papers. If you don't live in one of those states, it's still a good idea to have a real estate attorney review your purchase offer (and also the purchase-and-sale agreement, if that's a separate document) before you sign on the dotted line.

Purchase Price

This is the heart and soul of any purchase offer: how much you offer to pay for the house. (But the rest of the offer is just as important, as you'll soon see.) Remember that the offered purchase price is your opening gambit in the negotiating process. Few offers are accepted as made; instead, the seller is more likely to come back with a counteroffer.

Earnest Money

Earnest money is a good-faith deposit you make along with your offer to show that you're serious about buying the house. It's the real estate version of putting your money where your mouth is. You write a check and give it to your agent as part of the offer. Usually, your agent holds the check until you and the seller agree on a price and terms, and then the agent deposits the earnest money in a trust account. At the closing (see Chapter 13), the earnest money goes toward your down payment on the home or toward your closing costs.

How much earnest money should you include? Enough to show the seller you're serious but not more than you can afford to lose if a problem arises. Different areas have different customary amounts, but it's usually in the range of 1 to 3 percent of the purchase price. In some areas, earnest money may be a flat $1,000, and in transactions where the parties know each other, as in sales to family members, it may involve as little as $1.

If a deal falls through, you may get your earnest money back—or you may lose some or all of it. Laws vary from state to state. For example, some states allow a grace period during which you can change your mind about buying a house without forfeiting your earnest money. Beyond such laws, the fate of earnest money when a deal sours depends on what's in your purchase agreement. Both you and the seller must agree on how the money gets disbursed if the sale falls through, so it's important to write contingencies in a way that there's no penalty to you if, for example, the home fails to pass inspection.

 Tip Don't sign a purchase offer unless you understand how your earnest money will be held and under what circumstances it will be returned to you. This is one of the reasons that, even in states that don't require a lawyer to draw up purchase agreements, it's a good idea to consult a lawyer anyway.

Contingencies

A *contingency* is a condition that must be fulfilled for the purchase to move forward. Your purchase agreement isn't binding until all the contingencies it contains have been met. If a problem arises that prevents you or the seller from satisfying a contingency, you can cancel the contract and walk away from the deal. Contingencies protect you from losing your earnest money if something goes wrong and you can't go through with the sale. Here are common contingencies you might want to include in your purchase agreement (talk to your real estate agent or attorney if you have questions):

- **Appraisal.** Your lender requires an independent appraisal of the property to make sure it's worth what you offer. If the appraisal comes in below your purchase price, you can cancel the sale. But if you leave out this contingency, the seller might expect you to come up with the difference between the appraisal and the purchase price yourself.

- **Financing.** This contingency protects you in case your financing falls through. If the lender denies you a mortgage, you can cancel the purchase agreement without penalty. Include a financing contingency even if your bank preapproves you for a mortgage. If you lose your job, for example, and no longer qualify for a loan, you don't want to lose your earnest money as well. The more specific you can be in the financing contingency, the better. Spell out the maximum interest rate you'll pay and the number of points you want to buy on the mortgage, the name of the lender, and a clear definition of what you mean by "diligent efforts" to obtain a loan—for example, you should specify that you're making a diligent effort even if you apply for a loan with just one lender.

Tip The financing contingency should say that you may end the purchase agreement if you fail to get a written commitment for a mortgage loan from the lender named in the agreement.

- **Home inspection.** An essential contingency is the right to have the home thoroughly inspected by a professional home inspector of your choice. If the home inspection reveals problems that are unacceptable to you, like a cracked foundation or a leaky roof, you can cancel the contract (and get your earnest money back) or ask the seller to repair the problems or offer you a credit to pay for their repair. If the seller refuses, you can cancel the sale.

  You may want to specify one or more specialized inspections, such as these, as part of the home inspection contingency:

  — **Lead-based paint inspection.** If the home you want was built before 1978, it may contain lead-based paint, which is a health hazard if you inhale paint dust or a child or pet eats peeling paint. Federal law mandates that buyers have 10 days to inspect for lead-based paint. Page 140 tells you more about federal lead-disclosure requirements.

  — **Pest inspection.** In certain parts of the country, wood-destroying pests such as termites can cause significant, unseen damage to a home. Specify who pays for the pest inspection and make sure it includes all the buildings on the property, including garages, sheds, and barns.

  — **Sewer inspection.** You may need to have the property's sewer lines and (if applicable) septic system checked by a plumber.

  — **Well inspection.** If the property draws its water from a well (as opposed to a municipal water system), add a contingency that says the well water must meet health standards for drinking water.

  — **Roof inspection.** Because of safety and liability concerns, some home inspectors check the roof visually from the ground but won't climb a ladder and walk around on it. You might want a contingency that states that, if the inspector sees something "iffy" about the roof that needs further checking, you can have a roofing company inspect the roof.

— **Radon, mold, or asbestos inspection.** Your home inspector may recommend an additional inspection for one of these health hazards. For example, the inspector may spot some mold in the basement and recommend that you check the building for black mold—a toxin that can cause respiratory problems (and costs a lot to eradicate). This contingency should allow adequate time for these inspections.

• **Seller's disclosure.** As you learned on page 139, most states require sellers to disclose all known problems and material facts about a house to prospective buyers. If you live in a state that doesn't require disclosure (your agent can tell you if you do), make your purchase offer contingent on full disclosure.

• **Homeowners' association documents.** If the home you're buying is governed by a homeowners', condominium, or co-op association or board of directors, put in a contingency that lets you to review and approve of all association documents.

• **Title.** The seller must provide free and clear title to the property (no outstanding liens or claims), and your lender will require a title search to ensure this. Most purchase offers include a contingency that lets you cancel the contract without penalty if the seller can't deliver a clear title—make sure yours does.

• **Final walkthrough.** To avoid unpleasant surprises on moving day, make sure you have the opportunity to tour the home shortly before the closing. Page 287 tells you what to look for on the final walkthrough.

• **Sale of your current home.** If you already own a home, coordinating the sale of your existing home with the purchase of a new one can be challenging. If you find the home you want to buy while your current home is still on the market, this contingency protects both you and the seller. It gives you a specified number of days to sell your existing home before closing on this one. If you don't sell your home within that time frame, you or the seller can cancel the purchase agreement. This protects you from having to pay two mortgages at once, and it protects the seller from keeping the home off the market indefinitely, waiting for a sale that may not happen.

- **Final inspection of new construction.** If you're buying a brand-new home, you may think you don't need a home inspection contingency. Think again. Many homebuyers have moved into a newly built home to encounter major problems with shoddy workmanship and poor materials. Include a contingency that gives you the right to conduct an independent home inspection after the builder has finished construction. If there are problems, the builder can correct them before you move in.

- **Attorney approval.** This contingency gives you five or 10 days to have an attorney look over and approve the purchase agreement. It's a good idea if someone other than an attorney wrote the contract. If the attorney finds problems, you can renegotiate the affected sections.

The seller may also want to include some contingencies in the purchase agreement for the same reason you do—to protect himself if a problem arises. Here are some common seller contingencies:

- **Replacement home.** If the seller hasn't yet found a new home to move to, you may see a contingency that reads something like this: "This transaction is contingent on the seller finding a replacement home." Although it's understandable that the seller wants to coordinate selling his home with buying a new one, that one short sentence gives the seller the right to cancel the sale without penalty at any time—a big problem for you if you've invested time and money in the deal. If the seller insists on a replacement home contingency, be sure to give it an expiration date, such as 30 days. If the seller hasn't found a new home within that period, he must either release the contingency (letting the sale go ahead) or cancel the contract.

- **Time limits.** The seller doesn't want to wait around if you drag your feet applying for a mortgage or getting a home inspection. While you're checking such things off your to-do list, his home is off the market—and he may be missing out on other buyers if the deal falls through. So expect the seller to attach time limits to your contingencies. For example, the seller might give you a week to apply for a loan or two weeks to complete a home inspection.

- **Attorney approval.** Like you, the seller may want to get an attorney's stamp of approval on the language of the contract.

- **More earnest money.** Occasionally, a seller wants to raise your stakes by asking for an increase in your earnest money deposit before the closing, perhaps two weeks after you sign the purchase agreement, for example. From the seller's point of view, this kind of contingency, which is most common during a seller's market, shows the seller you're serious about the deal.

Contingencies, like everything else in your purchase agreement, are negotiable. You don't have to agree to a particular contingency, and neither does the seller. Some, like the financing, appraisal, and home inspection contingencies, are standard (so the seller would be foolish to try to reject them). Expect to spend some time going back and forth on contingencies. It can take a few rounds of negotiations to craft a purchase agreement that both you and the seller can live with.

What's Staying

If something is not nailed down (or sometimes even if it is), don't assume it comes with the home. This includes appliances, window treatments, light fixtures, and so on. These items are considered personal property, not part of the house, so you and the seller need to agree about which items stay with the home (called *conveyances*) and which move out with the seller. Unless your purchase agreement spells out that the refrigerator, washer and dryer, dishwasher, and so on stay with the home, the seller has no obligation to leave them for you.

Who Pays Which Costs

The divvying up of closing costs varies by area, and your agent will work with you to explain which costs are customary for you to pay and which the seller usually picks up. This section of the purchase agreement is where you ask for a seller concession (page 236) to help with closing costs or for the seller to pay for closing costs that are usually the buyer's responsibility.

Access

Between signing the purchase agreement and closing, you need get into the home several times: to inspect the building, measure rooms and windows, try out paint samples or fabric swatches, walk through one last time, and so on. You'd be surprised at how often buyers find it difficult to gain access to a home they're in the process of buying. Add a clause to your purchase agreement that gives you the right to reasonable access at reasonable times with a certain amount of advance notice, such as 72 hours. The key word here is "reasonable." Until you close on the property, it's still the seller's home, so don't go overboard with demands to get in and take yet another look around.

Closing Date

Several weeks—or several months—may pass before you're ready to close on the property. Your purchase agreement gives an outside date for the closing. Your agent can help you choose a realistic one. Thirty days is typical.

Possession

In most sales, the buyer takes possession of the home immediately after closing. Sometimes, though, you or the seller need to make special arrangements. You may need to move into the home before the sale because you've already sold your old home, for example, or the seller may need to remain there for a while afterward. If that's the case, include a rental clause that spells out the rent you or the seller will pay and the length of the rental agreement.

Acceptance

Your purchase offer comes with a time limit, usually 24 to 48 hours. If the seller fails to respond within that time, your offer expires. Although there may be situations when you want to give the seller more time (perhaps the seller is out of town and the listing agent needs more time to get in touch), 24 hours is usually plenty of time for a seller to accept or reject your offer or respond with a counteroffer. You don't want to spend several days tied to an offer that a seller might reject when you could be looking at other homes.

 Note If you're making an offer on a bank-owned home (an REO, explained on page 127), the bank may require up to four days to respond to your offer.

Negotiating: The Art of the Deal

After receiving your offer, the seller has three options:

- **Accept it.** If the seller is satisfied with the purchase price and conditions of your offer, you've got a deal. Your offer becomes the basis for a purchase-and-sale agreement between you and the seller, setting the wheels in motion for you to buy the house.

- **Make a counteroffer.** More likely, the seller will make a counteroffer. In a counteroffer, the seller changes anything in your offer she dislikes or doesn't agree to, including the purchase price, contingencies, concessions you've asked for, conveyances, or the closing date—everything is fair game. But a counteroffer also signals that the seller is open to negotiating (and now the ball's back in your court).

- **Reject it.** Sometimes, a seller will flat-out say no. This often happens when the seller feels your offer is unrealistically low. A rejection indicates that the seller doesn't want to negotiate (but see page 249 about responding to a rejection in a buyer's market).

It's rare for a seller to accept a buyer's initial offer, so be prepared for counteroffers, refusals, demands, and compromises. When you get a counteroffer, it's your turn to look over the suggested price and conditions and decide whether to accept them, reject them, or counter with adjustments of your own. It's very common to go back and forth for several rounds, crossing out numbers and clauses and writing in new ones before you and the seller reach an agreement.

 Although you and the seller have plenty to say to each other during negotiations, you probably won't sit down and discuss matters face to face. Negotiations almost always take place through your agents—and that's as it should be. Your agent is an expert negotiator who can explain terms and offer advice, so you have time to mull things over before you respond.

Negotiations can be stressful and frustrating, each side thinking that the other is being unreasonable and pig-headed. To make negotiations go smoothly, stay calm and professional. These tips help:

- **Know the kind of market you're in.** Different market temperatures call for different strategies. If you're in a hot seller's market, you won't have a lot of wiggle room for concessions and contingencies. But if the market is a cooler buyer's market, the seller's eagerness to close may work to your advantage. Page 243 tells you how to gauge whether you're in a buyer's or a seller's market.

- **Put a human face on the negotiations.** In most transactions, the buyer's and the seller's agents handle negotiations for you: Your agent presents your offer to the seller's agent, who gives it to the seller. The seller and her agent confer, and then the seller's agent presents the counteroffer to your agent, who discusses it with you. And on it goes. Usually, that's how you want things to work, leaving negotiations to the professionals. In some situations, though, being one step removed from the negotiations may feel too impersonal—the parties trying to agree can see each other as obstacles, not people. If you're comfortable with the idea (and your agent agrees it would help negotiations), meet the seller face to face, sitting down with your respective agents and talking about the purchase. Or write a friendly letter, explaining how much you love the house and the reasoning behind your offer, and ask your agent to deliver it to the seller. You and the seller will see each other as living, breathing human beings, and you may be able to finalize your agreement faster.

- **Understand where the seller is coming from.** The seller has goals and pressures related to the sale. If you know what these are, you're in a better position to negotiate. For example, a seller who's in a hurry to close might be willing to compromise on price or conveyances if this speeds up the sale. Ask your agent if she knows anything about the seller's situation that might aid you in negotiations.

- **Play your cards close to your chest.** Knowledge is power, so don't give too much away. For example, if you've been preapproved for a loan that's higher than your offer, you don't want the seller to know that; she might hold out for a higher price. Don't give away any information that the seller can use to her advantage.

- **Know your priorities.** Identify your must-haves and your deal-breakers. When you know what's important to you, it's easier to compromise on issues that aren't so high on your priority list.

- **Ask for something you could live without.** You might add a few terms to your initial purchase offer with the intention of using them as bargaining chips. For example, you might request the washer and dryer as conveyances or ask for more money than you're willing to accept toward repairs. If the seller balks, you can agree to drop that request—and insist on something you really want in its place.

- **Don't get too emotionally involved.** If you care too much about buying *this* particular house, you put yourself at a disadvantage in negotiations. Seasoned negotiators say the one who wins is the one who has the least to lose, the one who's ready to walk away from the table. So keep a cool head. Ask yourself, "What's the worst that would happen if this purchase falls through?" And keep looking at other houses as you negotiate, as a reminder that you have other options. That way, if things don't work out, you can move forward more easily.

- **Don't get too competitive.** The goal of negotiation is to arrive at an agreement that's satisfactory to *both* parties. Don't develop the mindset that you're out to "beat" the seller, or you might find that the seller stops negotiating. You're aiming for a win-win situation, not one where you win and the seller loses.

If Buyer's Remorse Strikes

I put in an offer on a home, and the seller accepted. At first I was ecstatic, but now I'm scared. How do I deal with buyer's remorse?

Buyer's remorse may pounce at any time as you go through the process of buying a house—even after you move in. It's the uneasy feeling, which might keep you up at night, that you've made a big mistake. You're not alone. Buyer's remorse is common among first-time homebuyers who worry about the amount of debt they're taking on, the lifestyle changes that come with owning a home, and even whether they might have found something better if they'd kept looking. If you feel that way, don't panic. You can work through buyer's remorse and go on to enjoy your new home.

The best way to deal with buyer's remorse is to avoid it in the first place. Do your homework at all stages of the home-buying process. That's why you bought this book, after all. If you set your budget (page 26), figured out how much home you can afford (page 31), come up with the down payment (page 146) and closing costs (page 234) you need, determined your housing needs (page 52), researched neighborhoods (page 72), and found a good agent to guide you (page 90), you did everything you could to find the right home. Remind yourself that you've done this groundwork and you're not rushing into the purchase blindly.

You can also duck buyer's remorse by avoiding situations that encourage second-guessing. For example, friends and family may be excited for you—but they're probably also full of words of "wisdom," criticism, and horror stories you don't need to hear. Whether you're hearing well-meaning advice or a flood of negativity, remember that these people aren't you, and their situation isn't yours.

Similarly, once you have a purchase agreement in hand, stop looking at other homes. Agreeing to buy one home can make every new home that comes on the market look like the best deal ever. Don't subject yourself to that. You had good reasons for deciding on this home. Focus on those—and stop checking new listings.

And if you *really* can't go through with the sale, the first thing to do is check your purchase agreement. There may be a cancellation clause that allows you to opt out of the deal without penalty if you cancel within a certain time frame. If you put together a good purchase offer (page 249), you have contingencies that give you an out under certain circumstances—from failing to get funding to an unsatisfactory home inspection to problems with the title—so you don't have to worry about being stuck with a lemon. Finally, if you're willing to say goodbye to your earnest money, you can always just walk away (be aware, though, that the seller may sue for damages and the agents may sue for their commissions if you do this).

But it doesn't have to come to that. Know that many, many buyers feel twinges of doubt on their way to becoming satisfied homeowners. If you're aware that buyer's remorse might hit you, you'll be able to work through it quickly and get on with the purchase of your home.

11 Prepare for the Closing

Congratulations—you've got a deal! Once the ink has dried on your new purchase-and-sale agreement and the fizz has left the celebratory champagne, you're probably left wondering, "Now what?" You've got a contract to buy a home, but the real work is just beginning. Now is the time to acquire financing (Chapter 8), arrange for a home inspection (Chapter 12), and work your way through a to-do list of other tasks to get ready for the closing—the official act of transferring ownership from the seller to you. Depending on the contingencies in your purchase agreement and when you want to close, you may have to move fast.

This chapter explains how to clear the way for the closing by removing those contingencies, initiating a title search, buying insurance and perhaps a home warranty, getting ready to move, and walking through the house to inspect it one last time.

Check Off Contingencies

Your purchase agreement contains a number of *contingencies* (page 251)—conditions that you or the seller must meet before the sale can happen. Some contingencies, such as the financing and home inspection contingencies, protect you if a serious problem arises that prevents you from buying the house. Others protect the seller, like a contingency that limits how much the seller will pay for repairs.

When you're satisfied that a contingency has been met, you remove that contingency from the purchase agreement. For example, when your lender sends you a commitment letter approving your loan, it's time to remove the financing contingency (see below). The seller also removes his contingencies as they're met. Although you can remove a contingency with a phone call to your real estate agent or lawyer, it's a good idea to do it in writing. That way, if problems arise later, you can prove when the contingency was met. Any contingencies either you or the seller doesn't release can become grounds for canceling the contract. For example, if your home inspection reveals problems with the home's structure, you can open a new round of negotiations with the seller to deal with those problems—or you can walk away from the sale because the house didn't meet the home inspection contingency.

Removing the Financing Contingency

You probably included a financing contingency in your purchase agreement to protect yourself in case you can't get a mortgage—if the lender denies your loan application, you can get your earnest money deposit back and cancel the purchase. When your lender sends you a commitment letter—its official approval of your loan—you've cleared that hurdle, and you can remove the financing contingency from the agreement.

 Tip Don't remove your financing contingency on the basis of a phone call from your loan originator. Wait until you have the commitment letter in hand. Until you've got a commitment in writing, something could still go wrong with your mortgage application.

The seller may agree to the financing contingency only if it includes a time limit—usually between two and six weeks—which protects the seller from taking the home off the market indefinitely if you have trouble getting a loan. If you don't get a commitment letter during that time, the seller has two options: extend the time limit or cancel the sale.

Tip Get preapproved for a loan (page 34) before you go house-hunting. Preapproval speeds up the final approval process, so you'll worry less about getting your commitment letter within the timeframe the financing contingency allows.

Removing the Appraisal Contingency

Your purchase agreement may include a contingency that says the lender's appraiser must find the home worth at least what you offered for it. In some states, you have a limited time to get the appraisal done—in California, for example, the standard is 17 days from the time you sign the purchase agreement. If all goes smoothly, the appraisal satisfies the bank, and you remove the appraisal contingency from your purchase agreement. If you and your agent have done your homework when you figured out the house's worth, you shouldn't have any problem with the appraisal.

Sometimes, though, an appraiser determines that a house is worth less than what you offered. A seller could overprice her house, for example, or multiple bidders could drive the price unrealistically high. Fast-dropping home prices or a flood of preforeclosures and foreclosures in the neighborhood can also affect a house's value—if most of the recent comparable sales are short sales, for example, your appraisal is likely to come in low.

If the house appraises for less than your offer, you have four options:

- **Get a second appraisal.** Sometimes the lender's appraiser covers a large geographic region and may be unfamiliar with the area where you're buying. If that happens, get an appraisal from a local firm and ask the lender to review the new appraisal.

 Tip If you decide to get a second appraisal, ask the seller to pay for it. The seller has taken the house off the market and invested significant time in selling you the home. If a second appraisal could salvage the sale, he might make the investment.

- **Negotiate for a lower price.** The seller may be willing to accept a price that's more in line with the bank's appraisal rather than lose the sale.

- **Pay the difference out of pocket.** If you *really* want the house and the seller won't budge on the price, pay the difference between the appraised value and what you offered. Your lender analyzes the home's loan-to-value ratio (page 39) because it doesn't want to lose money on your mortgage. If you put down more cash, thereby lowering the amount you need to borrow, the lender may move forward with the loan.

- **Cancel the sale.** The whole reason you put an appraisal contingency in the purchase agreement was to give yourself an emergency exit if there was a problem. You can take that exit if a low appraisal sours you on the house.

Removing the Home Inspection Contingency

You never know what problems lurk just out of sight when you walk through your future home for the first time. That's why a home inspection contingency is essential to every purchase agreement (it's so important that Chapter 12 is dedicated to showing you what a home inspector looks for). Schedule an inspection as soon as you sign your purchase agreement so you have plenty of time to go over the inspector's report.

Don't expect a "perfect" report. No home stays in newly built condition forever—and even new construction can have problems with workmanship or materials. It's up to you to decide which problems you can live with and which you want repaired as a condition of sale—or whether the problems are so severe that you no longer want to buy the home.

 Some states give the seller a chance to repair problems within a certain period of time before you can cancel a deal. Ask your real estate agent about your state's requirements.

Once you get the home inspection report (page 302), sit down and write up a list of repairs the house needs. Use this list as you review problems with the seller. You need to address important problems, but try not to go overboard. If you push too hard on minor issues, the seller might tell you to forget the whole thing. And if the seller has included a contingency that limits the amount he'll spend on repairs, you may have to prioritize your wish list of repairs.

When you talk with the seller, you want him to answer two questions: How will he address the problems (Fix them himself? Bring in a contractor?) and who picks up the tab? If the seller refuses to make all the repairs you want, you need to ask one more question: What do I do now?

How will the problems get fixed?

Some sellers might try to make the repairs themselves; lots of weekend handymen have a higher opinion of their do-it-yourself skills than they deserve. It's in your interest to make sure that you get high-quality workmanship that permanently fixes the problem. The bottom line: Insist that the seller use a professional to make repairs.

The seller may want to choose who does the agreed-upon work. Unless you can vet the person's work, don't agree. After closing, it will be your home, not the seller's. Remember, at this point, the seller wants to make repairs as quickly and as cheaply as possible. But you want repairs to be well done and long lasting.

 Tip Get estimates and have them in hand when you negotiate repairs with the seller. It's easier to discuss repairs when you know what they cost.

Who picks up the tab?

It seems only fair that the seller pay for any and all repairs, right? After all, these problems cropped up while he lived there.

To an extent, that's true. But a lot depends on the context of the sale, and you have to use your intuition when you negotiate repairs. A seller who's lowered his purchase price or is selling in a hot market may decide that the hassle and cost of extensive repairs aren't worth it and try to find a less demanding buyer. On the other hand, if you know the seller's eager to close the deal, you've got some bargaining power.

 Tip Check out the negotiating tips for making an offer on page 256. They apply to this kind of negotiation as well.

When you and the seller agree on which repairs are his responsibility, he can pay for them in one of three ways. He can:

- **Arrange and pay for repairs before the closing.** If you take this route, make sure the seller lets you approve the contractor before work begins. Then make sure the contractor shows up and keep track of his progress (if he doesn't finish the repairs in a timely manner, you might have to push back the closing). Double-check the work on your final walkthrough (see page 286).

- **Reduce the purchase price.** This option can save you money on interest (because you borrow less money), property taxes, points, and other closing costs calculated as a percentage of the purchase price. But, of course, you have to come up with the cash to make repairs yourself.

- **Give you a credit at closing.** Instead of receiving all proceeds of the sale that remain after he pays off his mortgage and other costs, the seller returns an agreed-upon amount to you. You can get the money in cash, or the seller may put it into a special account designated for repairs (your lender might insist on that second option to make sure the repairs get done).

What if the seller insists on selling "as is"?

You may find a seller who's uninterested in making or paying for repairs, essentially telling you to "take it or leave it." If that happens, you may decide to remove the home inspection contingency from your purchase agreement and buy the home as is. Before you do that, though, make sure you have a good idea of how much the repairs will cost and whether you can afford them. Or you can cancel the purchase agreement (thanks to the home inspection contingency), abandon the deal—and get back to house-hunting.

Removing Other Contingencies

You remove any other contingencies—like the preliminary title report and the final walkthrough—in the same way you remove the contingencies described above. When the seller meets a condition, say so in writing, and the transaction takes another step forward.

 Tip Many contingencies have a time limit, such as 7 days to apply for financing or 17 days to complete a home inspection. Keep a close eye on contingencies' expiration dates; if the date slips past and you haven't acted, you may no longer be able to enforce that contingency.

What if you find that you can't remove a contingency? For example, say your bank offers an interest rate that's higher than your financing contingency allows? Or you can't meet the appraisal contingency because the appraisal came in lower than expected?

In this situation, you've got three choices:

- **Negotiate with the seller.** You may be able to extend a contingency's time limit or revise the purchase price. Many sellers prefer renegotiating to losing the sale.

- **Waive the contingency.** You can remove any contingency you put in the contract, even if the conditions it describes haven't been met. You do this with a written, signed release stating you waive the contingency. Think long and hard before you do so. You put it into the purchase agreement to protect yourself in the transaction, and you should be reasonably sure that dropping the contingency won't cause problems for you down the road.

- **Cancel the sale.** You wrote contingencies into your purchase agreement so you'd have an out if the sale doesn't proceed as you expect. If a failed contingency makes the sale impossible for you—if you don't obtain financing, for example—you can cancel the sale. If that happens, you and the seller should sign a document that releases both of you from the purchase agreement. After that, you should get back your earnest money.

 Note The seller has to agree that the contingency can't be met and the sale is over for you to get your earnest money back. If the seller feels you're canceling the sale frivolously, he can try to get some or all of your earnest money—or even sue for damages or to try to make you go through with the sale.

All About Titles and Deeds

At the closing, money changes hands, and then the seller transfers ownership of the property to you. That transfer involves two elements:

- *Title* is a legal concept of ownership. When you hold title to a property, it means you own that property. As page 270 explains, there are several different ways you can hold title.

- The *deed* is a written document that records the title. It says in black and white who owns the property. The final step in the sale of a house is when your escrow officer or attorney records the deed with your local property office.

To prepare for this transfer of ownership, you need to do two things:

- Make sure that the seller is really the property's owner and has a legal right to sell you the property.

- Decide what you want the deed to say about your ownership of the property—that is, how you'll hold title.

This section explains what you need to know about titles and deeds to get ready for the closing.

Getting Clear Title

For your new home to truly be yours, the seller needs to give you a "clear" title; that means that no one has any claims on the property that could interfere with the seller's ability to sell it—or with your ability to own it. Soon after you sign the purchase agreement, your attorney or escrow agent starts the process of making sure that the seller has clear title by conducting a *title search*. This is the first step in getting *title insurance*, which offers protection if someone makes a legal claim against the title—perhaps a long-lost relative of a former owner or a contractor who never got paid for work done on the property. Your lender requires that you buy title insurance to protect the lender's interest in the home; you can also buy title insurance for yourself.

 Tip Many states regulate how much title companies can charge for title searches and title insurance. If your state doesn't, shop around to get the best deal for your money.

The title search

Before a title company issues you a title insurance policy, it does a *title search*, tracing the property's ownership and checking for claims against it. (Some states require that an attorney, rather than an insurance company, conduct the title search.) When someone researches a title, they look through decades' worth of legal records—deeds, tax records, divorce decrees, court judgments, wills, bankruptcy filings, and so on—with three main goals:

- **To establish that the seller has the right to sell the property.** Events like a divorce or a death in the family can affect who owns a home. It's also not unheard of for a distant relative of a past owner to lay claim to a property. The title search tries to prevent such surprises.

- **To discover any liens that must be paid off at the closing.** A *lien* is a legal claim made against a property, usually by someone to whom the seller owes money. Examples include second mortgages (where the bank places a lien against the property as collateral), tax liens (where the owner owes back taxes), mechanic's liens (for money owed to contractors or vendors), and liens for back alimony or child support. A lien may be consensual (the property owner agreed to it) or nonconsensual (a legal judgment against the property owner attached the lien to the property). If a property has liens against it, the money owed will most likely come out of the seller's proceeds at closing. But unknown liens can threaten the sale.

- **To identify restrictions and easements associated with the property.** An *easement* gives someone other than the owner the right to use the property for a specific purpose. For example, most properties have utility easements for electric and telephone lines so utility companies can plant telephone poles and string electric and phone wires across a front yard. Or there might be a view easement, which prevents the property owner from blocking a neighbor's view, or an easement that lets a neighbor use the property's driveway to access her property.

If the title search turns up a problem in any of these areas, the title has what's called a **defect** (or sometimes a **cloud**). About a third of all title searches uncover some kind of defect. Often, these are small oversights that are easily put right: a missing signature on a document or a paid-off lien whose holder forgot to file a release. The title insurance company or attorney conducting the title search prepares a preliminary report that lists any defects so you can get them corrected before closing. You get the final title search report at closing.

 Note If a search finds serious defects on the title, you have grounds to back out of the sale.

Title insurance

Title defects can turn up even after a successful title search. That's what title insurance is for—it protects the policyholder from losing money if an unforeseen title defect crops up. As part of your mortgage agreement, you have to buy your lender title insurance to cover their investment, and you have the option to buy an owner's policy as well. For either kind of policy, title insurance covers any costs you or your bank incur defending against a title challenge. In addition, here's what each covers:

- **Lender's policy.** If a defect turns up that voids your title to the property, lender's title insurance pays off your mortgage. Because it protects the lender's investment, the amount of protection the policy offers decreases as you make payments toward your mortgage, and it ends when you pay off the mortgage.

- **Owner's policy.** If you purchase an owner's title insurance policy (they're optional), it protects you if a defect results in the loss of your title to the home. Typically, this policy covers a property's full value, and it remains in effect for as long as you (or your heirs) own the property. Most policies protect against loss or damage from forgery, misrepresentations of identity, and liens in the public record that come to light after you've bought the home. If you have any questions about the policy, ask a real estate attorney.

Title insurance costs vary widely according to area (some states regulate title insurance pricing) and the home's purchase price. You pay for a title insurance policy just once, at the closing. There aren't any continuing monthly premiums.

Putting Your Name on the Deed

A *deed* is a legal document that, when recorded with your local government, formally establishes legal ownership of a piece of property. The deed is the instrument that transfers title from one owner to another, from the seller to you. Although recording the deed is the very last thing that happens in a sale, your attorney or closing agent needs to prepare the document ahead of time. For that to happen, you need to decide on the form of ownership you want, because it's recorded on the deed.

There are several ways you can hold title to a property. Each has different legal and tax ramifications, so discuss the options with your attorney and accountant.

 If your circumstances change, you can change the kind of title you hold. For example, you can start off with joint tenancy and later set up a trust and transfer title to it. If you want to change the way you hold title, consult an attorney who can draw up the paperwork for you.

Sole property

If you're a single person buying a home by yourself, you'll hold the title as your *sole property*. Sole property means that the house belongs to you and you alone—no one else has any interest in the title. If you're married or in a domestic partnership, you can still own the house as sole property. You might do this if your spouse has poor credit and wouldn't qualify for a mortgage, for example. In such a case, you need to talk to an attorney about whether sole property is the right decision for you and how to make sure that you retain sole ownership despite your marital status. Your spouse may have to sign a *quitclaim deed* to relinquish any claim to the property.

Sole property means sole responsibility. If you live alone, that makes sense. If you're married and you're the sole owner, you're responsible for all house-related expenses: PITI, maintenance, repairs, and so on. If your spouse contributes to these expenses, he or she may be able to claim an interest in the home's title later on.

Joint tenants with right of survivorship

Joint tenancy titles mean that each person listed on the deed owns an equal share of the property—if you buy a home with your spouse, for example, you each own 50 percent of the property.

If one of you dies, the full title automatically transfers to the other; because you have a joint tenancy with right of survivorship, you don't need to go to probate court (the kind of court that deals with wills and estates) to establish ownership.

You have to meet four standards (called "unities" in Realtor-speak) for joint tenancy:

- **Time.** Each of the joint owners must receive the title at the same time.
- **Title.** Each owner must receive title via the same instrument (the same deed).
- **Interest.** Each owner holds an equal share in a property.
- **Possession.** Each owner has an equal right to occupy the property.

With joint tenancy, both parties have equal benefits and responsibilities with regard to the property. For example, you can't rent out a guest house and keep the money for yourself; your spouse is equally entitled to it. And your spouse can't take out a loan using the house as collateral and then divorce you, leaving you to pay the debt; your ex-spouse is equally responsible for the loan.

Tenancy in common

Unlike joint tenancy, *tenancy in common* requires only one unity: possession. Under this arrangement, co-owners have an equal right to occupy the property, but you may own the property in unequal shares. For example, if you buy a house with someone and you put up 80 percent of the down payment and the other person contributes only 20 percent, tenancy in common allows you to own an 80 percent share in the home. Those shares apply to the entire house, not to certain rooms or areas. If you want, you can sell your share of the property without the other's consent (this works both ways, of course), unless you have a written agreement that says otherwise.

 Note If you want to split ownership into unequal shares, you must specify how you want those shares divided in the deed. Otherwise, the assumption is that ownership is 50/50.

Tenancy in common doesn't include the right of survivorship. Unless you specify in your will that you want your co-owner to inherit your share of the property if you die, your interest in the property gets divided up among your heirs.

 Note If a co-owner in a joint tenancy sells his or her part of the property, joint tenancy is broken and the title becomes tenancy in common.

Tenancy by the entirety

In *tenancy by the entirety*, the law treats the property's co-owners as though they were a single person. From a legal perspective, you and your spouse each own 100 percent of the property (not just 50 percent), and each of you has the legal right to sell the home but only with the other's consent. Tenancy by the entirety protects your home from creditors. If, for example, your spouse is in default on a credit card balance, the creditor can't come after your spouse's share of the home, because you each own the whole house. Each spouse also has the right of survivorship, so if one of you dies, the other automatically gets sole interest in the house without going through probate court.

Not all states recognize tenancy by the entirety (check with your real estate attorney), and only married couples (or, in some states, like Hawaii and Vermont, registered domestic partners) qualify.

Community property

Community property is another kind of title that's not available everywhere. And in the states that allow it, only married couples (or, in some cases, registered domestic partners) can own real estate as community property. If you and your spouse own your home as community property, each of you owns half the property. You and your spouse can will your half to anyone you please. While you're both alive, though, neither of you can sell or transfer your interest in the property to anyone else without the other's consent.

Currently, community property states include Alaska, Arizona, California, Idaho, Louisiana, Nevada, New Mexico, Texas, Washington, and Wisconsin. A few of these (Alaska, Arizona, California, Nevada, and Wisconsin) also allow *community property with right of survivorship*. In those states, if one owner dies, the other automatically inherits the property without going through probate—neither of you can leave your share of the property to a different heir.

Living trust

A trust is a legal structure where a trustee holds property for someone else (called the *beneficiary*). You can set up a ***living trust*** to own your home. You're the trustee, and you control the trust for as long as you live (or until you sell the property). If you die, the trust quickly distributes your home and any other parts of your estate to your beneficiaries. There's no need to go to probate court. Unlike a will, which becomes public information after you die, the details of the trust remain private. A living trust can also significantly reduce estate taxes.

Living trusts are revocable, so if your circumstances change, you can change the terms of the trust. You need a real estate or estate planning attorney to help you set up a living trust and transfer title to it.

Survey the Property

Your lender may require you to get a survey of the property to determine its boundaries and check for ***encroachments***—structures, such as buildings or fences, that cross the property line. Either you or your neighbor can be the one who's encroaching on the other's property. You may be able to deal with an encroachment by getting an easement in which the encroached-upon party grants permission for the encroachment. In some cases, however, you might have to tear down the encroaching structure.

 Tip Ask whether the seller had his property surveyed in the past. You may be able to save some money by having this survey updated or (if your lender will accept it) submitting it with an affidavit from the seller saying he hasn't made any changes to the property since the survey.

Homeowner's Insurance

It would be nice if someone could guarantee that disaster will never strike your new house, but that kind of guarantee doesn't exist. Insurance offers the next-best thing when it comes to peace of mind. Homeowner's insurance protects your investment in your home, so if your home is damaged or destroyed, you're covered. Your lender will require that you buy a homeowner's insurance policy, and you'll need to show evidence of the policy at the closing.

Homeowner's insurance has two main components:

- **Hazard insurance**, which covers physical damage to your property, such as from fire or wind. It also covers your possessions if, for example, they're stolen or damaged in a fire.

- **Liability insurance**, which protects you if someone is injured on your property by anything from slipping on icy steps to being injured by a pet or family member.

The sections below detail both parts of your homeowner's insurance policy.

Hazard Insurance

The homeowner's policy you buy must meet your lender's basic requirements for hazard insurance. What the lender wants, of course, is to protect its investment in your mortgage. Your home is the loan's collateral, and if some catastrophe destroys that collateral, your lender is out the money.

To you, however, your home is more than just an investment, and hazard insurance protects you, too. It's in your interest to buy a policy that's affordable and offers the coverage you need if the unthinkable happens.

Hazard insurance covers both the structure and contents (your personal property) of a home. If a grease fire breaks out in the kitchen, for example, the insurance company pays to fix the smoke and fire damage. If a hailstorm breaks a window, you're covered. If burglars steal your television, you'll get money to replace it. Most policies also cover personal property you temporarily remove from the home, like a laptop computer that's stolen from your car.

You may need supplemental coverage for these circumstances:

- **Structures and fixtures that aren't part of your house.** Examples include a separate garage or shed, barns or workshops, fences, walkways, and the driveway.

- **Landscaping**, including trees, shrubs, and other plants.

- **Loss of use**, which pays for your lodging and meals (beyond an established normal cost) if your house is so damaged that you have to move out while you have it repaired or rebuilt. Standard policies cover loss of use for a year; you can buy two-year coverage if you prefer. The latter is can be a good idea if you've got to rebuild from the ground up.

- **Personal property.** For some policies, you need to make a list of personal property, such as jewelry, computers, and artwork; they cover these items up to a set amount. If you want protection beyond that, you can buy additional coverage.

- **Property related to a home business**, such as office equipment and inventory.

Be aware that standard homeowner's policy doesn't cover some hazards, so look carefully. Damage from these causes is typically excluded:

- Flooding
- Earthquakes
- Mudslides
- War or law-enforcement activity
- Power outages
- Sewer back-ups
- Vermin
- Dry rot
- Poor maintenance
- Vacancy of 60 days or longer

You may be able to buy supplemental coverage for some of these hazards (the next two sections discuss flood and earthquake insurance), but it can be expensive and some insurers don't offer it.

Flood insurance

Standard homeowner's policies don't cover damage from flooding. Instead, you buy flood insurance from the federal government's National Flood Insurance Program (NFIP). You can learn about NFIP's residential coverage policies at *www.floodsmart.gov*.

If you're in a designated flood zone, your lender will require that you buy flood insurance. But you may want to consider buying a policy anyway, no matter where you live. Even areas that aren't at regular risk of flooding can end up flooded when a nearby river overflows, a deep snow cover melts quickly, or heavy rains fall day after day. NFIP covers up to $250,000 for house damage and $100,000 for personal property damage. If you want more coverage, talk to an independent insurance agent who can help you find a private company that sells supplemental flood coverage.

 Tip Not sure whether your new home is at risk of flooding? Use NFIP's One-Step Flood Risk Profile to check. Go to *www.floodsmart.gov* and fill out the profile form. Click Go, and you get an assessment of your property's flood risk, estimated annual premiums, and contact info for insurance agents in your area.

Earthquake insurance

Earthquake damage is excluded from standard homeowners policies, so if you live in an area where earthquakes are a concern, buy coverage. You can add a rider to your standard policy or buy a separate policy.

 Tip To assess the chances that an earthquake will shake you up, take a look at FEMA's earthquake risk table at *http://tinyurl.com/y99xbqt*. Also, check out the U.S. Geological Survey's earthquake maps at *http://earthquake.usgs.gov*.

Liability Insurance

When you become a homeowner, you're responsible for what happens on your property. Liability insurance protects you if someone is injured on your property or by a member of your household. Coverage is twofold:

- **Medical bills.** This pays the medical bills of "other people" (that is, people who don't live in your household) if they're injured on your property. It also pays other people's medical bills if a member of your household (including most pets) injures someone while *not* on your property. Policies cap medical liability at a certain amount, usually $100,000. With medical costs skyrocketing, it's a good idea to buy additional coverage—aim for at least $1,000,000.

- **Personal liability.** If someone sues you for personal injury or for damage to their property, this covers your legal fees and any damages you have to pay, up to a certain limit. Coverage includes incidents that occur on or off your property caused by any member of your household.

To protect yourself from any of the situations below, you have to get supplemental liability coverage:

- Injuries caused while driving (this is covered by your auto insurance policy, not your homeowners policy)

- Liability related to a home business you operate

- Injuries to domestic workers, such as a housekeeper or nanny

- Injuries to tenants

Liability related to pets is also a tricky issue. In some states, insurers can refuse to cover pets or can charge a higher premium for exotic pets or certain breeds of dog, including German shepherds, rottweilers, huskies, and pit bulls. In other states, insurers can't refuse coverage based on a dog's breed—they can only do so if *an individual* dog has a recorded history of causing injury or damage.

Types of Homeowner's Policies

Insurers use standard forms to write homeowner's insurance policies. Most commonly, they use the forms below:

- **HO-1.** This policy offers the most basic coverage, insuring against fire, lightning, windstorm, hail, vandalism, theft, damage from vehicles and aircraft, explosions, riots or civil commotion, glass breakage, smoke, volcanic eruptions, and personal liability. It protects your home's contents, but you must list items separately to receive coverage.

- **HO-2.** Called "broad coverage," this policy covers everything in HO-1 and adds these hazards: building collapse; freezing or discharge of water or steam from plumbing, heating, or air-conditioning systems; falling objects; damage from the weight of snow, ice, or sleet; and rupture of steam or hot water heating systems.

- **HO-3.** Your insurance agent may refer to this as an "all-risk" policy, and it offers the broadest coverage (it also costs the most). Instead of listing specific hazards it covers, as the two policies above do, it lists only the hazards it *excludes*, such as floods and earthquakes. You can, however, buy riders that cover most excluded hazards. (If you need flood insurance, you can buy it from the government, as page 275 explains.)

 Note Because it offers the most thorough coverage, most homeowners buy an HO-3 policy.

- **HO-6.** This is a policy designed for condominium and co-op owners. It covers the contents of your home, personal liability, and can fill in gaps not covered by your condo association or co-op's insurance policy.

- **HO-8.** This policy is designed for older homes. Their old-fashioned building materials, such as plaster walls and slate roofs, can be prohibitively expensive to replace if the home is damaged or destroyed. If replacing your home would cost more than its market value, this policy insures your home at market value. A "modified replacement policy" will replace old-fashioned materials with their current counterparts—dry wall instead of plaster, for example.

Shopping for Homeowner's Insurance

Before you choose a policy, shop around to get the most coverage for the lowest cost. These tips help:

- **Make sure you're insuring for the right amount.** Pay attention to your policy limit. This amount, which appears on your policy's declarations page, determines the maximum you'll get if your home is destroyed. For example, say you insure your three-bedroom, two-bath home for $200,000, the price you paid for it. A few years later, a fire destroys the home. Building costs have gone up, and a new home with three bedrooms and two baths now costs $250,000. Because your policy limit is $200,000, your insurer won't pay more than that, so you have to make up the difference or settle for less in your replacement home. Talk to your insurance agent about building costs per square foot to make sure you're buying enough coverage to replace your home. (Or ask about an extended or guaranteed replacement cost policy, described in the next bullet point.)

- **Insure the structure for extended or guaranteed replacement cost.** If a fire destroys your house, for example, these options insure that you can rebuild a home that's similar even if building costs are on the rise. "Extended replacement cost" covers the home's insured value plus actual building costs and pays out a certain amount above the policy limit—usually 120 or 125 percent. "Guaranteed replacement cost" is similar but comes without a cap. These options make your policy more expensive than actual value or plain-vanilla replacement cost policies, but if your home is destroyed, you won't have to settle for less than what you had.

- **Insure your possessions for replacement cost.** Most homeowner's policies cover your possessions, usually for up to 40 percent of your home's value. If your home is insured for $200,000, for example, the insurer covers your possessions for up to $80,000. This coverage is usually actual value coverage, which takes depreciation into account. Here's what that means: If you bought a computer for $1,000 a few years ago and the computer is now worth $200, your insurance covers the computer's loss for $200. For a little more money, however, you can insure your possessions for *replacement* cost. With this kind of policy, if something you own is damaged or stolen, the insurer pays the cost to replace the item at current prices—no depreciation involved.

- **Know exactly what's covered.** Although most policies cover the contents and structure of your home in case of damage from fire, hail, wind, explosion, and theft, standard homeowners insurance doesn't protect against flooding or earthquake damage. If you need that kind of coverage, you need to augment your standard policy with an addition to the policy called a rider (which will cost you more).

- **Consider a high deductible.** An insurance policy's deductible is the money you pay out of pocket when you file a claim—in other words, you have to pay the deductible before the insurance company shells out any money. Raising the amount of the deductible lowers your insurance premium because it reduces the insurer's risk. Of course, going with a higher deductible represents a gamble: If disaster strikes and you have to file a claim, you'll pay the high deductible first. But for many homeowners, the savings realized through years of lower premiums makes that gamble worthwhile. If you decide to go with a high deductible, check with your lender; many banks limit the size of the deductible.

- **Make your home less of a risk.** Install smoke and carbon monoxide detectors and a security system. You may be able to talk the seller into doing this as a condition of the sale. If not, make these improvements after you take possession of your home and present your insurer with evidence that you've done so.

- **Shop around.** All insurers are *not* created equal. Once you determine your insurance needs, check with several companies about the policies they offer and go for the best value.

- **Bundle your policies.** Many insurers offer discounts if you have more than one policy with them. If the company that insures your car also offers homeowners insurance, see if they can give you the best deal.

Get a Home Warranty

When you buy a new car, it comes with a warranty, a guarantee that the car and all its parts will function the way they're supposed to for a designated period of time or use. Your home is an even bigger investment, and many homebuyers want a similar guarantee—along with the peace of mind it brings. If that sounds like you, you're probably thinking about buying a home warranty.

Warranties for Existing Homes

Home warranties can cost anywhere from $250 to $900 a year (depending on the coverage you choose) but average from $300 to $400. They typically cover the systems and appliances that come with your home, including:

- Electrical system
- Plumbing system (including toilets but excluding private well pumps, septic systems, and fixtures such as faucets and shower heads)
- Heating and cooling system (including ductwork but excluding heat registers and in-window air conditioners)
- Water heater
- Telephone wiring
- Dishwasher
- Refrigerator (excluding ice maker)
- Stove
- Ceiling and exhaust fans
- Sump pump (which removes water from a wet basement)

If you want, you can buy additional coverage (at additional cost) for these items:

- Faucets and shower heads
- Well pumps
- Septic tank pumps
- Heating registers and grills
- Window-mounted air conditioners
- Refrigerator ice makers
- Smoke detectors
- Garage door openers
- Swimming pools
- Washers and dryers
- Roofs (limited coverage)

If an appliance breaks down or something goes wrong with a central system, you call the warranty company, which puts you in touch with a repair person. You pay a fixed service fee (usually $50 to $100), and the company picks up the rest of the tab. If a broken appliance can't be fixed, the warranty pays for a new one, including installation.

A home warranty sounds like a good idea, but in practice, the fine print in these warranties tend to exclude a lot: preexisting conditions, poor installation, hard-to-access areas, substandard maintenance, and anything beyond normal wear and tear. With all those exclusions, it can be difficult to get a claim approved—if you forget to have your furnace serviced once a year, for example, you might be out of luck when the furnace dies. Read the contract carefully before you sign it, keeping an eye out for loopholes. For example, many warranty companies require homeowners to update mechanical and electrical systems to current building codes (at your expense) before it will cover those systems.

Some states regulate the companies that offer home warranties; others don't. If you're thinking about buying a policy, find out whether your state does and check with the regulatory agency for complaints against specific companies. Otherwise, you can go online and check for complaints at consumer websites like Ripoff Report (*www.ripoffreport.com*) and ConsumerAffairs.com (*www.consumeraffairs.com*).

Often, a seller will pay for a one-year home warranty to entice buyers and give them confidence in the home. You can use the home warranty as a bargaining chip (instead of shelling out $300 or $400 for the home warranty, maybe the seller could install a new dishwasher), or you can accept it, since someone else is paying for it, and see whether you like it during the first year.

 Tip Emergencies happen. It's a good idea to set up an emergency repair fund of at least $5,000. Even if you don't have that much money to spare, make it a priority to build up a reserve so you have funds available if you need them. If you decide not to buy a home warranty, add the money you'd have spent to your emergency fund.

Warranties for New Construction

If the purpose of a warranty is to protect a previously lived-in home as though it's brand new, what about new construction? Do you need a home warranty when you buy a brand-new house? Yes, you do. A house that's never been lived in can develop problems with appliances and systems that haven't been tested by day-to-day use.

Although you should make sure your newly constructed home has a warranty, you shouldn't have to pay for it. In many cases, the builder warranties that, if a problem arises, he'll fix it. In other cases, the builder buys a traditional warranty for the first year (or for the first several years) you live in the house. When you buy new construction, a home warranty is a sign that the builder stands behind his work. Be suspicious of any builder who doesn't offer one.

A typical builder's warranty protects you against defects in the materials and workmanship of the structure and its systems, from foundation to roof, for the first year after closing. In addition, most warranties cover the building's central systems for two years and its structure for 10. Your builder may inspect the home during the first year—which is a good thing, because the inspection can find and fix small problems before they become full-blown emergencies.

As with any warranty, read a builder's warranty carefully. It excludes some things: appliances under a manufacturer's warranty, everyday wear and tear, normal "settling" of the building, soil conditions, and any drainage problems caused by landscaping you do (or have done). The warranty might also specify the hours and days when the builder will be available to address non-emergency problems the warranty covers.

 Many states have laws requiring warranties that all builders must comply with. This kind of implied warranty may be in effect in your state, even if it's not explicitly mentioned in your builder's warranty. Contact your state attorney general's office or Contractors Licensing Board to get the details on your state's requirements.

Prepare to Move

As if getting ready to close on your house doesn't already put enough on your plate, you also have to get ready to move into your new home. Whether you move across town or across the country, whether you pack and haul everything yourself or hire professionals, you need to make arrangements well in advance so that your move goes smoothly.

As soon as you know your closing date, pick a moving day. You might want to give yourself a few days to clean and prepare your new house before you move into it. Decide how you're going to move: Will you do it yourself or work with a professional moving company? Professional movers can do everything from packing your stuff to moving it to unpacking it in your new home and taking away the mountain of empty boxes—or you can pick and choose the services you want. Maybe you'd prefer to pack everything yourself, for example, and hire movers to get your belongings from the old place to the new one.

 If you decide to hire professional movers, ask your friends, buyer's agent, neighbors, and family members for recommendations. Even if you don't know anyone who's moved recently, a friend or acquaintance may be able to put you in touch with someone who has.

Avoiding Mover Scams

You may have heard horror stories about scam movers who demand a big deposit and then never show up on moving day or who hold people's possessions hostage until they pay an amount three or four times greater than the original estimate. Don't get scammed. If you plan to use a professional mover, follow these tips:

- **Choose a local mover.** Most scammers operate online only. Work with an established local company whose office you can visit.

- **Get in-person estimates.** Don't settle for an estimate that you get from a phone call or by filling out an online form. To get the most accurate estimate, have someone from the moving company look around your home to see what you'll be moving. Get written estimates from at least three different companies.

- **Be suspicious of lowball estimates.** If one estimate comes in much lower than the others, it's probably too good to be true.

- **Get referrals and references.** If you know someone who's moved recently, ask which mover they used and what they thought of the experience. And before you choose a mover, ask for references from previous customers, then call and ask whether those customers were happy with the mover's work.

- **Get a list of reliable movers.** The American Moving and Storage Association (AMSA) is the national trade association for professional movers. AMSA's website (*www.promover.org*) lists certified ProMovers, who must pass criminal background checks and agree to ethical standards (such as honesty in advertising and all business transactions). You can also use AMSA's referral service to request quotes from up to six prescreened ProMovers local to your area.

- **Check reviews.** Consumers use review websites like Yelp (*www.yelp.com*) and MoverReviews.com (*www.moverreviews.com*) to rate and write detailed reviews of moving companies they've worked with.

- **Ask for the FMCSA Rights and Responsibilities booklet.** By law, a mover must give you a copy of "Your Rights and Responsibilities When You Move," a publication of the Federal Motor Carrier Safety Administration (FMCSA). If a mover can't or won't provide you with a copy, look elsewhere.

- **Don't hand over a large deposit before the move.** Scammers often demand a big chunk of cash up front—and then never appear to move your stuff. It's not unreasonable for a mover to ask for a deposit of $100 to $200 to cover their costs if you change your mind, but if a mover wants more up front—like 25 percent of the cost of the move—don't pay it.

- **Get everything in writing.** Make sure the mover's estimate includes the cost of the move and any extra charges (for packing boxes, tape, wrapping materials, and so on). Don't ever sign a blank contract that the mover fills in later.

- **Check for past complaints.** Contact your local Better Business Bureau to see whether anyone has filed a complaint there about the mover. If you're moving from one state to another, you can also search for complaints filed with FMCSA (which regulates interstate moves) at *http://tinyurl.com/yajquhe*.

For a smooth move, think ahead. Unlike Dorothy in *The Wizard of Oz*, you're not going to look out the window one day and discover you're not in Kansas any more. A move happens in stages—and staying on top of those stages at the right time is the secret to a successful move. Use the to-do lists in this section as a starting point for your own, adding any tasks your situation requires.

 Tip This book's missing CD has a checklist you can print out that lists what you need to do to prepare for your move. Find it at *www.missingmanuals.com*.

Four to Six Weeks Before You Move

Start early. As soon as you choose a moving date, check these tasks off your list:

- If you handle the move yourself, compare prices from truck rental companies and reserve a truck. Buy moving boxes and start packing things you know you won't need for a while: nonseasonal tools and clothes, books you won't read in the next few weeks, and so on.

 Tip Preparing for a move is a great time to weed out possessions you don't really need or want. Hold a yard sale, list them in the classifieds, give them to friends, or donate them to charity.

- If you hire professional movers, contact three companies to get estimates. Each company will send a representative to your home to look at how much you've got to move and give you a ballpark of what it will cost to move it.

- If you plan to do any redecorating before you move to your new home, such as painting or installing carpets, get estimates and set up appointments to have the work done. If you plan to have the work done before you move in, consider how these appointments affect your moving date.

- If you're renting your current home, give your landlord notice that you'll be moving out. Depending on your situation, you may need to find a new tenant to sublet your apartment or pay overlapping rent and mortgage payments to avoid breaking your lease.

Two Weeks Before You Move

As moving day approaches, send out word about your new address and accelerate your preparations. Here's what you need to do:

- Call utility companies and arrange to begin service in your new home on the day of the closing and end service the day after you move out of your current home. Be sure to contact all of the following utility companies that apply:

  — Electricity

  — Heating fuel (natural gas, automatic oil delivery, automatic propane delivery)

  — Water

  — Telephone

  — Cable

  — Satellite television

  — Internet service

- File a change of address form at the post office or online (*www.usps.com*).

- Notify anyone who regularly sends you mail (credit card companies, student loan institutions, magazines you subscribe to, college alumni association, and so on) of your new address.

- Return library books and any locally rented DVDs.

- Order checks that display your new address. If you're moving to a new area, open a bank account there.

- If you're packing up your belongings yourself, start or continue packing.

 Tip House plants can be difficult to move. Some states regulate the kinds of plants you can bring in, and moving companies may transport plants with restrictions: only for moves of less than 150 miles and/or delivery within 24 hours, for example. Plants move best in a climate-controlled environment (such as your car) and in unbreakable plastic containers (as opposed to clay or ceramic pots). If you have houseplants you can't take with you, try to find them new homes at least a couple of weeks before you move.

One Week Before You Move

As moving day approaches, make sure preparations and plans are still on track and make your final preparations for the move:

- Check with your real estate agent, loan officer or mortgage broker and closing agent or attorney to make sure that everything is on track for the closing and to confirm the date.

- If you reserved a rental truck, double-check your reservation.

- If you hired professional movers, confirm the date.

- Set aside a couple of boxes and a suitcase or two for the essential items you'll need immediately in your new home: medications, toiletries, towels, sheets and pillows, some changes of clothes, and the items you'd pack for a short trip. It will take days to get everything put away and organized in your new home, so make sure essentials are accessible.

 Tip On moving day, transport the essentials yourself. You don't want to risk losing your medications, for example, among the mountain of boxes crammed into the mover's truck. If you're renting a truck and moving yourself, keep the essentials separate from the bulk of your stuff so you can easily find them when you need them.

- If you're doing the packing, take things one room at a time and clean each room as you finish packing it. Don't pack your cleaning tools, though—you'll want to give the place a final once-over after it's empty.

Take the Final Walkthrough

Weeks—or sometimes months—can pass between the time you make an offer on a house and the day you take possession of it. In between, things can happen that affect the home's condition—an appliance might go kaput, the owners' toddler could dump a half-gallon of grape juice on the white living-room carpet, the roof could spring a leak. That's why you put a final walkthrough contingency in your purchase agreement (page 253)— so you can check for last-minute problems before the house becomes yours. You can print out a checklist of everything you should look for in your final walkthrough from this book's Missing CD at *www.missingmanuals.com/cds/*.

If the home has been sitting vacant, problems might go unnoticed and unrepaired, until you have the bad luck to discover them after closing. You don't want to find that a burst pipe has flooded the house or that the seller has removed appliances or fixtures that were supposed to convey with the sale. If the seller is still living in the home or has recently moved out, check to make sure no recent damage has occurred—walls and floors can get pretty banged up when the seller moves his furniture and personal property.

What to Look for on the Final Walkthrough

Although a "walkthrough" sounds like a quick, casual check, dispel that notion. Take your time. Don't get distracted by deciding whether the sofa should go against the far wall or under the window—you'll figure that out later. Your priority is to make sure the house is in the condition you expect. If the seller made repairs and you haven't inspected the work, you might want to ask a professional to walk through with you, to make sure the repairs are complete. Also, bring a camera so you can document any problems.

 Tip If you took photos when you toured the home or during the home inspection, take them along to the final walkthrough. Use them to compare the condition of the home when you made the offer with its current condition.

In all likelihood, the next time you walk through the house, it'll be yours. Make sure it's in the shape you expect by doing a thorough check of all areas of the home, inside and out. Print out the Final Walkthrough Checklist from the book's Missing CD (*www.missingmanuals.com*) and bring it with you. Here's a summary of what you're looking for:

- **Outside the home:**
  - Visually inspect the home's exterior, including the roof, siding, shutters and trim, and so on, looking for any changes since you signed the purchase agreement.
  - Inspect the driveway and walkways.
  - Check the grounds—are the trees and landscaping the same as when you made the offer?

- **Interior rooms (general):**
  - Open, close, and lock/unlock all doors.
  - Open, close, and lock/unlock all windows, and check for missing or damaged screens.
  - In each room, inspect the ceilings, floors, and walls for physical damage (such as dings, gouges, or scuffs that the seller may have left when he moved out) and water damage (stains, dampness, soft spots).
  - Check the cleanliness of any carpets.
  - Make sure closets are cleaned out.
- **Kitchen:**
  - Open the fridge to make sure it works.
  - Turn on all the stove's burners and oven.
  - Test the light and fan in the range hood.
  - Turn on the dishwasher.
  - Run the garbage disposal.
  - Test any other appliances.
  - Run both the hot and cold water in the sink; check for clogged drains and in the cabinet underneath for signs of a leak.
- **Bathroom:**
  - Run water in sink to check water pressure.
  - As the water runs, check under the sink for leaks.
  - Turn on faucets in the tub/shower.
  - Check for clogged drains.
  - Flush toilet.
  - Turn on the exhaust fan.
- **Utility room:**
  - Turn on the washer and dryer.
- **Garage:**
  - Test the automatic door opener.
- **Attic and basement:**
  - Look for areas that are damp, wet, musty-smelling, or show visible mold.

- **Electrical system:**
  - Turn each light switch on and off.
  - Turn on ceiling fans and exhaust fans.
  - Test electrical outlets.
- **Heating/cooling system:**
  - Turn up the thermostat a few degrees and make sure the heat comes on.
  - If the home has central air conditioning, turn down the thermostat and verify that the air conditioner comes on.
- **Miscellaneous:**
  - Confirm that all conveyances remain in the home.
  - Make sure there's no trash or debris left behind.
  - Check that the seller removed all his personal property.
  - Check that the seller has made all agreed-upon repairs.

 Tip Bring along a list of issues that the home inspector found that weren't serious enough to require repairs. Check that these problems haven't gotten worse since the inspection.

  - Ring the doorbell.
  - If there's a security system, test it.

 Tip Before the final walkthrough, make sure the security service has your phone number as the designated contact. You don't want to set off the alarm and have no way to stop it.

  - Make sure you have the owner's manuals for all major appliances (furnace, central air conditioner, and so on).
  - Test railings on stairs, decks, and porches to make sure they're firmly attached.
  - Check that any built-in shelving is stable.
  - If there's a fireplace, make sure it's clean; open and close the flue.

If the seller has left junk behind on the property, find out how much it would cost to have it hauled away. Ask the seller to put that amount of money into an escrow account and get a written agreement that the seller will remove the junk by a certain date—if not, you can use the escrow money to pay someone to take it away.

What to Do If You Find a Problem

Most of the time, the final walkthrough is just that—a final look at the house before the closing. But if you find one or more problems you need to deal with, contact your real estate agent immediately so she can get in touch with the seller and open negotiations. When a house doesn't pass your walkthrough inspection, you have these options:

- **The seller returns money to you for repairs.** This can happen at the closing; the seller returns some of your purchase price so you can fix the problem. If it's a relatively small amount of money—say a few hundred dollars—the seller might give you cash. For pricier repairs, the seller may have the closing agent or your attorney put the money in escrow. As a contractor makes the repairs, your attorney pays for them with money from the account.

 For big repair jobs, get estimates before you negotiate. Know how much the repairs are likely to cost so you request enough money from the seller to cover them fully.

- **The seller reduces the purchase price.** Unrepaired damage to a house reduces its value, so you can renegotiate the final purchase price, reducing it by the amount of the repairs.

 Negotiations may delay the closing. If that happens, consider asking the seller to pay for any costs you incur because of the delay, such as furniture storage and hotel bills.

- **You cancel the sale.** If your purchase agreement has a final walkthrough contingency (page 253), you can invoke that contingency and cancel the sale if there's a significant problem. If the seller feels you're making a frivolous claim, though, he may try to keep some (or all) of your earnest money.

12 Inspect the Property

Your prospective new home looked great when you toured it with your agent, but you don't know what problems are hiding, waiting to jump out and yell, "Surprise!" once you move in. According to HouseMaster, a home inspection franchiser, a study of more than 2,000 home inspection reports found that 40 percent of inspected homes had at least one major defect that would cost several hundred to several thousand dollars to repair. Most problems arose in roofs, electrical systems, plumbing systems, central heating and cooling systems, insulation, and the home's structure. That's a long list of potential gotchas—and most homebuyers wouldn't begin to know how to search for them. That's why, before any money changes hands, you need an expert to evaluate these systems (and others). That's the role of your home inspector.

You probably put a home inspection contingency (page 252) in your purchase agreement. Now, it's time to get that inspection done. This chapter walks you through a typical home inspection, showing you, step-by-step, what a home inspector looks for. It also offers advice on finding a good home inspector and a list of specialized inspections you might want to have done. The last section tells you how to address any problems that come up (and they will—there's no such thing as a perfect home).

What a Home Inspector Does

A professional home inspector usually has a background in construction, engineering, or both. He gives your house a thorough going-over, checking its systems, structure, materials, and condition. He compares the condition of the house to current building standards and alerts you to potential problems. The inspector won't fix (or arrange to fix) anything, but his report shows you what needs repair—now and down the road—so you can decide whether to buy the house in its current condition, ask the seller for repairs or a credit, or cancel the sale (go to this book's Missing CD at *www.missingmanuals.com/cds/* to see an example home inspection report).

 Note A home inspector doesn't provide an assessment of your home's value, either, so don't even ask—that's an appraiser's job.

Home inspectors inspect only the parts of your house that he can access and view. For example, while he might suspect and report a potential problem with your foundation, he won't dig down to confirm it. (In a case like that, you need to hire a foundation engineer to do a specialized inspection—page 304 tells you more about specialized inspections.) Home inspectors observe and note the house's condition, but they don't guarantee that condition or provide a home warranty.

Find a Good Home Inspector

Because a home inspection is so important, you want the best inspector you can find. Your real estate agent, attorney, or lender may have a list of inspectors they recommend. Use this as a starting point. You should also check with friends, neighbors, and acquaintances for recommendations; someone who's had personal experience with a home inspector can fill you in on the results of his work. Even if they had the inspection done a couple of years ago, the homeowner can tell you how thorough and accurate it was.

Before you hire a home inspector, ask several about their rates, and interview the most promising ones (see page 102 for a list of questions).

 Tip Although you can begin looking for a home inspector with your agent's list of recommendations, look beyond that list, too. A tough inspector who has a reputation for warning potential buyers away from problematic homes may not be too popular with agents—but can be your best friend in making sure the home is structurally sound.

Some states license and regulate home inspectors. (Your state law library can tell you about licensing and other regulations in your state. For a list of law libraries, visit the American Association of Law Libraries at *http://aallnet.org/sis/sccll* and click the Libraries link.) In addition, home inspectors can join (and abide by the tenets of) several professional associations. Each has its own professional standards, a code of ethics, and educational and other resources for members. So if a home inspector belongs to one or more of the associations below, consider that a good sign:

- **American Society of Home Inspectors** (ASHI; *www.ashi.org*). With more than 6,000 members and 80 chapters across the U.S. and Canada, this is the largest professional association of home inspectors in North America. Full ASHI members have passed two written exams and have conducted at least 250 paid home inspections.

 Tip Visit the ASHI website to experience a virtual home inspection.

- **International Association of Certified Home Inspectors** (InterNACHI; *www.nachi.org*). To become InterNACHI-certified, a home inspector must pass a written exam, complete an ethics course, and take a standards-of-practice quiz. Renewing members must satisfy continuing education requirements.

- **National Association of Home Inspectors** (NAHI; *www.nahi.org*). Established in 1987, NAHI has more than 2,000 members, with chapters throughout the U.S. and Canada. To join, members must complete a 40-hour home inspection-training program or have conducted at least 20 home inspections for paying clients. As an inspector gains more experience, he moves up to higher levels of membership.

 Tip Check out the websites of these associations for resources for homebuyers, such as answers to frequently asked questions about home inspections, and to search for member inspectors in your area.

What Happens at an Inspection

After you choose an inspector and make an appointment for the inspection, clear the date and time with the seller to ensure your inspector has access to the house. Your real estate agent, the seller's agent, and the seller can all attend the inspection—and you should be there, too. While home inspectors report all the problems they find—large and small, urgent and not so urgent, being there lets you take a look, ask questions, and get a sense of whether you need to make immediate repairs. There's a world of difference between seeing with your own eyes and reading a report.

A thorough inspection of a typical single-family home can easily take two hours, longer if the house is old or large. Budget ample time and don't get impatient—you don't want the inspector to rush and miss something important. This section describes what the home inspector examines.

Exterior

 Note To see what a typical home inspection report looks like, check out the sample report on the Missing CD (*www.missingmanuals.com*).

Your home inspector will probably begin with the outside of the house. Here's what he's looking at:

- Wall covering materials (such as siding or stucco)
- Flashing and trim. Flashing is a weatherproofing material often found around structures that interrupt a house's siding or roof, like a kitchen exhaust fan or a skylight. It provides a seamless barrier between the existing siding or roof and the house itself, preventing water from entering at an angle or joint.
- Eaves, soffits, and fascias visible from ground level

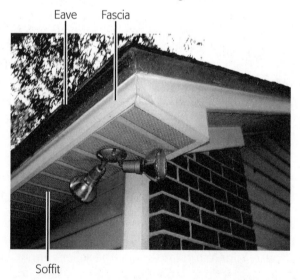

An *eave* is the edge of a roof that extends beyond the building. A *soffit*, the underside of an eave, often has air vents to ventilate a home's attic. And a *fascia* is the horizontal facing board that covers the ends of the roof rafters outside the home.

- Exterior doors
- Windows
- Structures such as decks, porches, and staircases that are attached to the home, along with their railings
- Exterior lights
- Walkways, driveways, and patios that are adjacent to the house or lead to its entrances
- Landscaping and vegetation (such as trees) that may cause problems, like roots that could interfere with water pipes
- Grading and surface drainage to see whether water flows toward or away from the home
- Retaining walls

Structural Components

You want to make sure the "bones" of your house—the structural components that hold it together—are sound, because these kinds of repairs are costly.

Your home inspector checks these components and probes any that show signs of damage or deterioration. He'll poke at wood that looks like it's rotting, for example. If there's no visual clue to a problem, the inspector won't do any probing.

Here are the elements the inspector checks:

- Foundation
- Crawl space (if applicable)
- Attic framing
- Floors
- Walls
- Ceilings

Roof and Attic

Water is the enemy of many building materials, including wood, metal, and masonry. It causes rot, rust, and crumbling. It makes a nice home for mold and mildew. And in cold climates, it freezes and expands, damaging pipes and any other material it seeps into (like a crack in a masonry wall). So you want to make sure water hasn't gotten into places it doesn't belong—particularly through the roof and around the foundation (page 310).

Some home inspectors will climb a ladder and walk around a low-pitched roof to inspect it. Others offer only a visual inspection, using binoculars (you can ask inspectors their method when you interview them). Either way, the inspector won't guarantee the condition of a roof or estimate how long it'll last (to find that out, have a certified roofing company do an inspection—read more about roof certifications on page 309).

But your home inspector will identify the type of roof construction and the materials that went into it. He'll also check:

- The roof's drainage system and gutters
- Any flashing
- Skylights, chimneys, and any other structures that go through the roof

If the house has an accessible attic, the inspector checks for damage from water or animals (such as squirrels, raccoons, or bats) and looks at these elements:

- The framing
- The underside of the roof
- The insulation
- The ventilation

 Note Poor attic ventilation is a major cause of roof damage. When air can't circulate, frost can damage the underside of the roof (in cold climates) and high temperatures can damage roof boards and the asphalt shingles that cover them.

Plumbing

The signs of a good plumbing system include water that flows easily (no banging or hesitation), good water pressure, and a lack of leaks. Your home inspector looks at:

- The materials and condition of all the pipes (including the pipes that carry drinking and waste water, drain pipes, and vent pipes)

- Sinks and faucets
- Showers and tubs
- Toilets
- Drains and traps
- Sump pumps and related pipes
- Water heaters and water heating systems

 Note Most home inspectors don't look at private wells, septic systems, solar water heaters, water softening or conditioning equipment, or lawn sprinkler systems. If you want any of these inspected, contact a company that specializes in the equipment.

Up to Speed

Polybutylene Pipes

If the house you're considering was built between 1970 and the mid-1990s (or had plumbing work done during that time), watch out for polybutylene pipes. These plastic resin pipes were cheap to make and easy to install, so they became popular with builders and plumbers who preferred them to pricier copper pipe.

The problem is that they degrade—and then they leak. If they were used in hot water systems, they can develop cracks. And the chlorine that keeps public water supplies clean makes the pipes brittle, leading to flaking and cracking. Eventually, the pipes can leak or break—and then you have an expensive problem on your hands.

Between 6 million and 10 million homes in the U.S. have polybutylene pipes. They're most popular throughout the southern states, the Pacific Northwest, and mid-Atlantic regions, but you can find them anywhere. If your home has them, consider getting an estimate of how much it would cost to replace them. You'll need that info whether you decide to negotiate with the seller about replacing the pipes now or whether you decide to buy the home with the pipes in place—because you may have to replace them some day.

Electrical System

A home's electrical system does more than run the TV and illuminate the house—it's vital to many core systems, like refrigeration/cooking and heating/cooling, so it needs to be maintained. In addition, an electrical system in disrepair is a potential fire hazard.

Your home inspector probably isn't a licensed electrician, but he knows about electrical source, circuitry, and general voltage and amp requirements. The inspector won't probe a home's electrical system but he will visually inspect it, including:

- The service drop—that's the power line that runs from the nearest utility pole to your home
- Conductors, cables, and raceways (covers that encase wires that run along the outside of walls)
- Grounding
- Ground fault circuit interrupters
- Main service panels and circuit breakers, along with any subpanels
- Wiring
- Light switches
- Light fixtures
- Smoke detectors

Heating and Air Conditioning Systems

To make sure your new home will keep you comfortably warm in cold weather and cool in hot weather, the inspector looks at the heating and cooling systems. This is important for more than physical comfort; a malfunctioning heating system can release poisonous carbon monoxide into a home. So a thorough inspection is important. If she suspects a problem such as overheating or inadequate ductwork, your home inspector may recommend a specialized HVAC inspection (page 299).

The inspector tells you the kind of heating system you have and what fuels it, and checks these components:

- Furnace
- Central air conditioner
- Heat distribution system, including fans, pumps, ducts, and piping, with supports, insulation, air filters, registers, radiators, fan coil units, and convectors
- Thermostat
- Chimneys, flues, and vents, when they're readily accessible

Insulation and Ventilation

Proper ventilation and insulation extends the life of a building. Your home needs to breathe, but you don't want it to be drafty. Ventilation makes sure that air circulates, preventing moisture from building up where it can cause damage. Insulation minimizes heat transfer between your house and the outside world, keeping you cooler in summer and warmer in winter. The HVAC industry uses a measure called *R-value* to measure the efficiency of insulation. The higher the R-value, the more efficient the insulation. To check for proper insulation and ventilation, inspectors check:

- Insulation and vapor barriers in unfinished areas, such as the attic and the basement or crawl space
- The material and R-value of attic insulation
- Exhaust fans
- Ventilation systems in bathrooms, the kitchen, and the laundry area

 Note The inspector may photograph your house with an infrared camera to get a thermographic image of the building, which shows where the insulation isn't working.

Installed Appliances

The inspector checks built-in appliances that convey with the sale, such as the:

- Dishwasher
- Oven, range, and/or cooktop
- Range hood fan
- Built-in microwave
- Garbage disposal
- Trash compactor

Other Interior Features

As an inspector walks through your house, they take note of the condition of these features:

- Stairs and railings
- Countertops and cabinets
- Windows

- Doors

- Fireplaces, along with their chimneys, fireboxes, and vents (if accessible)

 Note Your home inspector probably won't open and close all the windows and cabinet doors. They tend to look at a representative number of these features.

Basement

If your house has a basement, the inspector looks at any systems that have components there, such as heating, electric, and plumbing. Other than those systems, the inspector's main concern here is the presence of water—and the problems this can cause, such as rotting wood or crumbling masonry.

These are all signs of a wet basement that a home inspector will look for:

- Dampness

- Water stains

- Efflorescence, a sparkly white or gray residue left behind on concrete, brick, or stone when water evaporates

- Spalling, a peeling or flaking that occurs when water gets inside masonry

- Musty odors

- Mold or mildew

 Tip If an inspector discovers mold in your house, you might want to get a specialized inspection—especially for black mold (page 306 tells you why).

Garage

If your home has a garage, whether it's attached or detached, the home inspector examines the:

- Exterior

- Roof

- Slab or foundation on which the garage is built

- Walls and ceiling

- Doors

- Automatic door openers
- Windows
- Light switches and fixtures

What Your Home Inspector Won't Do

Home inspectors take a good, hard look at your house and report their observations, but they don't fix problems or offer engineering services (like redesigning the electrical or plumbing systems). They also don't assess the value of your house or whether it's suitable for specialized use, like a day-care center. ASHI guidelines state that certain activities are beyond the scope of what a home inspector does, including these:

- **A home inspector doesn't have to inspect any system or structural element not readily accessible.** Don't expect an inspector to get out a shovel and start digging up the back lawn to look at a buried storage tank or pipework. Nor will he move the current owner's personal property or furniture, or clear away snow or debris to inspect some element of the house.

- **A home inspector doesn't offer professional services beyond the inspection itself.** Some home inspectors work independently as contractors. But if you want repair work done, you have to hire them in that capacity—as a builder, not an inspector.

- **A home inspector doesn't evaluate the strength, adequacy, effectiveness, or efficiency of any system or component.** The inspector also doesn't speculate on the cause of problems or advise on their solution. And don't ask how long something is likely to last—the inspector may give you an informal answer, but it won't be part of the official report.

- **A home inspector doesn't conduct specialized inspections.** For example, the inspector won't check for wood-destroying insects or evaluate whether mold growing in the basement represents a health hazard. The inspector might, however, recommend a special inspection based on observations he makes during the general inspection.

 Page 304 explains the different kinds of specialized inspections you can get.

- **A home inspector doesn't estimate the cost of operating any of the property's systems.** If you want a sense of how much it costs to run the central air conditioner, for example, ask to see the owner's utility bills.

- **A home inspector doesn't evaluate anything that's not installed.** That includes standalone appliances (like refrigerators) and fixtures (like floor lamps). And the inspector won't inspect decorative fixtures like mini-blinds.

- **A home inspector doesn't evaluate structures that aren't attached to the home.** The exception is a garage or carport.

- **If you're having a condominium or a co-op inspected, the home inspector doesn't inspect common areas.** The inspector looks at the unit you want to purchase but not the lobby, hallways, elevators, laundry room, and so on.

 Tip Even new construction needs a general home inspection. The builder may have cut corners. Common issues in new construction include improper grading, sewer connection problems, and ventilation and weatherproofing issues.

Understand Your Home Inspection Report

Soon after your home inspector finishes peering, poking, and prodding, he'll send you a report that details everything he found (see the Missing CD at *www.missingmanuals.com/cds/* to see a sample home inspection report). It's a comprehensive list of major and minor issues—everything from cracked window panes and missing light-switch covers to structural problems like a deteriorating roof or a crumbling foundation. Look for the report a day or two after the inspection. (If you don't get it, give the inspector a nudge—some states limit the time in which you have to complete the inspection and deal with resulting issues.) If you attended the inspection, you should already have a pretty good idea of what the report will say.

During the inspection, your inspector probably carried a clipboard with forms he filled out as he examined the home or a used hand-held computer to record observations. These on-the-scene notes form the basis of his report. Some reports are little more than checklists that indicate whether each element is acceptable or needs replacing. The best reports describe the condition of the house in long form—paragraphs that take the time to explain the problems.

The Not-So-Top Ten

What problems and issues appear most frequently during a home inspection?

Be on the lookout for these problems, which, according to a survey of ASHI members, are most likely to turn up during a home inspection:

1. **Improper surface grading and drainage.** This problem, reported by 36 percent of home inspectors, can mean that water is damaging the foundation and getting into the house.

2. **Improper and undersized electrical wiring.** The second most-frequent problem shows up in the electrical system. Specific issues include insufficient electrical service to the house, aluminum wiring, inadequate overload protection, improper grounding, and dangerous amateur wiring connections. Because a faulty electric system is a safety hazard, put problems like these high on your must-fix list.

3. **Older and damaged roofs.** Deteriorating shingles or poorly installed flashing can result in a leaky roof.

4. **Deficient and older heating systems.** Heating system issues include broken or malfunctioning controls, blocked chimneys, unsafe exhaust flues, and cracked heat exchangers. As with the electrical system, a faulty heating system can pose a serious health risk.

5. **Poor overall maintenance.** This category reflects what happens when a homeowner doesn't take proper care of his residence: cracked or peeling paint, crumbling masonry and broken fixtures and appliances may signify an owner who hasn't paid much attention to maintenance.

6. **Structural problems.** Older homes are especially likely to have some damage to foundation walls, floor joists, rafters, or windows and door frames. These problems are often minor—but ask.

7. **Plumbing problems.** Old piping material, broken fixtures, and faulty water heaters are frequent issues in this category.

8. **Exterior items.** Outside the home, doors, windows, and wall surfaces sometimes let the elements in. Degraded weather-stripping or poor caulking is often the culprit.

9. **Poor ventilation.** Without proper ventilation, moisture can accumulate inside a home and cause rot, deterioration, mold growth, and other damage.

10. **Miscellaneous items.** This catch-all category includes problems found in the home's interior, from lead-based paint and asbestos insulation to windows that stick rather than open smoothly.

Most reports are several pages long and divided into sections. The first section is boilerplate, detailing the services the inspector provided and limiting his liability to the inspection fee you paid—in other words, if there's a problem with the report, you can get your money back, but the inspector doesn't owe you anything beyond that. Then he evaluates the house room by room, including all the structural components and systems listed earlier in this chapter. He may use digital photos to illustrate his findings. The report often ends with a summary of the major findings.

Read the entire report. It won't grip you like the latest bestseller, but it has more relevance to your day-to-day life. Write down questions that come to mind and make margin notes, then call your inspector. He can tell you which repairs you *have* to make and which are highest priority. But he won't tell you whether or not you should buy the house—that's your decision, and that's why it's important that you understand the report clearly.

After you talk with the inspector, contact contractors to get estimates of the high-priority repairs. You need these numbers when you sit down to negotiate with the seller (page 256).

Specialized Inspections

Aside from the general home inspection, you might want to contract for specialized inspections. If your home inspector recommends that someone take a closer look at, say, your electrical system, heed that advice. Your lender might require other inspections, such as those for termites or a septic system. Finally, you may want to get a special inspection for your own peace of mind.

Some sellers may pay for inspections to give the house an edge in the market. After all, a black-and-white document that says the roof is sound and the house free of toxic mold makes the property more attractive. Even if a seller paid for an inspection, though, you it's a good idea to contract for your own inspections. Think of them as second opinions to confirm previous inspectors' findings.

Septic System

Many homes, particularly those in rural areas, use private septic systems, which take solid waste and wastewater that passes through the house's plumbing, treat it, and release it into the ground around the system. Replacing or repairing a faulty septic system can cost tens of thousands of dollars, so you need to be sure that it works and that the current owner has properly maintained it. Inspecting a septic system is a dirty job, but be glad an inspection's available—it might save you from costly emergency repairs later on.

A mold inspector tests for the presence, amount, and type of mold. He also checks to see how good a host for mold your house makes. He analyzes the air quality and checks for moisture (mold loves damp spots), water leaks, and humidity levels. Some inspectors even use fiber-optic cameras to check inside walls.

Mold growing in a flood-damaged home

You can eradicate some mold, like the kind that typically grows on bathroom tiles, with bleach and a little effort. If you have a more pervasive problem—especially toxic black mold—you have to hire a mold-remediation company to get rid of it and ensure it won't come back.

Asbestos

Asbestos is a mineral fiber widely used in the past to fireproof and insulate homes. The fibers can lodge in your airways and cause cancer and lung disease, so if you buy a home more than 40 years old, check for asbestos.

Asbestos was also used in roofing shingles, ceiling and floor tiles, cement products, some textured paints and coatings, and insulation for pipes and water heaters, too. When a product that contains asbestos deteriorates or gets disturbed (during renovations or remodeling, for example), it releases fibers into the air that can lodge in your lungs and cause medical problems. You definitely don't want those fibers in your lungs.

If you suspect a home has asbestos (your general home inspector may point it out), consider a specialized asbestos inspection—especially in older homes you plan to remodel or update. The inspector will check for asbestos thoroughly and let you know if your house needs work. Professional asbestos remediation companies can remove or contain the problem while complying with safety laws. But asbestos removal can be expensive, so get estimates and think carefully before you go forward with your purchase.

Radon

Radon, a colorless, odorless radioactive gas, could lurk in any home—and the people who live there don't even know it. Radon is the second leading cause of lung cancer deaths in the U.S. (after cigarette smoking).

Radon occurs naturally in air, water, and soil, and it enters buildings through cracks and gaps in foundations, floors, and walls. To check for radon, inspectors leave an open charcoal canister or other collection device in the house for a couple of days, and then send it to a lab. If you want to check for radon (which is always a good idea), your home inspector may be able to do a radon test for an extra charge. Knowing that radon is a concern for potential buyers, many sellers test for radon, too—ask him if he's done (or is willing to do) a radon test and share the results with you.

Radon is measured in picocuries per liter (pCi/L). Fresh, outdoor air has about 0.4 pCi/L of radon. Homes with radon levels 10 or more times that amount—4 pCi/L or higher—require work by a certified radon mitigation contractor to reduce the radon to safe levels. If your radon test indicates you'll need to hire a radon mitigation contractor, get an estimate of the work needed to fix the home—and then negotiate with the seller about who will pay for it.

 Tip The EPA offers state-by-state information about radon (including information about qualified radon mitigation contractors) and maps that show radon levels by county. Go to *www.epa.gov/iaq/whereyoulive.html* and select your state to learn more.

Other Specialized Inspections

You can have the condition of just about any house component inspected. The health of trees, the integrity of a swimming pool, or the energy efficiency of a guest house are all candidates for inspections. So if sick trees or a cracked pool are deal-breakers for you, include a contingency in your purchase agreement that requires an acceptable inspection of those items.

- **Renovations.** If you plan to do substantial renovations on your house, discuss your plans with an architect or general contractor to see if you can make the changes you want (load-bearing beams or renovation restrictions in historic districts may scuttle your plans).

- **Lead-based paint.** The federal government banned the use of lead-based paint in 1978. If the home you're buying was built before that year, get a lead-based paint inspection and flip to page 140 to read more about federal lead-based paint disclosure laws.

Tip Don't try to remove lead-based paint yourself. Hire a certified lead-abatement professional.

- **Chimney.** Home inspectors look at chimneys but don't test them. A home's chimney can hide problems, such as crumbling interior bricks, a missing or cracked flue liner, or a build-up of creosote (which can catch fire). Make sure the chimney is sound, especially if you're buying an older home.

- **Heating and air conditioning system.** If your home inspector suspects a problem with the furnace or the central air conditioner, bring in an HVAC (heating, ventilating, and air conditioning) inspector. He can pinpoint the problem and estimate its repair.

- **Electrical system.** Older homes may have outdated electrical systems—your home inspector will let you know if yours is past its prime. To make sure an older electrical system complies with current building codes, your home inspector may recommend that you consult an electrician for a detailed inspection.

- **Plumbing.** A plumbing inspector checks pipes and fixtures for clogs, low water pressure, and other problems. You may be able to combine inspections for the plumbing, septic system, and private well to save money.

- **Private well.** For rural homes that rely on private wells for their water, well inspectors test the water quality, inspect the well's construction, and check the water table's depth (so you know if there's sufficient water to keep the well filled).

- **Roof certification.** If your home inspector recommends a roof inspection (or if your lender requires one), have a professional take a look. He'll check the integrity of the roof and estimate how much longer it will last. The inspector will certify his findings—this certification is usually good for one to two years (some roofers will certify a roof for up to five years).

 Tip Ask the seller to pay for a roof certification. It's traditional in many areas of the country. Some sellers automatically get the roof certified when they put the home on the market.

- **Foundation.** Your home inspector might notice cracks, bulges, or other abnormalities in the foundation. If that happens, call in a foundation engineer to check things out and estimate repair costs.

- **Swimming pool or spa.** Specialized inspectors check for leaks and estimate the life expectancy of essential pool equipment, like the filter and heater.

- **Trees.** A home inspector can tell you if a property's trees are causing (or likely to cause) a problem for the house, such as a tree that's too close to the home or a root system that may interfere with the septic system. If you want to know whether the trees are healthy, bring in a tree surgeon.

- **Energy audit.** Older homes can be drafty and expensive to heat and cool compared to homes built with modern materials and techniques. An energy audit rates the energy efficiency of your home and recommends improvements. The good news is you may be able to get a free (or low-cost) energy audit—many utility companies offer them. If not, go to the Energy Star website (a joint project of the Department of Energy and the Environmental Protection Agency) to find local Home Energy Raters qualified to do a professional energy audit. This web address will get you there: *www.tinyurl.com/ocf24b*.

If Problems Turn Up

First of all, don't panic. Any home that undergoes a professional inspection is going to reveal some issues. It's normal for a home to need some maintenance. And it's not necessary for a home to be in perfect condition when you buy it. In fact, it's not the seller's responsibility to sell you a perfect home. It's up to you and the seller to reach an agreement on what's acceptable for the sale to go through.

Your home inspection report is a tool for negotiating with the seller. Prioritize repairs—getting the roof certified is more important than replacing a damaged baseboard. Present the seller with a list of requested repairs, along with estimates of what they'll cost. You can ask the seller to have repairs done before closing to reduce the purchase price or to give you a credit toward repairs at closing (page 330 explains these options in detail). The seller won't be any happier than you are to hear about a need for repairs, so expect some back-and-forth before you agree. If you can't agree, you'll have to decide whether to go ahead with the purchase anyway or invoke the home inspection contingency in your purchase agreement and walk away from the sale.

Buying a Home "As Is"

What if the terms of the sale specify that the house is being sold in "as is" condition? Do I still need a home inspection?

An "as is" home means that the seller is unwilling to negotiate a lower price or make repairs if the home has structural or other problems. It doesn't mean that you give up your right to inspect the house, however. In fact, in an "as is" situation, it's more important than ever to get a thorough home inspection.

Sellers can list a home "as is" for several reasons. Banks sell foreclosed homes and bank-owned homes (REOs; see page 127) in "as is" condition as a matter of course. A seller may lack funds to pay for repairs or simply not want the fuss and bother of overseeing them. Often, the seller has listed the house at a discount to compensate for his unwillingness to negotiate over the home's condition.

A home that's listed "as is" isn't necessarily in bad shape. But it's up to you to find out. If you make an offer on an "as is" home, include a home inspection contingency in the purchase agreement. That way, if you find out that repairs or renovations are more extensive than you planned on, you can get out of the deal with your earnest money intact.

13   Close the Deal

All the time and effort you've invested in your quest for a new home are about to pay off. The closing, sometimes called the *settlement*, is when your new home finally becomes *yours*. You sign a small mountain of mortgage-related documents and pay the down payment and closing costs, your lender advances the money for your loan, an attorney or escrow agent distributes the funds, and the seller transfers title to you.

For a smooth closing, you need to do some prep work a day ahead of time. Of course, some glitch—a last-minute schedule conflict for the lender's attorney, a contractor who hasn't finished repairs—may delay the closing by a few days. There's probably nothing to worry about it; a delay isn't uncommon (see "What If the Closing Gets Delayed?" below).

What happens at the closing depends partly on where you live. In some states, all of the relevant parties go individually to an escrow agent's office to sign papers and pay funds; the agent holds these documents and funds in escrow, keeping them in reserve until all the documents are signed and all the money has been transferred, at which time escrow closes and the sale is complete. In other states, the parties meet simultaneously and close the deal together.

Whichever way the closing takes place, you'll have a lot of papers to sign, and this chapter explains them in detail. You'll also learn about the moment you've been waiting for: taking possession of your new home.

Countdown to Closing: 24 Hours to Go

In the day or two leading up to the closing, make sure you have everything in place for the big day. While your attorney or closing agent is busy doing behind-the-scenes work—preparing paperwork, getting information from the other parties—you can do several things to make sure the closing goes smoothly:

- **Take the final walkthrough.** Page 286 tells you what to look for as you tour the house one last time. And page 290 tells you what to do if you discover a problem.

> **Tip** Don't take the final walkthrough too far in advance of the closing, even if the house is vacant. Lots of things can go wrong in just a few days—from a sewer backup to a break-in to a cold snap that freezes the pipes. The best time for the final walkthrough is after the seller has moved out, and no more than a day or two before closing. That day or two gives you time to negotiate compensation if you notice any problems. And it's always a good idea to drive past the home on your way to the closing. If the seller failed to tow away the junk car he promised to remove from the driveway, you want to know that now.

- **Get the final amount for the closing costs.** The Good Faith Estimate you got when you applied for a mortgage has some teeth to it—federal law prohibits lenders from raising many of the costs listed there; others may go up by a maximum of 10 percent (page 328 tells you what can and can't change). So you should already have a good idea of your closing costs . But for the closing, you need to know the *exact* amount, including the fees you'll pay the seller for things like prorated property taxes and heating oil left in the storage tank. Call your attorney or loan originator and ask for a copy of your HUD-1 form, which, by law, lists *all* the fees you and the seller need to pay (page 325 tells you more about this form). Review the form to make sure it squares with your Good Faith Estimate.

- **Make arrangements to pay.** At the closing, you pay the down payment for your house and the closing costs with a certified cashier's check or by wire transfer. If you live in an *escrow state*, where an escrow agent holds funds and signed documents in trust until the transaction completes, you may be able to pay by personal check, but you have to submit your payment far enough in advance so that it clears well before escrow closes. (See page 319 to read more about how closings work in escrow states.) In non-escrow states, where the closing takes place during a single meeting, a personal check won't work for these major costs. Your lender wants you to pay instantaneously, using a method that won't take days to clear: usually with a certified bank check or cashier's check or by wire transfer.

If you pay with a certified or cashier's check, get the check from your bank the day before the closing. Make it payable to yourself; you'll sign it over to the closing agent or attorney when you close. If you pay by wire transfer, ask your bank ahead of time how it conducts wire transfers. Banks have different policies related to this payment method; make sure you know your bank's so you don't hold up the closing.

 Tip If you transfer money into your bank account from another source (such as an account at a different bank or a check from mom and dad) for the down payment and closing costs, remember that banks often put a hold on large deposits to make sure they clear. Allow plenty of time for processing so the money's available when you need it.

- **Wrap up any lingering issues.** You and the seller should have met the obligations in your purchase agreement by now. But read over that document to make sure the seller's met all the conditions of sale. Have you released all the contingencies? Has the seller taken care of all the agreed-upon repairs?

- **Review documents.** Often, the loan originator or attorney doesn't finalize the closing documents until the day of the closing. But ask them for a copy of any draft documents that are ready the day before. (If there are no draft documents, ask to see the standard forms used to prepare the documents.) Read over the documents, and ask about anything you don't understand or that looks wrong. Better now than at the closing, when you may feel rushed or intimidated by all the people and paperwork.

- **Make sure your real estate team has everything it needs from you.** Get those *i*'s dotted and *t*'s crossed. Call your real estate agent, your attorney, and your mortgage broker or loan officer to make sure that no one is waiting for you to hand in any of your paperwork and that there are no lingering details for you to attend to.

- **Gather what you need for the closing.** Here's a list of what you should bring:

  — **A government-issued photo ID.** Bring your driver's license or passport so you can prove who you are. One of the closing attendees is a notary public, a state-appointed public servant who verifies the authenticity of signatures. This notary will witness your signature.

  — **A certified bank or cashier's check.** This check pays your down payment and closing costs. (Of course, if you plan to wire the money at closing, skip the check.)

  — **Your checkbook.** Even though you pay the big costs with a certified or cashier's check or a wire transfer, you may have to pay for small adjustments—like increased homeowners' association fees or the final volume of heating fuel in the storage tank—so bring your personal checkbook. You might even walk out of the closing with a couple of checks made out to you.

  — **Your Good Faith Estimate.** When you applied for your loan, the lender gave you a Good Faith Estimate detailing the terms of your loan and estimating closing costs. You'll want to compare the GFE with the closing costs listed on your HUD-1 form.

  — **Your mortgage commitment letter.** This letter formally states the amount and the terms of your mortgage. Use it to correct any discrepancies in the loan documents.

  — **Your rate lock letter.** If you locked in your interest rate (page 204 tells you why you should), bring the letter that confirms that rate. If the interest rate on the loan papers is higher than your locked-in rate, you have proof of the correct rate.

  — **Proof of homeowner's insurance.** Bring along the binder you got from your insurance agent when you bought homeowner's insurance, along with a receipt that shows you paid the first year's premium.

  — **Home inspection reports.** Bring the general report and any special-inspection reports (page 304).

  — **A calculator.** If you want to double-check the math on your HUD-1 form before you sign it, a calculator comes in handy.

  — **Anything else the lender requires.** All closings are different. Call your bank representative, closing agent, or attorney and run down the list of what you intend to bring and ask if you forgot anything.

Take the day of the closing off from work—most closings take no more than an hour or two, but it's wise to be prepared for delays (page 330 lists some of the things that can slow down a closing). And get a good night's sleep beforehand. You want to be sharp for the meeting.

What If the Closing Gets Delayed?

Robert Burns, the Scottish poet who commented that "the best laid schemes of mice and men" often go wrong, could have been a real estate agent. No matter how carefully you plan, things can happen that delay—or even prevent—a closing. Problems may arise, for example, if the mortgage underwriter (page 162) requires clarification of or extra documentation for something in your loan application. It can take time to gather the information, submit it to the underwriter, and wait for a response. Delays like this can be harrowing. Submit the requested information and try not to get too nervous. Remember that, even though lenders want to close files as efficiently and quickly as circumstances allow, delays do happen.

Your mortgage broker or loan officer can give you the reason for a delay, but here are some common causes:

- Even if you're preapproved for a loan, the lender will check your credit report again. Any new debt or credit problems that appear on your report can slow or preclude final approval.

- Mistakes in your credit report can also cause delays—that's why it's a good idea to find and correct them before you apply for a mortgage (see page 48). A mistake can still pop up in your updated report, but you've taken care of the old ones.

- The lender may ask for updated bank statements or other financial documents.

- Your job situation changes. Lenders look for stable employment. If you change your job, they may want to look more closely at your employment history and current job status.

- The lender's appraisal comes in low. Page 223 tells you what to do if that happens.

- The mortgage underwriter may want a second appraisal to confirm the first. If the second-look appraisal is lower than the first one, the underwriter may refuse the loan.

- The title search turns up a defect (page 269). The seller will have to clear it before you can close.

- Even if the title search comes up clear, lenders will check it again before closing. Any interim liens or judgments on the home's title can delay or prevent the sale.

- You or the seller gets married or divorced. A change in marital status can complicate everything from your loan application to the way you elect to hold title to the house (see page 270) to whether the seller still has the right to sell the home.

 Tip If you're engaged to be married and you want to buy a home, talk to a real estate agent, loan officer, and attorney to find out whether you should buy before or after you tie the knot.

- The seller fails to make repairs. You may (and should, actually) decide to delay the closing until the seller makes agreed-upon repairs to your satisfaction.

- The seller requests to stay in the house after the closing. Imagine the seller comes to you a few days before closing and says, "I know we're closing on Thursday, but the moving company can't come until next Monday. You don't mind if I stay in the house through the weekend, do you?" If you don't want the seller living in the house after it's yours, you may end up delaying the closing until the seller moves out.

- You fail to supply complete insurance information. The bank will insist that you have all the required policies in hand before loaning you any money.

- Your mortgage preapproval commitment has expired—this may mean you have to apply for a mortgage starting from square one again.

If an event delays your closing, keep an eye on any deadlines in your purchase agreement and get an extension, signed by you and the seller. Also, check the expiration date in the bank's mortgage commitment letter. A delay in closing might void your locked-in mortgage rate. In that case, contact your mortgage broker or loan officer.

 Tip Because delays happen, it's a good idea to give yourself a few days' breathing room between the closing and the day you plan to move in. If you schedule things too tightly, you may have to reschedule the move or stay in a hotel for a few days.

What Happens at a Closing

Finally, you wake up one morning and the day of your closing has dawned. Whether you feel confident or a little nervous, it helps to know what to expect. Closing customs differ by geographic area. In addition to whether everyone involved signs papers individually or around a table, the location of the closing depends in part on local tradition (as well as what's most convenient for the parties involved). Most likely, your attorney or the title or escrow company will host the closing. But a closing can also take place at the bank, your builder's sales office (for new construction), the office of the lender's attorney, and sometimes even at the real estate agency.

This section explains what to expect at the closing, taking into account differences between regions. Whatever the local details and customs, the final result is the same: You become a homeowner.

Closing in an Escrow State

Some states—many of them in the west, including California, Oregon, Nevada, and Arizona—are *escrow states*, where you, the seller, and the lender choose an escrow company or agent to act as a neutral party to coordinate the house's sale. You (along with the seller and the lender) provide the escrow agent with mutually agreed-upon instructions for the transaction. The escrow agent makes sure that all the instructions' stipulations and conditions, as well as the funds and fees for the sale, have cleared before completing the sale.

In the days and weeks leading up to closing, the escrow agent collects the closing documents and money from all parties and holds them in escrow until the closing. This means that the escrow agent holds all the money and signed documents in trust until the sale instructions are complete—the seller may sign a document transferring title, for example, but the actual transfer won't happen until all of the necessary documents and funds are in the escrow agent's hands. Holding money and documents in escrow means that you and the seller each meet with the escrow agent, usually separately, to sign the necessary documents. You may make several trips to the escrow agent's office to take care of everything you need to do.

Here are some of the items escrow agents collect and hold in escrow:

- A fully executed purchase agreement, including releases or waivers of contingencies
- Your earnest money deposit
- Escrow instructions signed by you and the seller
- A lender-approved appraisal

- The home-inspection report or waiver
- The pest-inspection report (if required)
- The roof certification (if required)
- The home warranty (if applicable)
- Proof that the seller has made agreed-upon repairs
- A preliminary title insurance policy
- Proof you acquired homeowner's insurance
- Your lender's loan approval letter
- Your final walkthrough inspection report or waiver
- The home's deposit or the balance of your down payment
- Closing costs
- Your signature on all loan documents
- Funds that go from your lender to the appropriate parties (the seller, the seller's lender, real estate agents, and so on)
- Any agreed-upon funds that go from the seller to you
- The seller's signed and notarized deed conveying title to you

When the escrow agent has everything she needs, she conducts the closing: She disburses funds, transfers ownership of the property, and finalizes the sale. This is called "closing escrow." You may have to wait a couple of days after you sign the papers and hand over your money before escrow closes. When everything is final, the escrow agent notifies all parties—and you get to pick up the keys to your new home.

 Closing practices vary from one escrow state to another and sometimes from one county to another. To get a sense of how escrow closings in your area work, ask your real estate agent what a typical closing is like.

Closing in a Non-Escrow State

If you live in a non-escrow state (sometimes called a *title state*), a real estate attorney takes care of the closing. Title states include Florida, New York, Pennsylvania, Georgia, and many others in the eastern U.S. In such states, your attorney or lender sets a time and place for the closing. You and the seller get together with the other players (such as attorneys, agents, and the lender's representative) to sign papers, distribute funds, and transfer the property.

You may find most of your real estate team at the closing, along with some players from the seller's side. Some or all of these people will attend:

- **You.** You might want to give your writing hand a couple of good work-outs ahead of time, because you'll be signing *a lot* of papers.

 Tip What if you can't attend the closing? You should make every effort to be there—after all, it's your name on all those legal documents—but if you absolutely cannot make it, you can grant your real estate lawyer power of attorney to act on your behalf in this transaction. If you do, make sure it includes a clear expiration date, usually a few days after the closing.

- **Your real estate agent.** Your buyer's agent will be at your side, to encourage you, congratulate you—and pick up her share of the commission check.

- **Your attorney.** If you have any questions about any of the papers you're signing, your attorney should be there to answer them.

 Tip You can save some attorney's fees by not requiring your attorney to attend the closing. If you take that route, though, make sure your attorney reviews and okays all the documents you'll be signing a day in advance.

- **The seller.** Sometimes the seller's attorney or other authorized person may act on the seller's behalf—if, for example, the seller has already moved out of state. But usually the seller wants to attend the closing to make sure everything goes smoothly—and, of course, to collect whatever funds he's due after he pays his mortgage and other fees.

 Note The seller may arrive at the closing later than you do, because there are fewer papers for him to sign. You have to sign a stack of documents related to your mortgage; the seller mostly signs documents related to the transfer of the property. While your part of the closing can easily take an hour or two, the seller only needs to be there for about half an hour.

- **The seller's real estate agent.** Like your agent, the listing agent attends the closing primarily to collect his commission check, but he also offers his client support and guidance.

- **The seller's attorney.** If the seller has an attorney, that attorney may attend the closing to keep an eye on the proceedings and answer any questions the seller has.

- **Lender's representative.** The bank may send a representative, usually your loan officer or the bank's attorney. Often, though, someone at the bank prepares all the documents and sends them directly to the closing agent, who contacts the bank if any questions come up.

- **Notary public.** This person witnesses and certifies the participants' signatures.

 Note One person typically acts as the closing agent and oversees the proceedings, making sure all relevant parties sign all necessary documents and disbursing the funds. The closing agent is usually an attorney: yours or the lender's.

That's an awfully crowded room! Not everyone on the list attends every closing, but it gives you an idea of the players required to close a sale.

A Mountain of Paperwork: What It All Means

You've got two main responsibilities at the closing: to hand over money and to sign papers. You might feel a bit intimidated when you see the stack of papers. Don't worry, you'll get through them all. As the attorney or escrow agent passes each document to you, she'll explain what it means. If you have any questions, ask; the only question you're likely to regret is the one you don't ask.

If you got your HUD-1 and other draft documents a day in advance, you've had time to look them over and note any questions you have. But don't feel rushed. You have the right to read each document before you sign it. Don't sign anything you don't understand. Insist on a clear explanation, and make sure you're comfortable with what you sign.

The documents you sign depend on your state, your purchase agreement, and the terms of your transaction. But here's a description of some:

- **Final truth-in-lending disclosure statement.** When you applied for a mortgage, you received an initial version of this statement (page 214). Now that the bank has approved your loan, you get the final version, called the Regulation Z form. It details your payments, the loan's interest rate (page 153), and how much you'll pay over the lifetime of the loan. It also shows any modifications made to your rate for points you bought when you took out your mortgage. Take the time to read this form and confirm that everything is correct.

- **HUD-1 settlement statement.** This federal form, which you and the seller both sign, details the costs related to the sale. It spells out who pays how much to whom. The expenses listed include not only the cost of the property, but other costs as well, like property taxes and personal property included with the sale. Page 325 gives you an overview of what's on a HUD-1 form.

 By law, you have the right to review your completed HUD-1 form 24 hours before the closing. In practice, though, many people see this document for the first time at the closing itself. Let your attorney or closing agent know that you want your HUD-1 the day before the closing. When you get it, compare it to your Good Faith Estimate (page 215) to search for inconsistencies. That way, you can fix mistakes and resolve problems before the closing.

- **Mortgage note.** This document, also called a *promissory note* because it records your promise to repay your mortgage, states the amount you borrowed and the terms of the loan. It also spells out the lender's options if you fail to make payments.

- **Mortgage (called a *deed of trust* or *trust deed* in some areas).** This document secures your mortgage note—it gives your lender a claim against your house if you don't live up to the terms of the mortgage note. (Page 153 explains the difference between a mortgage and a deed of trust.)

- **Monthly payment letter.** This letter breaks down your monthly payments for the first year of your loan, explaining how much money you'll pay each in principal and interest. It also may say how much of your payment goes into escrow for taxes and insurance (including PMI if you have mortgage insurance).

- **Initial escrow statement.** This document (which may supplement the monthly payment letter) itemizes the part of your monthly PITI (principal, interest, taxes, and insurance) payments that go into an escrow account, breaking down how much goes toward taxes, how much toward homeowner's insurance, how much toward PMI, and so on. If you have to pay a lump sum in the first year to "cushion" your escrow account, it states that amount, too.

 The initial escrow statement covers only the first 12 months of your loan. Because the cost of taxes and insurance tend to increase with time, you should expect this portion of your monthly PITI payments to grow from year to year.

- **Mortgage servicing disclosure statement.** This document simply tells you whether your lender intends to service your loan itself or sell it to another lender on the secondary market. If your original lender transfers your loan to someone else, the second lender has to honor the terms of your loan.

- **Title insurance commitment.** This is a promise that the insurance company will issue you a homeowner's policy. You get the actual policy in the mail a few weeks after the closing.

- **Deed.** This document transfers the home's title from the seller to you (read more about that on page 267). The deed should contain an accurate description of the property and must be signed according to your local state laws. Check to make sure that your name is spelled right and that it describes the kind of title you've chosen (see page 270 for your options). After the closing agent records the deed with your local government's property recording office, she'll send it to you. Keep it somewhere secure, like a bank safe deposit box.

- **Bill of sale.** Just as a deed transfers ownership of the house and grounds to you, the bill of sale gives you ownership of any personal property that conveys with the home, such as appliances, drapes, fireplace accessories, and so on.

- **Affidavit of title.** By signing this document, the seller swears under oath that he knows of no title defects or liens against the property. The specific wording of the affidavit varies by state, but it typically includes:
    — The seller's name and address
    — A statement that the seller actually owns the property
    — A statement that the seller hasn't sold (or agreed to sell) the property to another buyer
    — A statement that no liens exist against the property
    — A statement that no assessments exist against the property
    — A statement that the seller hasn't declared bankruptcy

  A signed affidavit of title offers you some protection and legal recourse if a title defect or lien turns up later.

- **American Land Title Association (ALTA) statement.** Like the affidavit of title, the ALTA statement ensures that the property's title is clear and that the property is free of easements, encumbrances, and liens. Both you and the seller sign the ALTA statement. You need this document to buy title insurance.

- **Home warranty.** If the home comes with a warranty (page 279)—whether from the builder or a home-warranty company—you get the warranty at the closing.

- **Homeowners' or condominium association documents.** If the home you're buying is part of a homeowners' or condominium association (page 23), you have additional documents to sign, including covenants, conditions, restrictions, and the association's by-laws.

- **Certificate of occupancy.** If the house you're buying is new construction, this document certifies that the building meets building codes and is safe to occupy. Your local government issues the certificate of occupancy.

At the end of the closing, you get a complete set of documents for your records (except for the deed; you get that after the closing agent records it with your local government). Hang on to the paperwork, and store it in a safe place, such as a safe deposit box at the bank.

 Tip Save back-up copies of your documents by running them through a scanner and emailing the files to yourself. Keeping copies in your webmail account or your Internet service provider's email server gives you a secure backup and easy access to your paperwork if you need to review anything.

Your HUD-1 Form

One of the most important documents you get at the closing is the HUD-1 form, which itemizes all of the fees and charges paid by you and the seller in the transaction. Your lender fills out the HUD-1. Knowing what's on it can help you check it over and make sure it has no costly mistakes (go to this book's Missing CD at *www.missingmanuals.com/cds/* to follow along with the discussion of HUD forms below).

Basic Information

At the top of the HUD-1 form's first page, you'll see basic information about the sale: type of loan; the property location; names and addresses of you, the seller, and the person who's conducting the closing; the closing's date and location.

Summaries of Borrower's and Seller's Transactions

Sections J and K are side-by-side columns—your column is on the left and the seller's is on the right—that detail who pays what in the transaction:

- **Gross Amount Due From Borrower** (lines 100–120) takes into account the purchase price, the price of personal property (like appliances) included in the sale, your closing costs (taken from line 1400 on page 2), prorated taxes, and other charges.

- **Gross Amount Due To Seller** (lines 400–420) itemizes the funds that go to the seller. Most of these amounts (sale price, personal property) match what's in the borrower's column.

- **Amounts Paid By or in Behalf of Borrower** (lines 200–220) lists your earnest money deposit and the amount you're borrowing, along with adjustments for taxes and other charges that the seller hasn't paid. (If, for example, the seller pays property taxes quarterly and hasn't yet paid this quarter's bill, there's an adjustment here for the seller's portion of that bill.)

- **Reductions in Amount Due to Seller** (lines 500–520) itemizes charges that the seller pays out of proceeds of the sale: settlement charges, payoff of her current mortgage, and so on.

- **Cash at Settlement From/To Borrower** (lines 300–303) subtracts the money you've paid (and any that's being paid on your behalf) from the money you owe to come up with the amount you need to pay out of pocket: the down payment plus closing costs. This amount corresponds to the funds your closing agent asked you to bring to the closing as a bank check or wire transfer.

- **Cash at Settlement To/From Seller** (lines 600–603) subtracts what the seller owes from what you're paying the seller to show how much cash she gains from the sale. In some cases (in a short sale, for example), the seller may end up owing money if your payments don't cover everything the seller owes.

Settlement Charges

This part, called Section L, is the longest section of the HUD-1 form and takes up the entire second page. It details all costs related to the closing and specifies whether you or the seller pays each. Here's what it lists:

- **Total Real Estate Broker Fees** (lines 700–704) is about the real estate agents' commissions. It specifies the amount paid to each agent involved in the sale. The seller usually pays these commissions, but if you hired a buyer's agent, you may pay that agent directly.

- **Items Payable in Connection with Loan** (lines 800–811) lists what the lender is charging you for processing your mortgage. Each charge corresponds to a line from your Good Faith Estimate, and each corresponding line is labeled so you can easily compare the GFE to the charges listed here. They should match up—federal law prohibits lenders from increasing any of the fees listed here from what's on your GFE.

- **Items Required by Lender to Be Paid in Advance** (lines 900–904) itemizes charges that you must prepay, like interest that accrues between now and the date your first mortgage payment is due. Other prepaid charges may include private mortgage insurance (if your down payment is less than 20 percent) and homeowners insurance and property taxes (if you're paying those into escrow).

- **Reserves Deposited with Lender** (lines 1000–1007) details the escrow "cushion" you must pay in advance if you're paying taxes and insurance into an escrow account. The lender determines how big a cushion it requires—the amount may be six months' or a year's worth of charges—and tells you how much here. This section applies to PMI, other insurance, and property taxes.

- **Title Charges** (lines 1100–1111) gives charges related to transferring the title from the seller to you, including the title search and title insurance policies. The buyer usually pays the fees in this section.

- **Government Recording and Transfer Charges** (lines 1200–1206) gives you a list of the taxes and fees your state and local governments charge in relation to the sale: transfer tax, fees for recording the mortgage and the deed, city, county, and tax stamps, and so on. Taxes vary by state and municipality. The buyer normally pays these charges.

- **Additional Settlement Charges** (lines 1300–1305) includes miscellaneous charges related to the sale, such as a survey, home inspection, pest inspection, home warranty, and any other charges for third-party services. These charges are usually split by you and the seller, according to what you agreed on previously.

 Some fees, such as the home inspection fee, may be marked "POC," which means "paid outside closing." You've already paid these fees and don't have to pay them again now. They appear on the HUD-1 because it lists *all* costs related to the closing, whether you've already paid them or not.

- **Total Settlement Charges** (line 1400) gives a total for all closing costs you pay and all that the seller pays. These totals go on line 103 (for you) and line 502 (for the seller) to show how closing costs affect the bottom line for both parties.

Comparison of Good Faith Estimate and HUD-1 Charges

The top half of page 3 is set up to make it easy for you to compare what the lender told you about closing costs on your Good Faith Estimate with what you're actually paying at the closing. In three tables, it lays out, side by side, the numbers from your GFE with the numbers on the HUD-1 in these categories:

- **Charges That Cannot Increase.** This section shows what the lender is charging you for making the loan, any points you've agreed to pay (page 157), and transfer taxes. The numbers in the Good Faith Estimate and HUD-1 columns should match exactly.

- **Charges That in Total Cannot Increase More Than 10%.** This section lists government recording charges and any third-party services that the lender required and for which the lender selected the service provider, such as title insurance and the appraisal. Whip out your calculator to make sure that the amounts in the HUD-1 column are no more than 10 percent greater than the amounts in the Good Faith Estimate column.

- **Charges That Can Change.** Here you'll find third-party services that you shopped for yourself, rather than going with the lender's recommendation. This section might include your home inspection or title insurance (if the lender let you shop for the title insurer yourself). It also includes the lender's original estimate of your escrow cushion and daily interest that you owe between now and your first scheduled payment—the closing date wasn't definite when the lender prepared the GFE, so it's impossible to predict these charges precisely on that estimate.

Loan Terms

This section is the same as the "Summary of your loan" section of your Good Faith Estimate. Compare it line by line to your GFE to make sure that everything is the same.

Up to Speed

Co-op Closings

When you buy a co-op, you don't buy a piece of real estate, you buy shares in a corporation that owns the property. So co-op closings are a little different from real-property closings. Proof of co-op ownership is a stock certificate, and the current owner's lender holds his certificate as security against his mortgage. When you buy shares in a co-op, the co-op destroys the seller's old stock certificate, and you get a shiny new one that says you're now the proud owner of the shares.

When you close on a co-op, you meet with the seller (sometimes) and a representative of the seller's lender at the office of the co-op's attorney. Your lender's representative also attends, as do the real estate agents and attorneys for both sides of the sale. Co-op closings include these documents:

- Your stock certificate, which specifies how many shares of the co-op corporation you own.
- Your proprietary lease, which gives you the right to occupy a particular apartment
- A recognition agreement, signed by you, the lender, and a co-op corporation representative, in which the co-op promises not to cancel the stock or the lease or to allow additional financing without the lender's consent.
- A UCC-1 form, which provides public notice of the lender's lien on your co-op shares.

Unlike the sale of a house, where a new deed records the title transfer in public records, a co-op sale requires that you file a UCC-1 form to publicly declare you've borrowed money against shares in an incorporated entity (the co-op). Your lender will also require that you hand over the original stock certificate and a copy (with original signatures) of your proprietary lease.

If you locked in your interest rate after your GFE expired, the loan terms here may be different from the GFE. Compare them to your rate lock letter instead.

What If Something Goes Wrong?

By far, the majority of closings go smoothly. If you're a first-time home-buyer, you may be surprised at how easily the process flows and how non-chalant everyone seems. The pros in the room have done this many times before, and they're as eager as you are to close the deal. If you laid the groundwork properly—you met your obligations, got your questions an-swered, and gathered everything you needed for the closing—you'll be in good shape.

Even so, problems can and do arise. One of the most common is a lender who doesn't send over all the necessary documents or delays transferring funds to the closing agent. If the closing agent discovers that documents are missing, she'll contact the lender's office and ask someone there to fax them over. If the lender is slow to wire the money, you may have to wait for funds. Such problems usually result from tardiness, oversight, or a techni-cal glitch, not from any problem with your loan. But it can be annoying to wait for the lender to get its act together.

 A closing that is complete except for the final act of disbursing funds and deliver-ing documents is called a *dry closing*. In a dry closing, you've fulfilled all your ob-ligations, signed all the papers, and paid the promised deposit and other monies, but the funds from your lender haven't arrived. If all parties agree, the closing takes place anyway—but it's not final until the funds arrive from the lender and the clos-ing agent distributes them, usually later that day or the following day.

There can be more serious problems with loan documents as well, how-ever. You may find that the interest rate isn't what you expected or that the costs listed don't match your Good Faith Estimate. Snafus like this may take a day—or several—to clear up.

Last-minute title problems sometimes crop up, too. A lien or claim that didn't come up in the initial title search may become known at the closing. Or you may find that the seller hasn't paid back property taxes. Your lender won't want to proceed (and neither should you) until you settle these issues.

Sometimes, the closing agent may make a mistake and tell you the wrong amount of money to bring to the closing. If she asked for too much, no problem—you get the excess back. But if she asked for too little, everything comes to a grinding halt until you make up the difference. If it's for a small amount, you can probably pay the difference with a personal check (good thing you brought your checkbook!). If it's substantial, though—say, more than a few hundred dollars—you have to have the extra funds wired or go out and get a bank check or cash.

Issues that come up in your final walkthrough can also lengthen the closing. For example, maybe the seller has moved out but left the garage crammed with junk. Make sure you resolve such problems before the sale is final—in this case, for example, you could have the seller write you a check to have his junk hauled away—but dealing with issues like these at the closing takes time.

Usually, you can resolve closing problems the same day. Sometimes, you have to go through with a dry closing or reschedule the closing a day or two later. Most of the time, though, once you and the seller have released all contingencies, the escrow agent has fulfilled all of the escrow instructions , and the underwriter signs off on your loan, you're good to go. It's rare for closing-day problems to kill a sale.

After the Closing

All of the papers have been signed and all of the funds distributed. But the transaction isn't quite over yet. You might be ready to shout, "I'm a homeowner!" from the rooftops, but that's not how the world finds out that you now own a home.

To make everything official, your closing agent or attorney must record the deed in your local property records office. In some areas, the closing agent can record the deed electronically, which takes just a few minutes. In other areas, someone—the closing agent, an assistant, or a courier—goes to the records office to record the deed. Especially in the case of an in-person recording, it may take a day or so to file the paperwork. Once your local government has the new deed on record, you're done. The home is yours. *Now* you can shout from the rooftops.

 Note You'll receive the deed and your title insurance policy several weeks after the closing. Be sure to put them in the same safe place you keep the other documents related to the purchase of your home.

Even though the home is yours, depending on where you live, you may not be able to move in right away. Your purchase agreement probably has a clause in it defining when you can take possession. In most cases, that's immediately after the closing—the seller drops the keys in your hand, and you can start moving in.

But in some states, you may not be able to take possession right away. Massachusetts, for example, makes buyers wait until the deed has been recorded before taking possession—which may happen anywhere from an hour to a full day after the closing. New York sellers have a legal right to stay in their just-sold home for up to a week if they deposit funds in escrow to guarantee that they'll move out within that time. Make sure you know the law and how it affects your move-in date.

And you may have made special arrangements to let the seller stay in the home a little longer if, for example, he closes on his new house after you buy yours. In a situation like that, you and the seller work out the details ahead of time—how long the seller may stay and how much rent the seller pays you (make sure you get the details in writing).

 Note Your new homeowners liability policy protects you if the seller injures herself while living in your newly purchased home.

When you can take possession may also be affected by the kind of market you buy in:

- **In a buyer's market,** buyers typically insist on immediate possession. Sellers who can't provide a move-in-ready home at the closing may find it harder to sell their home.

- **In a seller's market,** the roles are reversed. Buyers are more likely to agree to a seller's demand to stay in the home for a period of time after the closing. In a situation where multiple buyers compete for the same house, buyers might sweeten the deal by allowing the seller to remain in the home at a very low rent (or even rent-free) for a week or more after the closing.

- **In a neutral market,** possession usually happens immediately or soon after closing.

Whenever you take possession, make sure that your purchase agreement (page 250) states—in clear, black-and-white terms—when the seller will vacate the house. This doesn't have to be tied to a certain date. In fact, the best phrasing is something like "on closing" or "two days after closing." This gives both parties flexibility if the closing date changes.

Taking possession means that you finally get the keys to your new home. And don't forget items like remote garage door openers and owner's manuals and warranties for appliances, the furnace, and the central air conditioner. It's all yours now.

 You did a lot of work and waited a long time to get those keys. But change the locks as soon as possible. This doesn't mean you don't trust the seller (although you might not). It's just common sense. You never know who might have a spare key that the seller didn't collect.

Index

Symbols

11th District Cost of Funds Index (COFI), **166**
80-10-10 loans, **150**, **187–188**
203(k) loan program, **182**

A

absorption rate, **248**
access contingency, **255**
Accredited Buyer Representative (ABR), **89**
adjustable rate mortgages (ARMs), **20**, **164–172**, **202–203**
adjustment periods (loans), **203–204**
ads
    online classified, **119**
    real estate, **110–112**
affidavit of title, **324**
A-frame houses, **53**
agency websites, **119**
agents
    insurance, **105**
    real estate, **80**
amenities, neighborhood, **74**
American Land Title Association (ALTA) statement, **324**
amortization, **155**
application fees (mortgages), **226**
appraisals
    contingency, removing, **263–264**
    fees, **227**
    lender-required, **251**
    online, **241–242**
appraisers, **104–105**
APR (annual percentage rate), **153–154**

ARM disclosure statement, **215**
"as is" home conditions, **311**
asbestos inspection, **307**
asbestos/mold/radon inspection, **253**
asking prices, **240–241**
associations, homeowners, **23**
assumable loans, **190–191**
attorneys, real estate, **99–102**
auctions, **126–132**
automated underwriting, **162–163**

B

balloon loans, **173**
bargain hunting, **121–132**
basement inspections, **300**
bill of sale, **324**
biweekly loans, **179**
break-even point (loans), **202**, **228**
bridge loans, **176**
brokers
    mortgage, **96–98**
    real estate, **80**
budgets, creating monthly, **26–31**
bungalows, **53**
buyer's agents
    defined, **81**
    finding one to work with, **90–94**
    signing with, **89–90**
    working with, **87–89**
buyer's contingencies, **252–254**
buyer's markets, **246–249**
buyer's remorse, **259**
buying vs. renting, **2–4**

C

calculators
  amortizations, **157**
  ARM, **167**
  online mortgage, **34, 158**
  rent vs. buy, **17**
Cape Cod houses, **54**
caps, rate. *See* interest rates
carryover practice (loans), **167**
cash sales, **191**
certificate of occupancy, **325**
Certified Exclusive Buyer Agent
  (CEBA, **89**
Certified Mortgage Consultant
  (CMC), **96**
Certified Residential Mortgage Specialist
  (CRMA), **96**
checklists, desired home features,
  77–78, 137–138
chimney inspections, **309**
classified ads online, **142**
clear titles, **268–270**
closing costs
  adding up, **233–234**
  agreements regarding, **255**
  government taxes and fees, **232–233**
  overview, **18**
  reducing, **236–237**
  related to mortgages, **226–231**
  related to transferring ownership,
    226–231
closing dates, **255**
closings
  conditions following, **331–333**
  co-op closings, **329**
  costs, **314**
  dry closing, **330**
  HUD-1 form, **325–328**
  in escrow states, **319–320**
  in non-escrow states, **320–322**
  paperwork required for, **322–325**
  potential problems with, **330–331**
  preparations for, **314–317**
  reasons for delaying, **317–318**
CMT index, **166**
collateral, **152–153**

colonial houses, **54–55**
commissions, real estate, **86**
commitment letters, **262**
community property titles, **272**
commuting to work, **75**
comparable sales, **240**
condominiums, **22, 60**
Constant Maturity Treasury (CMT)
  index, **166**
Consumer Handbook on Adjustable-
  Rate Mortgages, **215**
contingencies
  basics of, **251–255**
  removing, **262–267**
contractor estimates, **105**
convertible ARMs, **168**
conveyances, **255**
co-ops (housing cooperatives), **22,**
  61–62, 329
costs, closing, **314**
counteroffers, **256**
craftsman houses, **54**
Craigslist website, **119**
credit cards, **49**
credit checks, **226**
credit score and history, **39–46**
crime rates (neighborhoods), **76–77**

D

dates, closing, **255**
debt-to-income ratio, **36–38**
deed of trust, **153, 323**
deeds
  basics, **270, 324**
  defined, **267**
defects in titles, **269**
Department of the Treasury, **128**
digital cameras/camcorders, shopping
  for homes with, **136–137**
disclosure statements (sellers), **139–142**
discounted rates (loans), **169–170**
discount points (loans), **157, 201**
discretionary expenses, **28**
disposable income, **29**
documents and information, gathering
  (mortgages), **206–207**

down payments, **18**, **144–150**, **186–190**
dry closings, **330**
dual agents, **81**, **83**
duplex homes, **59**

E

earnest money, **250–251**
earthquake insurance, **276**
easements, **269**
economically stable environments, **76**
electrical system inspections, **297**, **309**
energy audits, **310**
equity, **12–15**, **146**
escrow funds, **230**
escrow officers, **105**
escrows, loan, **159**
escrow states, closing in, **319–320**
exclusive buyer's agency agreement, **89**
exclusive buyer's agent (EBA), **87**
expenses and income, calculating,
        27–31
exterior inspections, **294–295**

F

Fannie Mae, **128**
FDIC (Federal Deposit Insurance
        Corporation), **196**
fees
  condo (common charges), **22**
  homeowner, **22–23**
FHA (Federal Housing Authority), **148**
FHA-insured loans, **180–183**
FICO scores, **40–48**
fiduciary duty, **88**
financing
  contingency, **251–252**, **262–263**
  down payments, **143–150**
  rent-to-own, **189–190**
  seller financing, **188–191**
fixed-rate loans, **163**, **200–202**
fixed-rate mortgages, **163**
fixer-upper houses, **70–72**, **181**
flood insurance, **20**, **275**
foreclosed properties, **126–132**
For Sale By Owner (FSBO), **121–124**

FTC (Federal Trade Commission), **196**
fully indexed rate, **165**

G

garage inspections, **300**
General Mortgage Associate (GMA), **96**
Good Faith Estimate (GFE), **160**,
        199–200, **215–224**, **234–235**
government agency fees, **229**
government financing programs,
        180–186
government taxes and fees, **232–233**
Gulf War, **184–185**

H

halfplex homes, **59**
hazard insurance, **274–276**
health hazards, inspecting for, **306**
heating and air conditioning
        inspections, **298**
HELOC (home equity line of credit), **15**
home equity
  line of credit (HELOC), **15**
  loans, **14–15**
home inspection
  "as is" conditions, **311**
  basements, **300**
  electrical system, **297–298**
  exterior inspection, **294–295**
  fees, **229**
  finding professional inspectors,
        292–293
  garages, **300**
  health hazards, **306–308**
  heating and air conditioning, **298**, **309**
  inspectors, **102–104**
  installed appliances, **299**
  interior features, **299**
  limits of, **301–302**
  plumbing, **296–297**
  reports, **302–304**
  roof and attic, **296**
  septic systems, **304–305**
  specialized inspections, **308–309**
  wood-destroying pests, **305**

home ownership
  advantages of, 12–18
  disadvantages of, 18–23
homeowner's insurance, 273–279
homes
  comparing, 142
  determining values of, 240
  fixer-uppers, 70–72
  home inspection contingency, 252, 264–266
  home warranties, 279–282
  newly constructed, 66–68
  possession of, 256
  preowned, 69–70
  sales history of, 242
  styles of, 52–65
  touring, 108–110, 132–142
  types of markets, 243–249
HUD (Housing and Urban Development)
  homebuying programs, 185
  HUD-1 forms, 237, 325–328
  HUD-1 Settlement Statement, 160–161, 323
  overview, 128
hybrid loans, 164

I

income and expenses, calculating, 27–31
index, interest rate, 165
Indian home loan guarantee program, 186
Initial Escrow Statement, 161
inspection of homes. *See* home inspection
installed appliances inspection, 299
insulation and venting inspections, 299–300
insurance
  agents, 105
  costs, 230
  homeowner's, 19–20
  title insurance, 231–232, 269–270
interest
  defined, 19
  interest-only loans, 174

interest rate vs. APR, 153–154
  prepaying, 204–205
  prorated, 228
  rate caps, 166–168, 203
  rate locks, 204–205
  rates, overview, 33
  RateWatch website, 171
  researching rates, 197–203
Internet shopping for houses, 114–119
interviewing agents, 90–92

J

joint tenancy titles, 271

L

lead-based paint inspection, 252
lease option arrangement, 189
lenders
  finding, 194–197
  lender's title insurance, 231, 269
  mortgage lenders, 98
  viewpoint of, 36–47
liability insurance, 274
LIBOR index, 166
liens, 268
lifetime rate caps, 167
living trusts, 273
loan origination fee, 227
loans. *See also* mortgages
  80-10-10, 150, 187–188
  203(k) program, 182
  adjustable-rate, 164–172
  application processing, 162–163
  applying for, 161–163
  assuming seller's, 190–191
  balloon, 173
  biweekly, 179
  bridge, 176
  credit checks, 226
  escrows, 159
  FHA-insured, 180–183
  FICO scores and, 48–49
  fixed-rate, 163
  hybrid, 164
  Indian home loan guarantee program, 186

interest-only, 174
loan originators, 194
loan-to-value (LTV) ratio, 39
long-term, 177–178
low down payment, 148–150
for manufactured homes, 182–183
piggyback, 187
points, 157
preapproval process, 34–35
prepayment penalties, 170
prequalifying process, 34
reducing terms of, 178–179
rejected applications, 223
short-term, 177–178
teaser rates, 169
term of, 155
two-step, 173–174
Uniform Residential Loan Application, 208–209
Veterans Administration, 183–185
locks, rate, 204–205
London Inter Bank Offered Rates (LIBOR), 165
long-term home ownership, 16–17
long-term loans, 177–178

M

maintenance costs, 21
mansion tax, 232
manufactured homes
    basics of, 63–65
    FHA-insured loans and, 182–183
margin, interest rate, 165, 202
market inventory, 248
medical bills (liability insurance), 276
modular homes, 62–63
mold inspection, 306
mold/radon/asbestos inspection, 253
mortgage brokers, 96–98
mortgage lenders, 98
mortgages. See also loans
    adjustable rate (ARMs), 20, 164–172
    affordability of, 31–34
    application fees, 226
    basics of, 152–159

choosing terms of, 176–179
costs related to, 226–231
documents and information, gathering, 206–207
fixed-rate, 163
lenders. See lenders
Mortgage Servicing Disclosure Statement, 160, 222
online calculator, 34
private mortgage insurance, 229
seller-financed second, 150
from sellers, 188
underwriters, 162
moving preparations, 282–286

N

National Association of Mortgage Brokers, 199
National Guard, 185
NCUA (National Credit Union Administration), 196
negative amortizations, 168–169
negative equity, 23
negotiating deals, 256–259
neighborhoods
    choosing, 72–78
    touring, 120–121, 141
neighbors, 75
neutral markets, 243
nonexclusive buyer's agency agreement, 89

O

one-time costs, 18
online classified ads, 119
online home appraisals, 241–242
online lenders, 195–197
online mortgage calculator, 34, 158
open houses, 120–121
option ARMs, 172–173
origination points (loans), 157
originators, loan, 194
owner's title insurance, 232, 269

P

paying down principal, 178–179
payments, recurring, 19–20
periodic rate caps, 167
personal liability, 276
pest infection, 230, 252
phishing scams, 196
piggyback loans, 187
PITI (principal/interest/taxes/insurance), 36–38
plumbing inspections, 296–297, 309–310
points (loans), 157–159, 201, 227–228
policies, types of homeowner, 277
polybutylene pipes, 297
possession of homes, 256
prairie style houses, 56
preapproval process (loans), 34–35
preowned homes, 69–70
prepaying interest, 204–205
prepayment penalties (loans), 170
prequalifying process (loans), 34
principal, defined, 19
Private Mortgage Insurance (PMI), 19, 146, 229
processing loans, 162–163
promissory notes, 323
properties
    surveying, 229, 273
    taxes, 33, 232
prorated interest, 228
Public Housing Authorities (PHAs), 186
pueblo revival houses, 56
purchase price, 250

Q

quitclaim deeds, 270

R

radon/mold/asbestos inspection, 253
radon testing, 308
ranch-style houses, 56–57
rates, interest. *See* interest rates

real estate
    ads, 110–112
    agency websites, 119
    attorneys, 99–102
    Real Estate Disposition Corporation (REDC), 129
real estate agents and brokers
    commissions paid to, 85–86
    defined, 80
    firing, 95
    functions of, 82–85
    overview, 80–83
    providing information to, 94–95
    Realtor.com site, 114–115
    realtor, defined, 82
    working with, 108
recording fees, 233
references, checking agent, 92–93
rejected loan applications, 223
remodeling, 22
renovations, 308
renting vs. buying, 2–4
rent-to-own financing, 189–190
REOs (real estate owned properties), 127
repair costs, 22
reports
    credit, 39–40, 45
    home inspection, 302–304
RESPA (Real Estate Settlement Procedures Act), 159–161
roof and attic inspections, 252, 296

S

Safari Books Online, 9
schools, 72–73
second mortgages from sellers, 150, 188
seller-financed second mortgages, 150, 188
seller financing, 188–191
seller's agent (listing agent), 81
seller's concession, 236
seller's contingencies, 254–255
seller's disclosure, 253
seller's markets, 243–246
selling prices vs. asking prices, 241

septic system inspections, 304–305
services and shopping
    (neighborhoods), 74
Servicing Transfer Statement, 161
settlement fees, 232
sewer inspection, 252
shopping
  and services (neighborhoods), 74
  chart (GFE), 221
  for homeowner's insurance, 278–279
  Shopping for Your Home Loan booklet
    (HUD), 214
short sales, 124–126
short-term loans, 177–178
single-family houses, 52–58
sole property title, 270
spending, tracking, 30
split-level houses, 57
staging, defined, 134
starter homes, 17–18
structural components, inspecting, 295
surveying properties, 229, 273

T

taxes
  advantages of home ownership, 16
  government, 232–233
  transfer and recording, 232
teaser rates (loans), 169–170
tenancy by the entirety titles, 272
tenancy in common titles, 271–272
term of loans, 155–156, 176–178
TinyURLs, 8
titles
  defined, 267
  insurance, 269
  searching, 231, 268–269
  title states, closing in, 320–322
  title to property contingencies, 253
  types of, 270–273
townhouse homes, 61
tracking spending, 30
tradeoff table (GFE), 220–221
trading up, 17–18
transfer and recording tax, 232
tress, inspecting, 310

Trulia real estate search site, 115–118
trust deed, 323
Truth-in-Lending (TIL) disclosure
    statement, 214–215, 322–323
Tudor houses, 57
two-step loans, 173–174

U

underwriters, mortgage, 162
underwriting, automated, 162
Uniform Residential Loan Application,
    208–217
utilities, 21

V

Veterans Administration (VA) loans,
    183–185
Victorian houses, 58

W

walkthroughs
  final, 286–290
warranties, home, 279–282
well inspection, 252
wish list checklist, 77–78, 137–138
wood-destroying pests, 305

Y

Yahoo Real Estate site, 118

Z

Zillow real estate site, 118–119
zoning, 77

Get even more for your money.

Join the O'Reilly Community, and register the O'Reilly books you own. It's free, and you'll get:

- 40% upgrade offer on O'Reilly books
- Membership discounts on books and events
- Free lifetime updates to electronic formats of books
- Multiple ebook formats, DRM FREE
- Participation in the O'Reilly community
- Newsletters
- Account management
- 100% Satisfaction Guarantee

Signing up is easy:

1. **Go to: oreilly.com/go/register**
2. **Create an O'Reilly login.**
3. **Provide your address.**
4. **Register your books.**

Note: English-language books only

To order books online:

oreilly.com/order_new

For questions about products or an order:

orders@oreilly.com

To sign up to get topic-specific email announcements and/or news about upcoming books, conferences, special offers, and new technologies:

elists@oreilly.com

For technical questions about book content:

booktech@oreilly.com

To submit new book proposals to our editors:

proposals@oreilly.com

Many O'Reilly books are available in PDF and several ebook formats. For more information:

oreilly.com/ebooks

O'REILLY®